Riding the Storm
Strategic planning in turbulent markets

Riding the Storm
Strategic planning in turbulent markets

Gerald Michaluk

THE McGRAW-HILL COMPANIES

London · Burr Ridge IL · New York · St Louis · San Francisco · Auckland
Bogotá · Caracas · Lisbon · Madrid · Mexico · Milan
Montreal · New Delhi · Panama · Paris · San Juan · São Paulo
Singapore · Sydney · Tokyo · Toronto

Riding the Storm: Strategic planning in turbulent markets
Gerald Michaluk

ISBN: 0 07 7099354

Published by McGraw-Hill Professional
Shoppenhangers Road
Maidenhead
Berkshire
SL6 2QL
Telephone: 44 (0) 1628 502 500
Fax: 44 (0) 1628 770 224
Website: www.mcgraw-hill.co.uk

British Library Cataloguing in Publication Data
A catalogue record for this book is available from the British Library

Library of Congress Cataloguing in Publication Data
The Library of Congress data for this book has been applied for/is available
from the Library of Congress

Sponsoring Editor: Elizabeth Robinson
Editorial Assistant: Sarah Wilks
Business Marketing Manager: Elizabeth McKeever

Produced for McGraw-Hill by Steven Gardiner Ltd
Text design by Steven Gardiner Ltd
Printed and bound in Great Britain by Bell and Bain Ltd, Glasgow
Cover design by Simon Levy Associates

McGraw-Hill books are available at special quantity discounts. Please
contact the Corporate Sales Executive at the above address.

In memory of Jaroslaw Michaluk,
whose quiet words of encouragement live
with me always

Contents

Acknowledgements

This book summarizes my work over the last 14 years. It has been influenced by a great number of people; colleagues, friends, family, clients, managers, teachers, writers and reporters have all played a part. I have mentioned a few in the text, but there are numerous others who from the acorns of thought that they shared with me a tree of ideas has stemmed. Some of the most influential are those I have never met but through their work. To all who have shared their thoughts with me, I thank you.

In addition, I would like to thank those who helped me in the writing process by proofing work, making suggestions or simply keeping me working: Salma Abbasi of Lucent Technologies, Fumihiko Abe of Coca-Cola, Faisal Choudhry of MMSI, Chris Del Col, Dr Bill Donaldson of Strathclyde Post Graduate Business School, Paul Ellingstad of Compaq Computers, Carl Gardiner of the Chartered Institute of Marketing, Alan Gray of Compaq Computers, Prof. Susan Hart of Strathclyde University, Rikke Iversholt of MMSI, Terry Lamb of Scottish Management Projects, Stuart Patrick of Scottish Enterprise Glasgow, Claire Rutherford of MMSI, Jonathan Stone of MMSI, and a special thank you to my assistant Claire Thompson and to both Sarah Wilks and Elizabeth Robinson at McGraw-Hill.

In addition to those who helped me in the writing of this work, I would like to thank the team at MMSI plc for allowing me the time to write the book and for their not insignificant contributions to the individual GMAS modules and to the success of MMSI plc.

Thank you also to the following:

Comshare – Nicky Clark
Corvu – Mischa Zambataro
Hyperion – Claudine Caruso
i2 – Beth Elkin and Molly Fiden
Idons – John Galt
Inphase – Victoria Keogh
Market Modelling – Roger Singer
Oracle – Colin Addison
PeopleSoft – Alastair McGill and Katerina Sappia
Prodacapo – Alison Williams
SAS – Sheila Jones
Show Business Software – Morel Fourman
Siebel – Lucy Jacobs
Ygnius – Karen Reyes

Carolyn Blackburn at the New Lanark Conservation Trust for her assistance with historical information.

Tim Friesner and his website www.marketingteacher.com for assistance with the glossary.

Lastly, but most importantly, I would like to thank *you* for reading this book, without you it would all have been in vain. I hope I will give you a few ideas which you can grow and develop and that will benefit both you and your organization.

1

Executive Summary

WHAT IS GMAS?

Riding the STORM outlines a paradigm shift in strategic and operational planning. Using GMAS, a Global Marketing Advantage System, this book shows how a company can thrive in fast-moving, turbulent markets.

GMAS is defined as: 'the knowledge, experience, systems, processes, procedures, techniques, training, and software tools required to successfully generate and maintain a global marketing advantage'.

GMAS effectively links strategy with market reality. Strategy must be flexible. This is a lesson learned at great human cost in the First World War where the reality in the trenches and the invention of the machine gun made the planned strategy suicidal, resulting in such a waste of life as the world had never witnessed before. It is therefore essential to any organization where the market, technology or operational reality is at odds with the strategy, that these conflicts are investigated immediately to determine whether the situation has arisen from poor tactical execution or a more serious error in strategic thinking.

Figure 1.1 illustrates how and where GMAS is placed in relation to the Balanced Scorecard Model (BSC), Enterprise Resource Planning (ERP) and Customer Relationship Management (CRM). I will also demonstrate how the strategic planning process overlaps GMAS

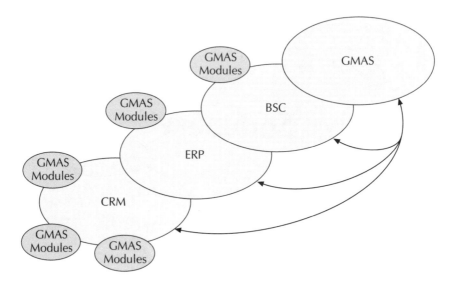

Figure 1.1   GMAS fit.

and its strategy monitoring role in the Balanced Scorecard model. All these models are discussed in Chapters 2 and 3.

Where organizations have not adopted the Balanced Scorecard model, GMAS is a tool that monitors the strategic plan and greatly reduces or even eliminates the need for strategic planning reviews. It still tests and monitors operational plan execution.

At the centre of a GMAS system is STORM, providing the links between Strategic Planning, Staff, Operational Planning and Execution, Real-Time Critical Assumptions, and Monitoring and Testing (Figure 1.2).

The STORM

The Strategic, Tactical Operational Review Meeting (STORM) is the name given to the systems and interactions required to maintain a GMAS system and therefore a global marketing advantage. The STORM is located at the heart of a GMAS system ensuring the oxygen in the life-blood, information, circulates around the organization.

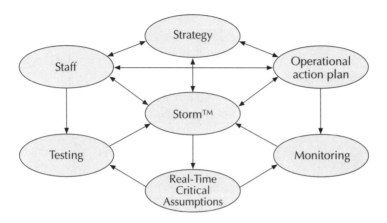

Figure 1.2 GMAS STORM model.

The Strategic Plan
The strategic plan and the process of its formulation and updating are the equivalent of the organization's brain. The human brain requires inputs from the senses and links to the muscles to be effective. If a nerve in a finger detects pain, the brain causes the muscle to move the finger away from the source of the pain. Likewise strategy cannot function effectively in isolation from the senses (monitoring and testing) nor from the muscles (operational plans).

Operations
If strategic planning is the brain then operations are the muscle, it is what makes things happen. When muscle movements get out of sync with the brain, a human cannot function effectively. Therefore, it is logical that the two are linked closely and that it is possible to tell when action is being taken in the correct way and that it achieves the desired goal.

A baby struggling to develop its coordination can be compared to the building of an effective organization. You can see the baby knows what it wants, but just cannot yet coordinate its muscles to reach its objective. Managing a company can be very similar: strategically you know what must be done, but operations are uncoordinated and wasteful. As the child grows it increasingly becomes able to coordinate its muscles and achieve its goals. Unfortunately, not all organizations manage to get past the first phase of muscular development.

The Staff

The staff are the life-blood of the organization providing the vital oxygen and nutrients needed for the whole body to function. Oxygen carried in the blood is required for all the functions of the cells and likewise within an organization the knowledge and skills carried by the staff allows the company to function. Knowing that your staff's goals, key performance indicators and rewards reflect the strategy is vital if a strategic focus is to be maintained throughout the firm. It is vital to know who is affected and by which critical assumption they are affected. To this end, Enterprise Neural Trails (ENT) are used to link individuals to the strategy so that at a glance the impact of a challenged critical assumption can be determined and a team brought together from the affected groups to think through possible scenarios and develop solutions or grasp opportunities.

Monitoring and Testing

Monitoring and testing are the senses of the organization and, like the five human senses of sight, hearing, smell, taste and touch, there are many ways to monitor and test the environment in which the organization is active. Using the five senses provides us all with 3125 different ways of sensing our world. In the same way, market research can provide us with almost as many options in the organizational context.

Monitoring involves the tracking and comparison of expected with actual. For example, press and media are monitored to ensure that the critical assumptions on which the strategy is based do not turn out to have been fiction, while testing ensures that systems, staff and consumer reactions are as forecast. For example, mystery shopping visits are used to determine whether staff live up to the company values, and focus groups are used to determine the acceptance of a new product's features or distribution channel.

The Real Time Critical Assumptions

All operational and strategic plans consist of the three ingredients of Fact, Faith and Fiction. By extracting the critical assumptions the plans are based upon, it is possible to separate these three elements over time. As Socrates said: 'The only true wisdom is in knowing you know nothing.' What we presume to be facts are open to interpretation, and are often not as robust as we had assumed. Take your bank balance. If you look at a bank balance and find £500, it sounds like that is a fact, but is it? Have you deposited a cheque recently that is in your account waiting to clear? What if that cheque bounces? What about the interest that has been accrued but not yet added to your account? Often what we think we know turns out not to be so. Thus, plans looking forward are full of Fact, Faith and Fiction. GMAS determines whether a critical assumption derived in the planning process is becoming more solid indicating it is a fact or whether it is turning into fiction. Critical assumptions that become fiction may have a major impact on the success of the organization and will in most cases need the planners to look again at their plans and assess them in the light of the new information. This will have one of three outcomes: (a) the plan or strategy will need to be changed, (b) the plan or strategy can proceed without change or (c) further research is required to determine whether action is needed or not.

Components of GMAS

GMAS consists of many different systems and tools linked together. Deployments are quite different in every instance because GMAS deployments are as individual as the companies they serve. Your company has its own uniqueness. The effectiveness of a GMAS module is based on matching it to a known environment, i.e. best practice is only best practice in certain circumstances. The GMAS modules match best practice to the environment or market conditions to ensure a high probability of success.

The core strategy elements of GMAS monitor and defend the company strategy which is linked to the organization via a Balanced Scorecard system (BSC), Enterprise Resource planning system (ERP) or Real Options. The GMAS modules supply information to and take information from these systems. Because GMAS was designed with the goal of marketing advantage in mind, it has many modules which link to Customer Relationship Management (CRM) systems. However, GMAS principles can be utilised on their own without the need for these other systems, but is most effective when integrated.

2

The Beginnings of GMAS

THE BACKGROUND

The story begins way back in history in 1989—before ERP's acceptance, the Internet or CRM. For example, leading strategist Henry Mintzberg was writing about *The Rise and Fall of Strategic Planning* in 1994 describing the dangers in strategic planning and pointing out pitfalls such as how a badly managed strategic planning process can destroy commitment, promote tunnel vision, discourage change, and generate an atmosphere of politics. All of these destroy shareholder value. He left no stone unturned and delivered a harsh critique of some of the most sacred cows in strategic planning. He described the three most common fallacies of the strategic planning process: 'discontinuities can be predicted, strategists can be detached from the operations of the organization, and the process of strategy-making itself can be formalized (Mintzberg, 1994).

The gauntlet had been thrown down. I set out to show that discontinuities could be predicted, that strategy making can be systematized and how strategic planning and operational planning could be symbiotically aligned in order to ensure that the strengths of both are intermingled to produce a strategy focus that would respond to what was happening operationally and within the marketplace.

As an academic the challenge was exciting and I had soon developed a plausible model. However, there were considerable challenges to overcome if it was ever to become a reality. For instance, information would have to be gathered in real time and delivered at the right time to the right people so they could make the right decisions. It must be remembered that this was pre-ERP, so accounts were not available at the touch of a button for a widespread organization; pre-CRM, so anticipated sales could not be predicted let alone displayed as a sales pipeline; pre-Internet, so information was too slow to collect and often out of date—if you were lucky enough to find it in the first place. So, a concept was born and shelved.

Time passed and in 1996 Thomas Siebel wrote a book with the help of Michael Malone entitled *Virtual Selling* which described a method of achieving total sales quality. Meanwhile, in Germany, SAP-AG was evangelizing an accountancy package that would give the global company instant access to its financial position regardless of location and currency. In addition, the Internet was revolutionizing information access. By 1998 all the missing pieces to turn theory into practice had been developed and GMAS was taken off the shelf, dusted down and work began in earnest to make it a reality. There are several theoretical models that I will discuss in terms of how they are incorporated into GMAS. GMAS depends on a number of researchers' work and I will now cover some of the most important building blocks, which have shaped its design.

Strategic and Tactical Alignment

The 1980s brought together McKinsey and Company, the world-renowned strategic consultancy firm, Harvard Business School and Stanford Business School professors to identify the best way to manage and organize a firm. This team developed the 7-S Framework, a model for organizational alignment often called the McKinsey 7-S model. From this model, which I will discuss in more detail in Chapter 3, it is clear that strategy, systems, style, staff, skills and structure are all linked to the organization's shared values.

The research resulted in five main findings. These were:

1   There is no 'best way' to organize. This was not really surprising, but considering the objective of the research was to find the best way, this must have come as somewhat of a disappointment. This is even more of an issue for ERP systems such as SAP, which tend

to believe one fit fits all, and strives to include 'best practice' in its modular R/3 system. Clearly, if there is no one 'best way' there can be no one 'best practice'.

2 The most likely success in organizational design comes from the organization most closely aligned with its environment. My take on this was, if there is 'best practice when linked to a specific environment, then 'best practice' can be documented. However, it must be remembered that it will only work where the environment is also documented and you find yourself in the same or similar environment. This I built into GMAS. Think about what this means. If the environment/market changes, then your 'best practices' may cease to be just that. Therefore, there is a need to revisit what is best practice, regardless of how well that practice may have served you in the past, if there is an environmental or market condition change. The old saying 'If it ain't broke, don't fix it' should now read 'If it ain't broke, it's probably obsolete, but if it's not, don't fix it'.

3 Organizational systems are complex and interlinked. Complexity and inter-linked systems suggest Newton's law 'for every action there is a reaction' may apply. Managers should be prepared for a reaction from any changes in the organization, market or environment.

4 There are seven key elements you need to consider if you want to understand an organization and what makes it effective or not: strategy, structure, systems, staffing, skills, style and shared values (the 7-S model).

5 Internal alignment is as important as external alignment with the environment. To be most effective the organization must have a high degree of fit between the 7-S internally. Misalignment and associated disharmony arise where one of the 7-Ss is clashing with another. For example, new systems are introduced that reduce the technical skill required in the staff. This change and its impact, you may well have already experienced in your own organization. Not only does the 'simple' system change impact staff, it also affects skills, style, structure, strategy and shared values.

Many companies have great difficulty creating and maintaining shared value while others make it a competitive advantage. For example, the

Hard Rock Café is famous throughout the world for its staff's attitude. Its food is similar to competitors such as Planet Hollywood, but what the Hard Rock Café does is to ensure, with considerable effort, detailed training and evangelical fervour, that its shared values are instilled into its employees, regardless of their locations throughout the world. This has been one of the main reasons for the global success of this company, which is now part of the Rank Group.

Alignment Tools and Ideas

The tools for aligning an organization behind a single strategy are now well developed and are reported by Robert L. Howie Jr, co-founder and vice-president of the Balanced Scorecard Collaborative, to have been installed in 60 per cent of the world's top 1000 companies. These software tools are certainly readily available with ERP, BSC and Activity-Based Costing (ABC). Appendix 1 discusses software available from a variety of vendors.

The basic strategy, adopted by the company, is fed into these systems and thereby the whole organization can be focused on its achievements with each individual getting their own Key Performance Indicators (KPI) tied to the strategy. However, with such a powerful model for focusing your organization, you had better be sure that you have the strategy right and have considered the other elements outlined in McKinsey's 7-S model. In addition, you need to ensure that you have understood the market, how it is changing and where it is going, otherwise you may land up charging over a cliff, if the market has moved or the landscape is not as you imagined it would be.

Overcoming the Difficulties in Strategic Planning

GMAS uses a breakthrough method of marketing and business planning to ensure you have the right strategy in the first place and that it is adaptable to market changes. By synergistically aligning strategic and operational planning, GMAS allows users to identify and thereby avoid or exploit paradigm shift. Paradigm shift has seen the downfall of some of the greatest names in a variety of industries such as Apple, Tandem Computers, Lucent Technologies, Digital, Xerox, Sears and IBM. All these organizations were stranded, unable to move forward or go back, without massive organizational upheaval. Many of the names survive today, but mainly as shadows of their former selves.

GMAS enables strategic decisions to be made at the right time by monitoring the critical assumptions used in formulating the original strategy and in real time. Consequently, there is no need for the customary annual planning cycle because GMAS makes small changes to strategy throughout the year at the optimal time. These small changes are reflected instantly in modifications to the KPI which can very quickly take effect in companies running a BSC or having an ERP system.

GMAS clearly changes the function of the strategic planners in your organization who in a GMAS company spend the entire year modelling, testing, responding to warnings, scenario planning the results of critical assumptions being challenged and studying real options.

The simple idea behind GMAS is that strategy is only as good as the assumptions made in its formulation. Therefore, strategy is only valid while the assumptions remain intact. If the assumptions are compromised, the strategy is compromised and may need to be modified or changed—not at the next planning cycle but immediately—if global marketing advantage is to be had. This is not to say that strategy will change every five minutes because if the critical assumptions are not challenged then the strategy will continue to be effective without requiring modification.

The majority of critical assumptions being challenged result in none or very minor strategy changes. However, where a paradigm shift is detected major changes have to be made. In the late 1990s Microsoft made such a change when it realized that it had ignored the Internet while Oracle, Sun and others were moving to exploit the situation. Overnight, Microsoft's entire strategy and KPIs were changed to reflect the new strategic direction. With the right tools it is quite possible to change strategic direction with little more than a ripple being created in the course of the direction change.

Why Should You Consider Deploying a GMAS System?

There are many excellent reasons. Here are three in each of the four BSC areas of financial, customer, internal, and learning and growth that all apply whether you build your own GMAS system, buy from an approved vendor or use MMSI's GMAS.

Financial

1   Increased stakeholder value because the company can deliver more often on its promises and be more accurate in its planning and forecasting.

2   Increased sales because the company has a better situational awareness of unfavourable or favourable market conditions, which it can exploit at the right time and sooner than competitors using a traditional planning cycle. This is coupled with the ability to continuously monitor the market opportunities.

3   Increased profit because, by understanding the market better and by having a more flexible strategy model, profit opportunity can be maximized.

Customer

1   Increased customer satisfaction because you understand their needs better and are able to anticipate their future needs with a higher degree of accuracy.

2   Increased loyalty because you understand the elasticity of loyalty and can model competitor offerings against your own and predict acceptance by channel and market segment.

3   Increased trust because, by identifying and acting upon natural paradigm shifts, you can ensure your customers' satisfaction by providing them with products and services that meet their current as well as future requirements.

Internal

1   Increased control because failures in execution can be separated from failures in strategic thinking, both of which can be fixed quickly and effectively.

2   Faster decisions because more reliable information is available faster.

3   Better execution because with a clearer strategic focus, managers can be given more tactical freedom.

Learning and Growth

1   Increased organizational learning because by not being able to pass

the buck, reasons for poor execution can be investigated, corrected and documented. The same mistakes need not be made twice.

2   Increased feelings of empowerment because with a clear understanding and confidence in the strategy being right, staff can make better decisions closer to the customer.

3   Increase cooperation on strategically important issues because by making smaller changes to strategy, more frequently, major changes are avoided and there is much less fear in the organization.

In a nutshell GMAS provides:
1   The potential for global marketing advantage.
2   A lowering of risk across the whole organization.
3   A more empowered, strategically focused organization.

GMAS provides a clear and simple view of strategic planning in turbulent markets that when combined with existing systems or simply implemented alone, provides a framework for 'real time right time' strategy that responds to market reality and can distinguish between operational and strategic errors. Thus, it offers your company increased stakeholder value, cost-effective implementation and enhancement of existing investments in enterprise systems.

3

Riding the STORM: Why Strategic Planning Must Change

THE CHEQUERED HISTORY OF STRATEGIC PLANNING

Strategic planning and, specifically, long-term planning, has moved in and out of favour over the years, while the development cycle has continuously condensed (see Figures 3.1a and b). I am sure you, like me, have heard it said there is no effective means of predicting the future and therefore it is not worth the effort to do so. On the other hand, you will also have heard it said that because of this increase in tempo there is more need than ever to undertake strategic and long-term planning.

The arguments for and against strategic planning are outlined in a great many books but if you only have time to read two, they should be Mintzberg's *The Rise and Fall of Strategic Planning* (1994), and Michael de Kare-Silver's *Strategy in Crisis* (1997). Both outline why strategic planning and, in particular, long-range planning have been ignored by managers and warn of the consequences.

Michael de Kare-Silver reports in his book that chief executives and even corporate planning vice-presidents have a variety of definitions for strategy. Had he logged on to Amazon.com and looked for books on strategic planning he would have found 5513 books listed. It is of little surprise, therefore, that there are a variety of definitions. One definition I especially like is from Michael Porter's book entitled *Competitive Strategy*: 'It is a combination of the ends for which the firm is striving and the means by which it is seeking to get there' (1980).

Figure 3.1a   Speed of change.

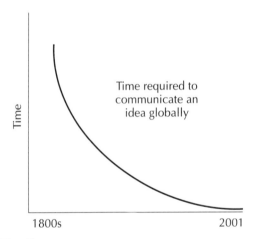

Figure 3.1b   Timeline.

The various schools of thought and definitions of planning are discussed in Mintzberg's work (1994), but I will opt for a rather more simplistic definition: Planning is the process of discovery of what is required to be done in order to achieve a specific goal. If you have a Specific, Measurable, Achievable, Realistic and Timed (SMART) objective, then how you think you are going to achieve your objective is your plan. The process of thinking, deciding between options and articulation is planning.

The Rise and Fall of Strategic Planning

Henry Mintzberg's (1994) work clearly described the dangers in strategic planning. Mintzberg writes about how, if badly managed, even the strategic planning process could undermine commitment, create myopia, destroy innovation, and generate a Machiavellian atmosphere of politics and intrigue. All these do not just damage shareholder value, but also destroy the company's ability to be managed effectively with inevitable consequences.

These are good reasons to be cautious and extremely careful in the strategic planning process and partly explain why some firms have given up on the process. However, when managed effectively and inclusively these dangers can be minimized. Bear them in mind and be on your guard for any tell-tale indicators that the process is going off track.

Mintzberg came to three conclusions:

1   Discontinuities cannot be predicted.
2   The process of strategy making itself cannot be formalized.
3   Strategy cannot be detached from the operations of the organization.

The GMAS contradicts two of these three Mintzberg Laws:

1   Discontinuities or paradigm shift cannot only be detected, but can be predicted.
2   The strategic planning process can be formalized, but will need to be a continuous process to avoid becoming obsolete.

Mintzberg's third law, that strategy cannot be detached from operations, is confirmed by GMAS. What is interesting is that strategic planning becomes ineffective if the rule is ignored. However, the closer the two (strategy and operations) can be linked, the more effective the strategic plan becomes.

Henry Mintzberg was right in that, in the past, discontinuities (paradigm shift) could not be detected and strategy making could not be formalized. Both are possible in the 21st century using GMAS. However, one point of Mintzberg's theory remains true even in the 21st Century: strategy cannot be detached from operations. What is clear now is that it is a two-way street. Just as operations cannot be detached from strategy, strategy cannot be detached from operations and neither may be isolated from the reality of the market regardless of how well conceived the strategy is. Only by monitoring and testing the strategic assumptions and having a fast mechanism to communicate and keep the strategy aligned throughout the organization, can firms compete and dominate markets in the information age.

Fact, Faith and Fiction

Global Marketing Advantage Systems consider the importance of the three Fs of planning—Fact, Faith and Fiction. All plans contain a mixture of Fact, Faith and potential Fiction. For example, we know when the company was registered (Fact); we have projections and budgets that we will use to build our business and these are based, one hopes, on a sound understanding of the market and our cost structure (Faith); when we begin to execute the plan, where we end up may not be where we intended and therefore the plan has the potential to contain Fiction.

The majority of large company initiatives fail to start on schedule and to complete on time. This is surprising considering the experience of most companies involved in major initiatives. Bain & Co, the strategic consultants, reported that at any one time as many as 11 major management approaches were being implemented simultaneously within the same company.

This is almost like Management By Bestseller (MBBS) where management simply introduces the approach suggested by whichever book happens to be the bestseller that quarter. This constant change has created, in most companies, a feeling of apathy towards new initiatives. This must be overcome if the synergies and benefits from the various management approaches are to be gained or the alignment behind one approach is to be achieved.

Being able to distinguish between Fact, Faith and Fiction is critical for the successful implementation of any plan. As soon as fiction becomes apparent, action must be considered. For example, if we are in the CRM software business and we have assumed that the CRM market will continue to grow at 40 per cent per annum over the next two years, our strategy will be impacted if it comes to light that the market is growing by less than that amount. Sales, manufacturing capacity, inventory, etc. will all be affected. GMAS measures the extent of the impact and offers management the opportunity to change tactics or strategy to cope with the new marketplace much faster than with traditional planning models. In traditional planning models market growth figures may not be considered until the next round of annual planning or until sales have failed to make the forecast and inventory and/or manufacturing overheads are too high. Without GMAS, all of this can come too late and the victim company has already entered into firefighting mode in which strategy and long-term development are sacrificed to solve the immediate problems which, in fact, could have been avoided with a more dynamic planning model as provided by GMAS.

The Need for Intelligence

> 'The only true wisdom is in knowing you know nothing.'
>
> Socrates

If you imagine you are a general about to invade a foreign land, what would be your first actions? What would you want to know? The first thing, I suggest, would be to search for a map of the area to be invaded, determine the accuracy of the map and then undertake some reconnaissance.

In the context of business, the map is a representation of a market. The difference in business is that the map keeps changing: what products are available, what consumers want to buy, fashion trends, etc. Therefore, the first difference, we have to realize, is that there are no accurate maps and whatever we are able to map is not accurate for very long. A good analogy would be trying to map the sand dunes of a desert. As soon as you think you have it mapped, a sandstorm comes along and moves the dunes. Even in a desert there are certain features, such as coastlines and oases that stand out and resist change in the short to medium term. These must be found and from these landmarks we can determine where we are.

If we accept that we do not know where the dunes are, we had better invade in vehicles that can cope with dunes turning up where we least expect them. In business, the business units have to be capable of recognizing a dune and routing themselves either over or around it as our maps cannot identify these dunes nor their location.

Individual business units must therefore understand the strategy of the organization and their role, but remain adaptive to local conditions, taking advantage of opportunities that will help them achieve the corporate goal without having to wait for orders from the top.

The next item for reconnaissance is to examine the opposition. What are their strengths, deployment, equipment, leadership, resources and morale. Like any army, the opposition will try to disguise its weaknesses and exaggerate its strengths, it will try to stay hidden and surprise you, outmanoeuvre you or ambush you.

In business our competitors are just as diligent as enemy troops and will exploit our weaknesses and mislead us whenever they can. Thus, the first battle to win is the intelligence battle. We must know more about how the land lies, what the weather forecast is and what the competition is up to. GMAS starts by winning the intelligence battle and maintains the advantage over time and changing circumstances.

Competitive Intelligence, edited by Larry Kahaner (1996), outlines just how effective competitive intelligence can be and illustrates how it has been used by some of the world's largest corporations including Nutrasweet, AT&T, Procter and Gamble, Corning and Motorola. However, in many companies, business intelligence gathering is at best haphazard. For example, a sales team knows that regular review of the press will generate sales opportunities, but when they get too busy they stop reviewing it and only return to their monitoring when business begins to slow. Market intelligence gathering must be ongoing, never ignored or forgotten about.

The Major Strategic Planning Tools

There are a wide range of strategic planning tools available to help formulate your strategy and prepare plans. Some of these you will be familiar with, others not. How many do you recognize from this list? Arthur D. Little's Life Cycle Matrix; the Boston Consultancy Group's Growth Share Matrix; Citicorp's Interaction Analysis; Dow-Corning's Strategy Matrix; General Electric's Matrix; Harrigan-Porter's End-Game Analysis; King's Strategic-Issue Analysis; the Orchard Matrix of Market Attractiveness; Porter's Value Chain Analysis; and Real Options.

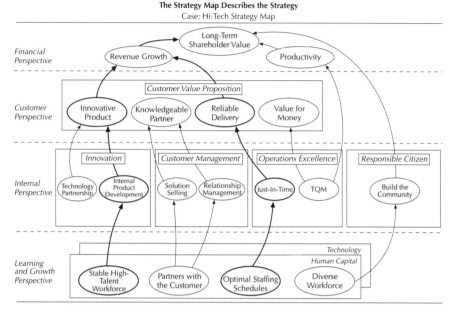

The Strategy Map Describes the Strategy
Case: Hi-Tech Strategy Map

Figure 3.2 Strategy views. Copyright © 2001 Balanced Scorecard Collaborative, Inc. (bscol.com).

This multitude of differing approaches, along with your particular
favourite, can be built into GMAS with just a few modifications. Each
of the tools mentioned above are described in the Glossary at the back
of this book.

Recent Strategic Planning Models

The Balanced Scorecard approach developed by Kaplan and Norton
has been widely adopted by many of the world's largest companies,
and software to support its deployment has been developed by some of
the world's leading names in the software industry. The model featured in Figure 3.2 involves the strategy being viewed from four
different perspectives, namely, the financial, the customer, the internal
and from learning and growth.

The Financial View

The ultimate objective of this view is to 'improve shareholder value'. Improved shareholder value comes as a consequence of the offsetting of income growth against increased productivity within the company. The factors of income growth and productivity both consist of two main subsections. Within income growth, the contributing factors are the expansion of the market and the increasing of income from the present client base. The two factors that lead to increased productivity are increased efficiency and better use of current resources combined with large investments being replaced by gradual investments.

The Customer View

Kaplan and Norton describe this section as 'the heart of the strategy'. This area outlines the exact strategy for gaining new custom or for enlarging the current customers' division of business.

The Internal View

This view outlines the corporate processes and exact actions that a company must perfect in order to maintain the customer view, which as has already been said is fundamental to the model.

Learning and Growth View

Kaplan and Norton (2001) outline the 'unquantifiable' resources that are necessary in order to allow the goals of organizational actions and client–company interaction, carried out at increasingly sophisticated levels, to be achieved. There are three main sections to be considered within the learning and growth view. The first is that of strategic capabilities. This section encapsulates the knowledge and abilities demanded from the staff in order to maintain the strategy. The second section is that of 'strategic technologies' (Kaplan and Norton 2001: 93). This part is concerned with the technological requirements that are necessary to maintain the strategy. The third and final section that contributes to the learning and growth view is that of environment for activity. Within this the effect of shifts in the social atmosphere of the organization are taken into account as the optimum environment in which to maintain the strategy is examined.

This model is very powerful and where organizations have adopted a BSC approach to communicating strategy throughout the company, then GMAS is a great add-on. What GMAS does, that is not covered in the BSC, is to ensure that the strategy is right and detects when it needs to be modified in the light of market conditions.

This, coupled with the ability to detect and respond to operational execution errors, means that the risk in a company using this system can be substantially reduced when it is paired with GMAS.

Short Termism and Quarterly Horizons

Perhaps the biggest single hindrance to strategic planning and the long-term shareholder value proposition is the quarterly reporting feeding frenzy. The analysts, press and day traders speculate on results, encouraging executives to promise more each quarter and punish the share price of those who cannot deliver. The pressure on the chief operating officers (COO), chief finance officer (CFO) and (CEO) is enormous. As much as 50 per cent of the CEO's time can be absorbed in dealing with the markets and providing information that is often competitively sensitive, to keep the share price high.

There are some great examples of companies forced to disclose intentions to keep shareholders happy only to find that a competitor is able to beat them to the market. One example in the Internet browser market: the prize for innovation goes to Netscape who are often first to announce a new service only to find Microsoft brings it to market quicker. Why does Netscape announce its intentions? Shareholder pressure.

Loyalty Key to Getting the Shareholders Off Your Back
In 1996, Frederick F. Reichheld wrote a book entitled *The Loyalty Effect: The Hidden Force Behind Growth, Profits and Lasting Value* in which he describes types of shareholder. The basic argument is that if you want to reduce share price volatility then plan to have loyal investors. Actively pursue investors with a high loyalty tendency. Reichheld names Leo Burnett, MBNA and A. G. Edwards, among others, as examples of companies that have experienced and benefited from high levels of loyalty.

Others seeking to dispel market volatility always give warnings. For example, Chambers, CEO of Cisco was warning of a downturn in his sector a year before it occurred. The result was that Cisco was the last to be hit when the downturn finally came in 2001.

Gaps in the Product Life Cycle

Moore (1995) points out in his book: *Inside the Tornado* that the product life cycle has a gap —the 'chasm'. Moore describes the chasm as a stage that exists when 'the early market's interest wanes but the mainstream market is still not comfortable with the immaturity of the solutions available' and describes strategies high tech companies can adopt to successfully cross the chasm.

What Moore fails to tell us is that there are chasms throughout the product life cycle and the higher the company climbs the deeper the chasms. I suggest that in addition to Moore's chasm between early market and mainstream there are chasms between growth and maturity, and another between maturity and decline. These chasms are littered with the bodies of CEOs who failed to appreciate that they were near the edge, or who simply did not want to believe it until they had marched the company up and over the cliff. This 'lemming thinking' is unfortunately all too common; you just have to look at most markets' growth projections for evidence.

Accepting that companies grow and decline just as their products do means that strategic planning is more important than ever for long-term success and there are at least a few investors interested in long-term growth that can claim to have out-performed the market with their strategy. So how come so many companies fall into these chasms and have to be rescued by the 'downsize kings'? Why was there no indication of the problems? Why was no one listening to reports from the field? Why were sales returns rapidly rising just after the end of each quarter? The answer may be summed up in the old adage of 'there are none so blind as those who do not want to see, and none so deaf as those who do not want to listen'.

Here is a story you may find interesting. MMSI was once brought in to investigate quality issues in a global company. Once there we found that there was a backlog of some 600 units returned from customers apparently awaiting fault testing. Each unit had a value ranging from $10 000 to $50 000—that equated to a potential of $30 million lost revenue. We initiated a short-cut process to have returns units checked for faults so we could get to the source of the problem. To our surprise the majority came back as 'no fault found'. On investigation it was clear that there was nothing wrong with the returned units,

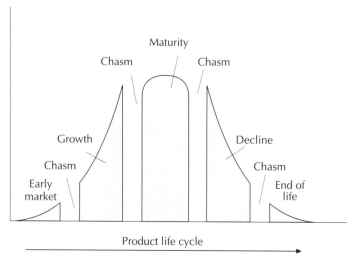

Figure 3.3 Product life cycle showing multiple chasms.

they had simply not been ordered. Having been delivered to large organizations it took them a few weeks to determine that they had not ordered them and to return them. The sales targets were met in the quarter, presumably the sales commissions got paid and there was a hope that things would be better next quarter. Of course, things never got better, and this fraud was what was allowing the company to reach its quarterly sales targets, the scale getting bigger each quarter. Who wanted this information uncovered? Not the CEO: we got fired!

There are profit opportunities at all stages of product life cycles and companies such as Atlas Copco, who in the 1980s prided themselves on being the last man in the market, can capitalize on this. Their CEO of 1985 said words to the effect of: 'If we had been blacksmiths we would have had the largest market share and be making the last horse shoes for the last people holding on to their horses, but boy would they have had to pay some money for the horse shoes they needed'. High market share in a mature or declining market is, after all, a cash cow position. So why are companies so reluctant to accept their market position and plan accordingly? Probably because the focus has always been on this quarter's results and with firefighting resulting from a lack of a strategic focus, they are simply not in control of their own destiny.

Real Time Wrong Time

Regis McKenna (1997) outlines the need to utilize real-time data in his book *Real Time: Preparing for the Age of the Never Satisfied Customer*. In developing GMAS it became quite obvious that real-time data has its limitations. The problems arise from two sources: reliability and volume, which lead to apathy or procrastination.

Data is not always reliable and, like plans, are full of the three Fs of Fact, Faith and Fiction. If data is taken in real time then there is a danger of it being accepted as fact when it is actually fiction if data collection is incomplete. Therefore, while you can collect data in real time it is most effectively judged in combination with other sources, some of which are likely not to be available in real time.

Managers subjected to real-time data feeds quickly stop looking at the data, often because of its questionable reliability, but more often because of the sheer volume of data that can be gathered. There is no effective filter process to sift out erroneous, incomplete or irrelevant data. Thus, the managers get swamped with data that they cannot use at that time, and the sheer volume makes it difficult to find if needed at a later date.

However, there are considerable advantages to having information in real time in fast moving markets, but these advantages are dwarfed by the benefits of having data at the right time. That is to say, we should gather data in real time, but deliver it at the right time. This can only be done effectively by understanding why the data is needed in the first place; what the data is being used for, how reliable it is and who and how decisions will be made based on the data collected. By answering these questions data can be delivered that is accurate, at the right time and given to the right people to make the right decisions.

GMAS incorporates the philosophy of gathering only needed data, making that information irrefutable, utilizing its 'real-time-right-time' methodology to turn data into market intelligence, and disseminates the information quickly and effectively using the Enterprise Neuron Trails (ENT), a GMAS module described in Chapter 4. This effectively avoids the danger of swamping managers with data they do not really need, or cannot use, and ensures when data is supplied that it is taken seriously and acted upon.

WHAT NEEDS TO BE DONE TO MAKE PLANNING WORK?

Planning in today's environment is more critical than ever. However, the old, and even some of the most recent models, fail to deliver an effective solution to the ever-increasing fast market-cycle times. Quarterly horizons make us vulnerable to avoidable chasms, while failure to consider all the publics means that there are gaps in the corporate strategy in relation to investor loyalty planning. All this means that short-term operational issues dominate management's agenda. Rather than start afresh and throw out the models developed to date GMAS has taken the best elements from each and modified them to fit into today's environment.

The principle used was simple: if it works find out why, when, where and how and then only apply that model when you can identify similar conditions.

Because models do not work every time they are often discredited and a search for a new better model is undertaken, but it is not surprising models stop working or do not work every time they are applied, this is because the environment in which they are being applied may be different. Understanding the why, where, when and how of strategic planning and operational initiatives allows failure of some models to be predicted and more suitable models to be recommended that better fit the environment being encountered by the organization. There is more on this in Chapter 7, which describes how GMAS modules are designed and built.

The following section discusses the theories and ideas that have been incorporated into GMAS.

McKinsey's 7-S model

The McKinsey 7-S model is an effective aid to understanding the factors that make up an organization, how they interact and how changing one element has a knock-on effect on all the others.

Cobbler's Shoes

I have recently performed a relatively straightforward (or so I had envisaged) change of taking MMSI from being a private limited company (Ltd) to a public limited company (plc). I found myself caught

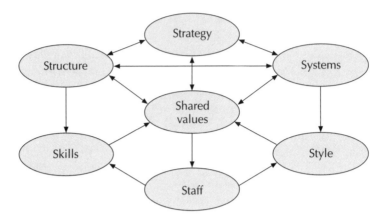

Figure 3.4 McKinsey's 7-S model. Copyright © 1979 McKinsey & Company.

up in a major change process instead of the simple change in name and a few more accountancy reporting requirements I had imagined the process would involve. Inadvertently, because of the new legal reporting requirements, I was upsetting the style and structure of the company and this had knock-on effects in the skills required, staff attitudes, systems and produced a major misalignment in shared values within the company almost overnight. This resulted in staff changes and loyalty being tested to the limit. This was a relatively minor change that had major consequences. How firms like KPMG and Accenture are faring, moving from partnerships to partial flotation, I am watching with interest. This process, I am sure, will provide Harvard Business School's course on heading professional service firms with years' worth of case study material and will illustrate the difficulties, even within the top consultancy firms, of making a change to the elements of the 7-S model.

Freeing the Mind Creativity

Having an open mind is essential for effective strategic planning, as is astute situational awareness, the ability to identify and understand patterns in data and the ability to be creative.

These are two quite distinct traits that are not naturally associated. If the old stereotypes are to be given credence, creative people cannot be analytical and analytical types cannot be creative. There are some interesting companies that have exploited this niche offering courses for business analysts on how to be more creative and creative people how to be more businesslike. These two activities, often referred to as right- (creative-) and left- (analytical-) brain activities, can be developed and right-brain dominated individuals can find that by becoming good at left-brain activities they enhance their right-brain skills and vice versa. Both Tony Buzan and Edward De Bono provide a wealth of literature on how the mind works and on how to benefit from whole brain thinking (e.g. Buzan, 2000; DeBono, 1970). Anecdotal evidence suggests that some of the best minds in history have excelled in more than one discipline. Take Leonardo de Vinci and Albert Einstein for example: both of these notable figures excelled in creative and analytical activities.

With an increasing need to understand patterns in information and gain meaning from multiple sources, often containing conflicting data, it is not surprising that software tools have been developed to make this activity easier.

These tools generate logic paths that allow people not present during strategy discussions to understand the logic of the strategy and how it has been derived. These tools are used in the building of a GMAS strategy as the critical assumptions on which it is based must be understood and clearly defined. Appendix 1 provides a list of the software tools available to make strategic planning easier by assisting the effective handling of multiple data streams.

Breakthrough Marketing

Breakthrough marketing was developed from the work of Gerald Nadler and Shozo Hibino who described the concept in their book entitled *Breakthrough Thinking* (1994). This is a complex but highly rewarding read. Their model provides a methodology with which multiple stakeholder groups can effectively address intricate problems/issues. By following the process, breakthroughs can, quite literally, be achieved to what at first appear to be insoluble problems.

Nadler and Hibino present seven principles that provide a practical framework that can be employed to solve complex issues. As production of an effective strategy for a large or growing company in a turbulent, ever-changing market is a complex issue, the theory and practices recommended by Nadler and Hibino have been adopted by GMAS simply because they work. The modifications made by GMAS are minor compared to the power that the seven principles bring to a strategic planning process. This will be discussed in greater detail in Chapter 4.

GMAS provides a framework that enables the use of Nadler's and Hibino's concepts in the context of strategic and operational planning.

Publics/Stakeholder Maps

One of the fundamental mistakes of many plans is that they do not consider the customer's perspective. However, the old question still arises rather quickly: Who is the customer? In order to answer this question you must first map the organization's interactions with the world around it. We soon find a multitude of connections.

The British Red Cross (BRC) helps the needy by providing, for example, volunteers. There is therefore a relationship between the BRC and the volunteer. Similarly, there is a relationship between the volunteer and the needy. In addition, there is also a need for the BRC to get the funds required to help the needy and in this case the funds come from the public, you and me, therefore we also have a relationship with the needy. The great success of Live Aid was a direct result of the public seeing the needy literally dying in front of them. All of these relationships, or interactions, have an exchange process attached to them. For example, the volunteers give up their time, learn new skills and provide a service for the BRC. What does the BRC provide them with in exchange? If you have ever been fortunate enough to work with these exceptional people, you will know that they have a mixture of motives for working for a charity. Motives can range from guilt—perhaps not having been able to help at the scene of an accident—through enhanced self-image to truly altruistic motives. The BRC caters for a wide range of needs. Similarly, there is an interaction between the volunteer and those being helped, the public and the BRC. Each one has a complex set of interchanges, which, if mutually beneficial, will continue. However, when a volunteer is asked to give too much then the relationship breaks down. Each year some of the elderly in our society die from hypothermia rather than ask for help. Help at the cost of loss of pride may be too high a price for them to pay. Therefore, in order for an agency such as the BRC to help it must first ensure that it considers each of these interchanges.

Publics maps draw out these relationships and allow the nature of the exchange and the balance to be considered. Put simply, you have a customer if you profit from the relationship. Thus the BRC has three customer groups: the public, the volunteers and the needy. The BRC profits from the work of the volunteers, it achieves its mission by helping the needy and it gains its funds from the public. In all three relationships the BRC profits. Therefore it is in the BRC's interest to treat each of these groups as customers, to understand and monitor the relationships and to strategically plan for the long-term so that it can maximize its 'profit' from the publics or stakeholders.

The second advantage of publics maps is that you can determine where the relationship is not profitable from your company's perspective; these are areas where you can make savings.

Ideally, you will want relationships to be mutually profitable. By this it is meant that both sides of the exchange believe they are achieving profits. This has been done very effectively by the BRC, because profits are multiperspective items. Labour may be considered by a volunteer to be less valuable than the sense of achievement they gain from helping. While, for the BRC, giving a sense of achievement to its volunteers may be relatively easily achieved when compared to the cost of employing, managing and motivating staff to undertake work carried out by the volunteers. With both parties treating each other as the customer, a mutually beneficial partnership is born.

A third benefit is what you do not see when you draw up your publics maps. On a creative thinking course one of my clients was running, one of the exercises was to draw a plant. Art was not my strong point at school and you can imagine the outcome—I think a five-year-old could have done better! What they then said was to stop trying to draw the plant, but instead draw the spaces around the plant. What a difference. I produced a much more recognizable drawing of the plant. This came as a great surprise. Often the spaces are more important than the object that fills your view and what is missing from the publics map is just as revealing, what should I see? What relationships are we missing out on?

The publics mapping is a vital ingredient in gaining a true under-standing of the relationships between your organization and its stake-holders and should be drawn out early in the planning process.

Real-time Right Time

I have already discussed the limitations of real-time information flows. What differentiates GMAS from real-time strategy models, is that it accepts that real time is not relevant but right time is. Getting even partial information at the right time can be more helpful than com-plete information at the wrong time. In the 2001 high tech stock falls on the worlds markets, knowing the history and watching the share prices fall in real time was too late to prevent value loss. However, leading indicators foretold the crash, and numerous high tech com-panies not meeting their projections throughout 2000 should have given prudent investors enough warning of pending problems. Thus, knowing what is critical to confidence and monitoring that results in leading indicators of problems ahead. This information delivered to the right people at the right time means that they can take the right action or be prepared for real-time data to trigger action that has been previously modelled.

The challenge is to keep real-time data flowing, but to understand its meaning, using trends and history to predict events. By modelling various scenarios it is possible to determine the sequence of events that are required to trigger the scenario. Thus, by monitoring the real-time data for these triggers and only reporting when triggers are active, managers can access as much data as is available on which to make a decision. This, of course, does not prevent managers from making the wrong decisions, but it should provide them with enough advanced warning for them to get it right at least 80 per cent of the time.

In research there are two types of error known as type 1 and type 2 error. Type 1 occurs when you reject a hypothesis that is true and type 2 error occurs when you accept a hypothesis that is false. It is important to understand this in the context of real-time right-time decision making.

If we make a decision based on what we believe to be fact and in reality the information is true, then we have made no error. This is also the case when we believe the information to be faith and it is true or when we believe information to be fiction and it is. However, life is not that simple—there are dangers lurking. It is possible that what we believe to be fact and faith can turn out to be fiction and we can therefore make the wrong decisions. Likewise, what we consider to be fiction can turn out to be true and again this can lead us to make the wrong decisions.

We can reduce the probability of error by combining data sources and by commissioning further research to reduce the risk of being mislead by false information or information we disregard because we believe it to be fiction. It is therefore imperative to have access to research methodologies that can be believed and verified speedily and accurately. GMAS provides systems to do this and thus allows real-time–right-time information to be verified in hours, or at most a few days, 80 per cent of the time. There is more detail on these methodologies in Chapter 6.

Methodical, Boring, Plodding but Effective Systems

One thing I should point out is that most of GMAS is really dull, boring, plodding routine and so it should be. To detect change and opportunity you need to have a very strong handle on what is normal. Fortunately, there are computers to get rid of most of the tedium of monitoring and reporting, but they still have not invented a computer that is better than a human at distinguishing patterns in unrelated data and thinking outside the box. So while 80 per cent of GMAS is routine, 20 per cent calls for the talents of your best thinkers and strategists to ensure that your organization achieves its full potential. Unlike those concerned with annual planning or the five-year planning cycle, the team which utilizes GMAS has to be available at short notice and be able to produce the goods quickly. Therefore, there are two sets of individuals needed in GMAS teams: the first is a group of very talented perfectionists who can pay attention to detail and the second a group of generalist visionaries who can think well and truly outside the box. A strategy team consisting entirely of out of the box thinkers will not provide the right balance nor will having your team full of perfectionists. The balance is crucial, as is an understanding of each other's role because these two groups normally do not interact well unless carefully managed. However, the benefits from being balanced will allow your company to gain a global marketing advantage, making the effort of bringing such groups together extremely rewarding.

SUMMARY

- We have reviewed the issues in strategic planning and have concluded that planning can be effective if we tie it to operational planning, that it can detect paradigm shift and that some of the strategic planning process can become formalized under GMAS.

- Plans contain the three Fs of Fact, Faith and Fiction that can be difficult to determine, therefore we have to make assumptions and monitor and test them to detect the three Fs. There are a number of strategic planning tools at our disposal and usually a number of initiatives active in the organization at any one time.

- We have seen how short-term horizons can impede strategic planning and that shareholder loyalty will become a major issue in the 21st century.

- The product life cycle has been shown not to be a continuum and that it has several chasms that will trip up the unwary company.

- Finally, we have seen how too much information delivered at the wrong time is counter-productive and real-time–right-time information is the ideal model.

4

Creating the Perfect STORM

THE GMAS PLANNING PROCESS

GMAS is highly adaptable and can be used in conjunction with your preferred planning model. Where it differs from other strategy tools is in relation to breakthrough marketing, the acceptance of the three Fs and the need for the meticulous gathering of the critical assumptions upon which the strategy is being developed.

Fast-Moving Market Issues

In fast-moving markets, it is often difficult to find anything that does not appear to be changing. Finding a feature that you can get a bearing on is a challenging task. Historic trends are dismissed because the past does not appear to be any kind of predictor of the future, paradigms change constantly and speed to market is king. Predicting the future appears to be futile. Yet, on closer examination, the old adage comes to mind: 'There is nothing new under the sun'. Fast-moving markets are as much about perception as reality. Yes, the speed of change has quickened, but our forefathers were probably as shocked by the speed of change in their time that came with the expansion of the railways, telephone and road building. The pace of life would have appeared, in their day, to represent immense change at breakneck speed; and it was, from their perspective.

Speed to market and the rate of change has increased significantly but so has the general pace of life for the majority of the countries of the world. We deal with a constant 24 hours a day, 7 days a week (24-7) world yet mills in the 18th and 19th century in Scotland, e.g. New Lanark Mill from 1820–21 were running 24-6, staff including children, working as much as 84 hours a week, while sailing ships raced around the clock to bring tea and fine porcelain from China to Europe and America. Perhaps we can therefore relax a bit more about the speed of change in the certain knowledge that our grandchildren will consider our rate of change to be nothing compared to what they have to deal with.

When dealing with such dynamic markets it is necessary to adopt the KISS principle (Keep It Short and Simple). Events will happen or they won't, information is Fact, Faith or Fiction and therefore we can create scenarios for each one of the most likely outcomes. To adopt a simplistic model is not to ignore all the complexity of the markets or your organization, lead times and supplier contract. However, before considering them, cut to the core of the business and deal on, at first, a simplistic level, before building the flexibility into your strategy to cope with the dynamics of your market.

Flexibility is built around a few core elements. Take for example, Cisco systems. How does it manage such a diverse range of businesses and deal with, up until the 2000 high tech stock 'downturn', a phenomenal growth rate and yet maintain command and control? Well, it appears to have a simple set of guidelines for managers that apply whatever type of business. If you are doing the following: making us a profit, satisfying our customers and increasing the rate at which we can grow, then you are doing the right thing. If you are not: STOP, because you are doing the wrong thing. Cisco realized long ago that it needed to do things smarter than its competitors because its scenarios showed that there would always be a shortage of the kind of skills its business required. In order to maintain the technological lead that it was building on it knew it would have to be more innovative than its competitors, yet in-house development in large firms would be too slow, and in any case it did not know in which area the next breakthrough would emerge.

Starting simply with a core set of values that any manager can judge and be judged upon is essential to maintain control on a very rapid growth company. [Cisco grew from nothing to $23.6 billion revenue (last four quarters to March 2001) in 17 years, that is what I call growth].

Cisco accepted the market reality, made its business aware of the issues, and designed a way around its problems. As one manager told me when I asked him if it had ever failed to achieve what it set out to do, 'We never fail, sometimes it takes us longer than expected to get there, and we learn a lot on the way'. This reminded me of the old saying 'Experience is the name given to one's mistakes'. It solved the skills shortage it anticipated by building some of the most advanced web-based support systems on the market today. This effectively multiplied its 'corporate knowledge'. Cisco solved its 'innovators dilemma' by developing the ability to select and help fund innovative ideas, by spotting innovation, acquiring a share and learning how to integrate that knowledge and then exploiting its ability to scale and bring new technology to the market quickly. This, coupled with an internal and external model of measuring customer satisfaction, ensured that it enhanced the customer experience and value perception.

Therefore, do not reject scenarios planning. It is vital to understand the future and using GMAS, the scenario that eventually comes into being can be anticipated. Keep the core philosophy simple by determining what is truly critical and putting that in a simple format so that everyone can understand the priorities and measure themselves against it.

Most companies have mission or vision statements that are either the same as every other company, or which get so complex no one in the organization can remember them, let alone apply them to the day-to-day running of the business.

Paradigm Shift

The example of Cisco Systems showed its strategy for dealing with paradigm shift. The alternative, as one manager from Cisco told me, is simply to back all new technology. From the way he said it, I was not sure whether he was saying that that was the strategy of Cisco or that it had developed a better way of finding the next wave. A small bet on all new innovations, might be a very good way of keeping a finger in all the pies and providing yourself with the knowledge about what to eventually buy into. Perhaps this option is cheaper than running an R&D department in-house.

Real Options analysis is perhaps the real secret. GMAS uses Real Options analysis to determine what investments are justified.

The *Innovators Dilemma* by Clayton Christensen (1997) is an essential read for anyone in new product development or in a company that has an R&D function. With Cisco's experience in mind and having read Christensen's work, Marketing Management Services International plc set aside some $3000\,\text{ft}^2$ ($300\,\text{m}^2$) for a hothouse facility which was given the name Exploiting Global Opportunities (eGO). Christensen (1997) points out that in-house R&D is great at providing incremental innovation, but consistently fails to generate paradigm shift, even when the technology is understood.

Christensen gives the example of the 3.5 inch disk drive, among many others. He highlights how the market leader in disk drives prior to the invention of the 3.5 inch drive had chosen not to proceed with its development and as a result, it lost its market lead. New entrants soon succeeded where it had failed. Why had the market leader not detected how important the 3.5 inch disk drive would be? It was market leader for good reason; it had an excellent reputation due to incremental innovations on the large disk drives and its marketing team was first class. Perhaps it did everything too well? It had surveyed its customers, IBM being the largest of them at that time, and found that they did not want smaller disc drives. Instead they wanted more capacity and size was not an issue with mainframe design. The customer research considered that the technology was not going to be useful to their customers and naturally it dropped further development.

What had it done wrong? It conducted market research—surely that was the correct thing to do? GMAS has many modules dedicated to customer satisfaction research. Are they wasted? No. The answer is that there are two types of innovation; incremental and discontinuous (paradigm shift type). Incremental improvements are predictable, can be measured by customer research and are relatively easy for internal R&D departments to produce. Discontinuous innovation is not easy for R&D departments to recognize, even when they have invented the potential innovation, because the basis of the end-user purchase will differ from that in the current market. Therefore, researching the current market would only find that there was not a market. This problem has long been understood by artists and is in my opinion why many are so poor. If Picasso, Miro or Dali had conducted re-search prior to painting, they would have been portrait or landscape painters and the world would, creatively, be a poorer place for it. Artists who want to be different must effectively create a paradigm shift. They must convince the community, patrons and critics to view art in a different way. They start with a vision and a great deal of faith. They believe against the odds in their idea and drive their vision into the marketplace. The same is required in discontinuous innovation in other fields. It has to be driven, it may not follow traditional distribu-tion channels, pricing models and risk profiles as housed in traditional R&D departments. If the concept is not driven, it is easily lost. I often visit the technology marketing divisions of some of the UK's former nationalized industries. With the innovations there left sitting on the shelf, it is no wonder some of the world's leading companies have hundreds of staff trawling through patents for the gold that lies there undiscovered. New types of research and market monitoring techniques have been developed within GMAS to locate, test and exploit these latent ideas. While detection of a developing paradigm shift with GMAS market monitoring a relatively easy thing to do, traditional companies find it difficult to first accept what is happening around them and secondly, to take the actions required until it is too late. Take Compaq Computers and Dell. Compaq was not blind, it could see what Dell was doing, it read the press, and it could see the impact on sales. Yet, it did nothing. Only after the CEO was replaced and several downsizings later, did things start to change. Why? The reason was that Compaq was locked into the old paradigm. It had too much invested in the old way and thought it had too much to lose if it changed. Dell overtook Compaq in market value and it had a market capitalization of $63.61 billion compared to Compaq's $27.18 billion according to the 9 July 2001 edition of *Business Week*.

Contrast this with Microsoft, who got caught out just by how fast the Internet was developing. Subsequently, it successfully fought off Oracle and Sun systems to maintain its position as number one.

Therefore, the GMAS eGO module was developed as a centre to help spin-outs from R&D departments develop paradigm shifting innovations, free from their corporate masters. The rationale being, for discontinuous innovation to develop, it must be free from the parent company and free to develop outside the required return of capital of its mature parent or their suffocating administration and rules. However, a 'golden share' provides a means by which, should the innovation become successful, the parent can buy it back and using the parent's ability to scale, drive the innovation to levels of very high market share, very quickly. For example, if Compaq had used the eGO centre to develop a competitive brand and distributed it in the same way as Dell, then there would have been two companies sharing the market. Compaq would have, in effect, denied Dell half its market which would have resulted in the situation of Dell at $32 billion and Compaq at $59 billion. The eGO offers a means by which market leaders can maintain their lead even when faced with paradigm shift.

Too many companies, perhaps yours, behave like Cronos, the Greek god, and eat their own children fearing they will become greater than themselves only to let someone else take the crown in the fullness of time.

Fact, Faith and Fiction

Fundamental to all decisions is the knowledge that is used to help a management team reach a decision. There are many, pure and not so pure, motives for providing a management team with information that may not be entirely accurate. Take profit, for example.

I remember the shock I got on asking my accountant after my first year in business: 'What was my final profit for the year?' To which he replied: 'What would you like it to be?' Depending on how you handle things like depreciation, cross charges, etc. you can easily manipulate profit figures quite legally! Therefore, the profitability of one business unit might be at the expense of a huge loss in another. Do not try to tell me it could never happen in your organization, I have heard that one too often!

Information *per se* is Fact, Faith or Fiction. It is imperative to try to distinguish between the three and where that is not possible make an assumption and monitor that assumption against real-time information to identify anything that strengthens your assumption or weakens it. GMAS has a range of complex monitoring tools to monitor the

Web, press, etc., but there are simple ways of monitoring your critical assumptions, the simplest being just to write them down and look at the list regularly, asking yourself: 'Have I heard anything that contradicts any of these assumptions? If so, how does that impact my strategy?'

In larger companies the sheer number of critical assumptions made during the planning process requires automated monitoring systems. George Orwell wrote in *Animal Farm* that 'All animals are equal but some are more equal than others'. The sentiment of this statement can be applied to critical assumptions; 'All assumptions are critical but some are more critical than others' and it is these that the management team needs to keep in the forefront of its mind.

STARTING THE GMAS PROCESS

The process of starting a GMAS plan is very similar to the typical strategic planning process. The main differences are:

1 A breakthrough marketing model is used.
2 Critical assumptions are discussed, assessed and recorded.
3 A spherical vision approach is adopted and public/stakeholder maps are produced.
4 Research must be irrefutable or have a full explanation of the inherent assumptions.

Breakthrough Marketing Model

As mentioned previously, breakthrough marketing is an approach to planning based upon 'breakthrough thinking', a model first developed by Gerald Nadler and Shozo Hibino (1994). There are seven principles you need to accept in breakthrough marketing. They are:

1 Your organization is unique and from that uniqueness you can derive a unique selling proposition (USP). By using the McKinsey 7-S model you can determine the unique make-up of your organization. Not only is your organization and selling proposition unique, but the strategy you derive will also be unique. I accept that you may borrow strategies from other fields or markets, but

they should only be utilized if you are sure the environment you are operating in is conducive to the working of borrowed strategy. Keep in mind what works in your unique circumstance and organization is likely to be itself unique.

2   You will have a spectrum of purposes (not a single purpose) and everyone involved in a complex organization may not all share the same ultimate goal. This is especially true if you are working in partnership with other organizations and developing a joint strategy. Having a spectrum of purposes will allow you to match your spectrum with others and identify the common ground quickly and constructively. This match will result in an agreement of a common purpose which, while not being your ultimate goal, will be beneficial to all and take you closer to your ultimate goal. This exercise is dependent on an accurate determination of publics. Publics are the business relationships or exchange processes that occur in and around the organization. Spherical Vision and associated publics maps are discussed later in this chapter.

3   There are always more decisions to be made in the future. Therefore, you must consider the impact of your strategy on future strategies aimed at achieving higher level goals in the purpose spectrum. In any plan, strategic or tactical, it is imperative to be aware that there will be other plans following, perhaps aimed at achieving higher purposes in the spectrum or necessitated by changing market conditions. Therefore, it is essential to consider future requirements within the context of planning today so that nothing is done that will hinder the future prospects for the organization or achievement of a future goal. This is particularly important in GMAS because purposes shift in line with market opportunity and it is already known that the strategic plan will, at some time, change and the mechanism to change strategy quickly and effectively is built into to the original plan.

4   Systems and metrics should be behind 80 per cent of any operational plan you produce. Only by developing systems can we consistently deliver faultless quality, ensure compliance from staff and that you have something solid to measure performance against. Customer service is considered a soft measure, yet customer service is considerably more predictable in companies that have adopted systems such as McDonald's, Pizza Hut and Taco Bell.

It is in effect what makes franchises and organizations scaleable and capable of ensuring quality control during rapid growth.

5   You do not need most of the information gathered during a traditional planning process therefore gather only *needed information*. There is no shortage of information in today's society. We are bombarded by information; the secret is turning that information into market intelligence. This is done by first being selective about what information you need. We continuously receive enquiries for market reports asking questions such as: 'What is the size of the market?' 'What is its growth rate?' 'What are competitors doing?' All these can be needed information, but in the majority of cases it is merely 'nice to know'. Huge amounts of time and billions of yen, pounds and dollars are spent gathering information that is not needed. Perhaps as much as 75 per cent of the world's total expenditure on market research is a waste of money simply because the information is not truly required and therefore never fully utilized. Unless there is a clear and actionable reason for gathering information it should not be gathered as only needed information is required. This has two very positive effects: (a) it reduces the amount of data required to be understood and therefore makes it much more user friendly when discussing strategy because vital information is not lost in the sheer volume of data and (b) it reduces the tendency for information paralysis where the sheer amount of information causes no action to be taken or analysis becomes so complex that management fails to understand what it means.

6   You must involve the people who will implement your plans in the planning process. People must be designed into the process of planning. This is the single most common factor in plans failing to be implemented. The plan may be quite brilliant in conception and have faultless, detailed system designs attached, but because the staff who will implement the strategy do not feel a part of the plan it fails to be effectively implemented. This is a danger, even when great care has been taken to involve the staff through strategy implementation planning initiatives and corporate communication reviews. This is because as new staff join the company or take up new roles they are often not embraced by what has become, by that time, a one-off planning exercise long passed. Hence

they start, slowly at first, questioning the plan and why things have to be done in a particular way and soon they have made 'minor adjustments'. Before long the plan is no longer aligned with the strategy of the organization. This can be avoided by having a continual planning process backed by effective organizational induction programmes providing new entrants with 'buy in' to the strategy. Therefore, changes they feel necessary are considered within a change management process, and, where beneficial, are adopted by the whole organization, leveraging the benefits of new knowledge or expertise.

7 A date stamp and betterment time line should be attached to all plans. Nothing lasts forever, no matter how well conceived, therefore every element of a GMAS strategy must have a date stamp indicating at which time it needs to be reviewed or bettered. This is especially true of systems that can quickly become obsolete in a dynamic market. Take Ascend Communications, a company making access products for the Internet Service Providers' (ISP) market in the 1990s. The new ISPs were interested in the latest features and locking out competitors was core to their success. That is to say that speed to market was the most important determinant of success. Users of the Internet, at that time, were mainly 'computer nerds' who were capable of spending hours fixing problems with the service and software provided and getting fun out of doing it. Reliability and new software, after all, tend not to go well together. Ascend became very successful at getting the product to market early, but the consequence of this was that its products often had bugs and were not too reliable.

The strategy of early release was very effective while the market was small, however, the consequence of early release was a need for high levels of field engineer support and as the market matured, engineers became a very expensive commodity. Internet customers wanted increased reliability because they were no longer 'computer nerds', but were increasingly becoming the general public who were used to telephones, televisions and other electrical goods that worked. They had no interest in unreliable connections or in spending hours finding work around options.

Ascend started to have problems, the strategy that had made it so

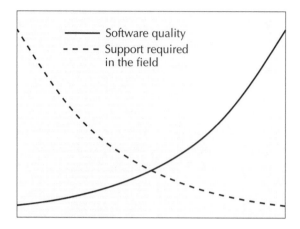

Software quality
Support required
in the field

Figure 4.1   Software quality and field engineer support required.

successful was not sustainable in a maturing market. As luck would have it, Lucent Technologies—famous for its Bell Laboratories—bought Ascend, some might say just at the right time. Lucent well respected for its 'Carrier Class' and quality was able to bring the new product development discipline to Ascend and improve quality and reliability at the right time for the maturing market.

By working within the framework discipline of the breakthrough marketing model, more effective and innovative strategies can be developed that are more focused, inclusive, measurable, flexible and adaptive.

Critical Assumptions

In the process of strategic planning a great deal of care must be taken to uncover and understand what are the truly critical assumptions, on which the thought process behind the strategic planning exercise is based. These must be monitored in real time to determine whether they are Fact, Faith or Fiction. If Fact, then more confidences may be justified, if Faith then proof may be needed, and when Fiction, a change in strategy may be called for.

Spherical Vision and Publics Maps

In order to understand the nature of the organization and its relationship with its stakeholders a publics map needs to be produced.

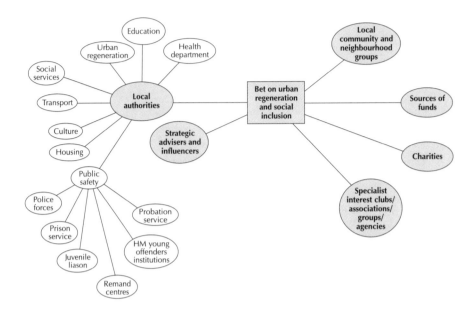

Figure 4.2   Map for work in inclusion and urban renewal projects.

Figure 4.2 shows a simplified publics map. The maps go into increasing detail ultimately linking to databases containing the contact details of key individuals in each stakeholder group. These maps are used to ensure participation of key individuals in the planning process from outside the company, e.g. suppliers and channel partners, and to ensure common purposes can be established between the most important stakeholder groups and the purpose of the organization.

Irrefutable Research

If we are going to gather only needed research, we can spend more time, care and attention to its collection and interpretation. New innovative research methodologies have been developed by MMSI with the aim of ensuring that, as far as it is possible, the research gathered from primary sources such as focus groups, face-to-face interviews and telephone interviews is absolutely irrefutable. Great care must be taken to ensure the quality of the market intelligence, and using a research company that does not have BSEN ISO 9001 registration, BS7911 (1998) registration, IIP accreditation or similar quality assurance procedures should not be considered. The old adage commonly used in computer circles is just as true in strategic planning: 'garbage in, garbage out'.

MARKETING PLANNING GMAS STYLE

As an example of a GMAS planning task I am going to use a marketing planning process. It represents, in most commercial organizations, a major part of the business planning process and is instrumental in seeing the business plan move from faith to reality.

Like all the elements of GMAS, you can choose to use your own preferred planning outline provided you follow the GMAS rules. I have taken the specific GMAS marketing planning module outline and will discuss the process.

Internal Review

Like most planning exercises the first port of call is the information held within the organization such as sales records, customer lists, market reports, etc. This was traditionally called a 'marketing audit'. However, the term 'audit' has fallen out of favour and you may prefer to refer to it as a 'review'. Audit, review, call it what you will, is the starting point. There is no point reinventing the wheel, if the information is already at hand (*needed information only* remember).

The information is held in two principle places within an organization, the filing system and/or in the heads of the staff. There has been a lot of developments in providing corporate knowledge bases and even appointing corporate knowledge managers, but what I have seen 'on the ground' has a few years' work ahead of it before it will replace the CEO's PA as the centre of knowledge within an organization. I am convinced they know more than the CEO! If they do not know the answer to your question they can always direct you, accurately, to a person who does.

By far the easiest to access is the staff and they are usually the fastest route to reports or previous work done. Therefore, information is divided into three types: formal, informal and managerial.

Formal information is the information found in hard copy, computer files, etc. This should be reviewed where it is likely to contain

needed information or can lead the researcher to the source of needed
information.

All reports should be catalogued so that three important things are
drained from them:

1   The date range for which the report is current and when it is due
    to be replaced. For example, there are league tables of the UK's
    top strategic marketing consultancies published annually pro-
    duced *Management Consultancy* magazine in the July/August
    2001 edition. We expect to maintain our position within the top
    10 and much of our marketing materials make claim to that pos-
    ition. Much of what we plan to do is based on that position and if
    we fail to achieve a top 10 rating it has implications for our strat-
    egy. Therefore, in our 2002 marketing plan we assume that we will
    remain in the top 10 and on publication of the magazine, we can
    reclassify our 'faith' that we will be in the top 10 with the fact that
    we are.

    Thus, each year the magazine issue must be reviewed and our
    position verified. If we remain at number 8 we do nothing, if we
    slip back or move up the table we report at the STORM meeting.
    The article is valid for one year.

2   The critical assumptions, on which the findings in the report have
    been made, must be teased out. These should be monitored for
    changes during the valid period of the forecast. If a report sug-
    gested that the market for CRM systems is growing at 40 per cent
    per annum, we must ask how that figure has been derived. Is it
    based on an extrapolation of the cumulative sales of the principal
    suppliers of CRM systems or on customers buying intentions or
    the wishful thinking of some CRM providers? If it turns out to
    have been based on the cumulative sales, any profit warnings and
    quarterly reports will support or refute the assumption. However,
    if it was based on buyer intentions, overall buyer confidence
    monthly surveys would be a good source of confirmation during
    the period of the forecast.

    Where a forecast is a combination of factors, perhaps including
    gut feeling, then the assumptions being used may in isolation not
    be critical, but the combination of factors is. For example, in the
    court case concerning the killing of Jill Dando, a journalist shot

dead in London, her murderer Barry George was convicted on a combination of evidence. Each individual item in isolation was not enough to convict a man of murder but when combined, was sufficiently compelling that a jury could find him guilty. Using GMAS fuzzy logic models (I will explain more in Chapter 6), what leads to a combined critical assumption can be modelled and the elements monitored. By monitoring the environment, the computer can judge whether the combinations of assumptions are changing sufficiently to require a change in the forecast.

3   The authors of the reports or forecasts should also be monitored for new reports that they may issue in the same field, which may or may not reinforce their earlier work. In 2000 and 2001 the US Federal Reserve chairman Alan Greenspan made statements about the economy and, in particular, interest rate cuts. If your strategic plan had a critical assumption regarding interest rates, taking an opinion at one point in time would be acceptable only if you monitored Greenspan's ongoing statements and they did not contradict his forecast of the US economic performance. If they do, the assumption made that interest rates would continue to be cut would be compromised. Therefore, you may require a speedy rethink of your strategy.

Combining Real Options with this model provides very powerful tools for strategic decision making. More on this in my next book.

Publics maps

Publics maps need to be produced to ensure that from the internal and external audits you understand all the stakeholders and wider publics that will have an impact on your business and in this example specifically the marketing function.

The publics maps give a guide as to the groups that you should survey. In this context, candidates will include competitors, new customers, existing customers, lapsed customers, bid analysis, trade or industry influencers. The map further allows the balance of the relationships to be judged and various scenarios considered, helping to identify prospective areas for strategic partnerships.

External Review

The external review is where the company collects needed information not held within the company. This can involve you in the whole spectrum of market research techniques, but must above all provide you with reliable data and preferably irrefutable data.

Like the police detective trying to solve a case, one piece of research or evidence can often generate more questions than it can answers. It can also appear to contradict other data, and when involving perceptional research provide a complex mixture of information that contains a good mix of the three Fs. If you are using grounded theory, you are more like the detective than ever as the method quite closely follows the model of how a detective would work. It can be highly effective at delivering needed information in a short time frame compared with the more traditional research approaches.

SWOT/PEST

The results from the audits, are analysed in some kind of framework. My favourite is still the SWOT analysis, although we never report it in that order. We prefer SWTO as the last thing you want to leave your audience with is a threat. Instead we leave them to consider the opportunities. There are a great many options for how to conduct this analytical phase of the planning process and a number of software packages, discussed in Appendix 1, which can help.

Active Strategy Facilitation

I have often been present when boards are meeting to discuss their plans and a facilitator has been brought in to help ensure open, fair and frank discussion. Where this works well is where the board itself can challenge each other and their respective thinking and have a good understanding of all areas of the business. However, all too often the facilitator is weak, but intelligent enough to know who is the boss. Instead of ensuring a robust discussion which results in an action plan that all board members subscribe to, they simply ensure that the will of the dominant directors is documented for the passive directors to implement.

Perhaps I am being unfair, but I feel the best facilitators are those that have a good knowledge of the industry and are in their own right of the same calibre as the board itself. They then challenge from a position of knowledge and respect and are not frightened to go head to head with the tough nuts on the board. Ultimately, they are diplomats, good communicators and effective facilitators in that action items are recorded and plans are produced. Most importantly, they ensure that all the board members have been involved and contributed their best.

It is too easy for the board to get detached from what is happening on the ground when you consider that they may be spending most of their time with investors. When companies grow, the dictatorial drive needed, some may say, to drive a rapid growth business must give way to a more professional approach. All the rapid growth companies I know are lead by strong CEOs, as well as most of those I do not know, after all you do not get to be the CEO of a global company by being weak and timid; in the same way as you cannot lead the armies of workers for long without a degree of magnetism and drive. Whatever the personality, strong or weak, the best strategy comes from one which is understood and communicated throughout the organization and to which all the stakeholders can subscribe. This cannot be achieved without true communications and the meeting of minds, and therefore the choice of facilitator is vital to the success of the strategic planning process.

More needed Research in Quick Time

After the initial phase of the set of strategy meetings there are inevitably more questions that need to be answered. These questions have to be answered quickly if the excitement and enthusiasm generated by the strategy meetings are not to be lost to intrigue and politics.

Therefore, as it is inevitable that there will be questions to answer, a small team of researchers should have previously been convened, and if previous primary research was conducted, a research pool established (more on this in Chapter 8). A research pool consists of respondents who have agreed to take part in further research and have stated a preferred method of contact. These groups are vital if opinions are to be gathered between strategy planning meetings, as there is not normally the time to go through a typical *ad hoc* research programme to answer the specific questions raised during the planning process.

The majority of questions asked would relate to beliefs, gut feeling or perceptions expressed by the strategic team members. These can normally be dealt with in one of two ways. Simply commission the required research and report the outcome or add to a testing list. The testing list is a list of assumptions that at some time will need to be tested but have not been classified as urgent and important. All assumptions are ranked by importance, even when they are all classified as critical. There are three categories colour coded, red, blue and green. Red assumptions are considered both urgent and important and therefore confirmation is a priority. Blue assumptions are considered important but not urgent, these are usually placed on the testing list and scheduled for testing at some time during the life of the strategy. Green assumptions are everything else that would be nice to know, but if they were never investigated it would not have a large impact on the company.

Let me give you an example. In a railway engineering company, knowing the projected spend by Railtrack (the track owners) on track maintenance was considered red (urgent and important) and knowing the likely location of the spend was also considered red. Knowing the nature of the work likely to be done was considered blue (important but not urgent), while knowing the buyers' profiles was considered green (nice to know). This is because without knowing the size of the market, the geographic proximity estimates could not be made on what Railtrack would need to invest in. Knowing the nature of the work allowed the most appropriate equipment to be purchased, while knowing the profile of a buyer was more tactical. If the company knew what was to be spent and where, and had the best equipment for the job, not having the profile of the buyer was acceptable. A critical assumption about the profile of the buyer had to be made: 'They would be inexperienced in buying in a free market, honest and fair but lowest price focused'—this was a critical assumption but it did not require to be tested immediately.

Items on the testing list are programmed for testing as part of the GMAS system and an appropriate method of testing is derived and a timetable produced when a complete list has been compiled.

Where a definitive answer to an urgent and important critical assumption cannot be found, it has to be accepted as such and where it is used it has to be documented as well as those decisions that have been made based on the information, gut feeling or assumption. In this way should, at any point in the future, evidence come to light that compromised this assumption then decisions taken and plans made that include this as a basis can be reviewed in the light of the new information and changes made if required.

Decision choice criteria

Perhaps most importantly in a GMAS design is a clear understanding of the decision-making process. How were the decisions and choices made during the strategy discussions? By understanding the rationale it is possible to tease out the critical assumptions. Therefore knowing which decisions were made based on which critical assumptions means that when a critical assumption is compromised, the decisions on which it will impact are easily determined.

Mission, Vision and Values

I still like to see mission, vision and value statements, but I can fully understand the cynics who feel it is a sham. I found Timothy Foster's (1993) book *101 Great Mission Statements* very amusing, especially his spoof of the Maxwell Communications plc's mission. Robert Maxwell was a British tycoon who misappropriated millions of pounds from pension funds and vanished off the side of his yacht in suspicious circumstances.

> *We aim, through the consistent and creative application of double dealing, contempt, bullying, lying, subterfuge, connivance, theft and fraud, to cheat our investors, our employees, our pensioners, our suppliers and other business partners and the regulatory bodies of the countries where we choose to operate, or die in the attempt!*
>
> (Foster, 1993)

The company's actual mission statement was:

> *We aim, by excellence of management and preeminence in technology, to grasp the great opportunities created by the ever-increasing worldwide demand for information, prosperity and peace.*

Clearly it would not have been interested in untangling its three F's.

This is one of the areas where managers and investors can differ as GMAS provides an early view of the reality in the organization and thus greater levels of protection for investors, but managers may feel threatened. In reality GMAS works for both these stakeholders in that by helping to identify and secure more stable, understanding, loyal investors GMAS rewards them by allowing better insight and more safeguards. Thus the investors, for their loyalty, get a safer investment. Managers, by not having to concern themselves as much with the swings of the market and each individual quarter's results, are freer to do what is in the best interests of the company and to secure longer term success, so both parties win.

Clearly where the investors are in for a fast buck and the managers have something to hide neither party will be interested in implementing GMAS.

Where a mission statement is skilfully crafted it acts as a guiding light for the company, a reminder to stakeholders of what and where the company is going and it facilitates the meeting of minds of the company's staff. In effect, it becomes the flag that all the stakeholders can rally around.

The mission statement should be short, flexible and I believe, unique. Care must be taken to get the balance right between flexibility and providing stability in the STORM. Mission statements often fail by not being flexible enough or are too flexible and thereby fail to provide the stability needed in the organization and as a result, the organization capsizes. I particularly like the following two mission statements:

The Scout Movement

To promote the development of young people in achieving their full physical, intellectual, social and spiritual potentials, as individuals, as responsible citizens and as members of their local, national and international communities.

McKinsey & Co Inc USA (1993)

To help our clients make positive, lasting and substantial improvements in their performance and to build a great Firm that is able to attract, develop, excite, and retain exceptional people.

Compare McKinsey's mission above with that of Coopers & Lybrand's (1993), prior to its merger with Price Waterhouse.

Our mission is to be the leading business advisor.

Which would you rather have given your custom to, or worked for?

I think the best mission statements make your stomach churn just a little, instil a feeling of pride and provide a noble cause for us to work for that we can be proud of. But if they are to be real, they must be meant and not just a statement for the shareholders or to cover your real intent. The ethical investment lobby is making many companies in the Global 1000 consider SA 8000, which is a voluntary code of conduct for companies seeking to make the workplace more humane. If SA 8000 were adopted it would have to be considered in any product sourcing plans as it prohibits a company from buying from firms using child labour, but not providing educational facilities. Thus, even if a cost advantage could be gained by buying from such a supplier, this option would be ruled out and another strategy would require to be developed. It is imperative that the image the company projects matches the reality or true aspiration of the organization. If a company proclaims one set of values but lives by another then the workforce know the mission, vision and values are merely a veneer.

Options and Choice

All through the planning process there is the need to decide between options and just how these decisions are made is important to record so that they can, as they would say in quality speak, provide 'traceability'. Thus, like a properly run quality assurance system, the marketing or business strategy has a full set of document control procedures. This ensures that the whole organization is working to the same strategy and plan. This is a very important feature of GMAS as after the initial, more or less traditional planning process, planning is done when it needs to be, not at a given date or time. Strategic thinking is integrated into the day-to-day activities and as GMAS detects problems with the strategy or plan, or if critical assumptions are compromised, then action is taken immediately to rectify the situation.

Sign-off

I like to have, after the plans are produced and a few days have passed to let everyone involved reflect on the decisions and scenarios considered, have each member of the planning group sign the plans. It is funny how the process of having the team sign the plan flushes out the malcontents and ensures a more detailed look at the strategy.

Marketing Plan, Action Plans and Budgets

From the sign-off of the strategy and the objectives to be achieved, planning passes on to those who have to make it happen. This is the stage that GMAS best practice modules come into their own. The GMAS uses relatively simply SQL databases to match the market environment, the company's 7-S profile, its objectives and customer profiles to generate a list of marketing tactics that have been known to work in similar conditions. These are then considered by the marketing teams who make the decisions on which to use, and when to use them. They also decide which should be dropped. The system has the partial costing and then calculates the work-hours required. Using project planning software, GMAS produces an action plan with resources etc. allocated and budgets set. The plan has detailed implementation guides and can be traced back to the critical assumptions associated with the promotion or tactics being effective and is also linked to the strategic objectives and their associated critical assumptions. As the plan is implemented, it is monitored. If it shows signs of failing to deliver as forecast, assumptions can be tested and a diagnosis routine then determines whether the fault lies with the strategy or tactical deployment and appropriate action can be taken to bring things into line or to modify the tactical or strategic plan.

GMAS planning can be applied to the marketing function but is equally valid for other departments within a global company and strategic business units. How GMAS modules can be applied to everything from manufacturing fault impact on customer satisfaction models to country risk assessment using 'Fuzzy logic' is discussed in later chapters.

In researching the applicability of GMAS, I personally visited 26 countries around the world and met with 130 companies speaking mainly to managers and strategic planners. All, except one group, found that the principles behind GMAS had a place in their organization. The group that could not see any benefit were contract manufacturers, where they basically had four or five customers for whom they made items. These can be huge organizations in their own right, but because of the low number of customers and no contact with the end market, this group felt they survived by being flexible and anticipating the needs of their small number of intimate customers. I felt they were wrong but I can fully understand their position as they are living in the shadow of their customers and as long as their customers do well so do they. However, if their customers catch a cold they will get pneumonia. I put this argument to the CEO of one of the world's largest producers of PC monitors based in Singapore. He replied that they have such long-term contracts, they know well in advance before their profits are impacted if things are going wrong and they have the time to find new business. Any expenditure not resulting in a reduction in the price their customer pays is considered a dangerous waste of resources. I must say I was almost convinced. When interviewed, they could not make monitors fast enough for the world demand, but perhaps now the computer industry is revising its forecasts he can see the point of GMAS.

SUMMARY

- We have looked over the GMAS planning process and established that it fits with most existing models. Fast-moving markets need not be intimidating provided we accept the three F's of planning.

- We have explored strategies for dealing with paradigm shift and have been through the breakthrough marketing model that will allow us to create the paradigm shift.

- The importance of identifying and documenting critical assumptions and obtaining irrefutable research has been explored and a typical planning illustration showed how GMAS thinking could be applied to a marketing plan.

5

Riding Out the Storm

THE GMAS STORM

At the heart of GMAS is the STORM. This is a meeting chaired by the strategic planning team which provides the human input into the interpretation of both real- and right-time market intelligence and supplies the initial decisions. Figure 5.1 shows the STORM (Strategic Tactical Operational Review Meeting) as the central key of the principal GMAS module groups: Strategy, Operations, Staff, Real-Time Critical Assumptions, Monitoring and Testing.

STORM

Let me now take you through the various groups and specifically, how the STORM works. At the core of GMAS is the STORM. This is the central focal point for all the data internal and external to the organization. This is where alchemy happens: the base metal of data being turned into the gold of market advantage. Please do not view the STORM as a simple meeting; it is much more than that and involves both prior- and post-meeting work. STORM not only utilizes people, but also makes use of modern expert systems that interact along with the most advanced thinking support tools. The objectives behind the STORM are:

1 To act as an information clearing house.
2 To monitor strengths and weaknesses.

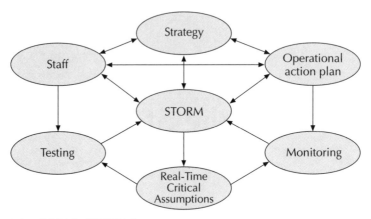

Figure 5.1 GMAS STORM core.

3   To identify and assess opportunities and threats.
4   To commission research and other test activities.
5   To recommend changes to strategy, operational or tactical plans.
6   To monitor performance and analyse data.
7   To communicate.
8   To action and police changes.

Information Clearing House
Data is not in short supply but quality is variable. The importance of
being able to separate the three Fs has never been more important.
The huge growth in the PR industry, investigative journalism and
lobbying groups has increased the data pool, but has had the effect
of increasing the 'selective reporting' bias in public domain information. The importance of reading such texts as Darrell Huff's humor-
ous, but deadly serious book, *How to Lie with Statistics* (1991) today is
unquestioned. If you have not yet read that book, you are at a significant disadvantage in interpreting the information that flows across
your desk each day. His book has been described as 'a sort of primer in
ways to use statistics to deceive', and while I am sure you would never
use this knowledge to deceive, it tells you how to look out for those
who do.

Segmenting information into Fact, Faith or Fiction is one of the
key roles of the STORM. The aim is to take data and by analysis
generate information, combine this information in the STORM to

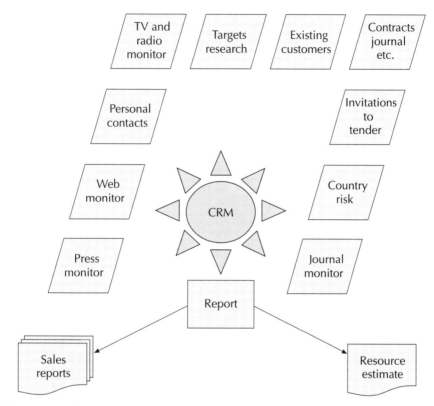

Figure 5.2   STORM typical market monitoring data sources.

produce market intelligence then add this market intelligence to management's expertise to produce competitive advantage.

For this process to work, the data must be valid and the most important criteria for assessing the validity of data are: its source, its consistency, its trend over time and corroborative information. Figure 5.2 shows the multitude of raw data sources for a typical STORM. Information is the collection of pertinent data from various sources. The STORM meeting effectively filters, distils, interprets and analyses this information, turning it into market intelligence upon which decisions can be effectively made.

The STORM, like any decision process reliant on research information, is not immune to type 1 and type 2 errors and that is why GMAS logs and monitors the decisions and if necessary, tests to verify data accuracy using primary research surveys.

Type 1 error 'Fact taken as Fiction error' and type 2 error 'Fiction taken as Fact error' is present in any system which has a degree of uncertainty present. If we take action on information, believing it to be true, when it was fiction then we have committed a type 2 error. Where we choose to ignore market intelligence because we believe it to be fiction when it was fact then we have committed type 1 error.

Taking raw data on the journey to knowledge requires constant separation of the three F's as you transform data into information, then intelligence, and finally to knowledge. Knowledge is the category where we can accept it as Fact that there is none or very little possibility of type 1 or type 2 errors.

Monitor Strengths and Weaknesses
In most planning models the strengths and weaknesses of the organization are identified, and in GMAS the firm's progress in eliminating its weaknesses and building upon its strengths are monitored. The issue of what are considered strengths and what are considered weaknesses depends on the environment the company is operating in. While strengths and weaknesses are internal to a company, they are strongly influenced by the market and general business environment: take size as an example. If you are in a small company, you may view your size among your strengths, as you can give a more personal service to your customers. However, it can also be considered as one of your weaknesses in that it limits the size and number of the contracts you can take on, even when demand is growing. In this light, strengths and weaknesses should be monitored and if the strategy favours rapid growth, then current size becomes a weakness. If, on the other hand, the strategy is organic growth through a secure loyal customer base, size becomes one of the organization's strengths.

The STORM meetings make sure strengths and weaknesses are classified correctly in the changing environment. What at first is one of an organization's strengths can, because of the market or environment, become a weakness overnight. For example, being a dot.com company in 1999 was a major strength in getting financial investment, while in 2001, being a dot.com is a positive hindrance in gaining investment. GMAS's constant checking ensures that the relative strengths are growing while the weaknesses are being eliminated and that both are classified correctly.

Other external factors impact a company's internal strengths and weaknesses: take competitors' activities. A unique strength of the company can be matched and bettered by a competitor. During the 1960s, the US car industry had a technological advantage over the Japanese car producers but by the 1990s, Japanese technology had matched that of the US and the strength of their technological 'know-how' had been equalled. The US industry has perceived their technology as their strength. The Japanese countered this 'know-how' strength with the strength of 'their rate of learning'.

The Japanese car industry did not catch up with the US industry overnight, and observers such as Christopher Meyer (1996), in his book *Fast Cycle Time*, writes, 'a sustainable FCT capability can be achieved only by learning faster, not by working faster'. The Japanese car industry was learning faster than the US industry with the result that it has now exceeded the know-how of the US automobile makers. It is therefore important to understand the critical strengths in an organization. In this case, it was not speed of production or current know-how that was the critical factor, but the rate of learning. You must ensure that you know your company's critical strengths and ensure new strengths emerge in line with what is needed to maintain and develop competitive advantage.

Identify and Assess Opportunities and Threat

There is a well-known saying: 'As one door closes another one opens' meaning that as one opportunity closes some other will always come along. While I have always believed this, I have found that opportunities tend to come around faster if you look for them and, like British buses, they tend to all come together after having kept you waiting at the bus stop for some considerable time. By constantly monitoring your market for opportunities and threats, you can take appropriate action to secure the best opportunities and you will have time to deal with the threats, or even transform them into opportunities.

What at first often appears to be a threat can often be a major opportunity. I remember when MMSI plc was a small, local consultancy firm generating most of its business from companies in and around Glasgow (Scotland) and was reliant on these firms receiving grant assistance to pay for their consultancy. When the government withdrew the grant scheme MMS (Marketing Management Services)

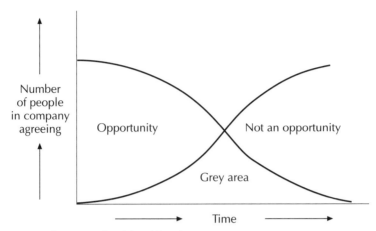

Figure 5.3   Opportunity identification spectrum.

as it was then, had to find new markets, and we found them in the world's Global 1000. This resulted in massive growth and, despite still being based in Glasgow, MMSI plc has, at the time of writing, no local Scottish clients. Its clients are all global multinationals based around the world. What I have learnt from that experience is that you should not wait for one door to close before opening another. Using GMAS allows many doors to be open at once and provides users with opportunity options. As one of our clients once said, it provides 'optionality'.

As with strengths and weaknesses, opportunities and threats need to be monitored in real time and the STORM meeting is used to filter and sort the data into market intelligence. In order to be sure just what is important and represents an opportunity, you have to be sure what you are looking for. This is not as straightforward as it might seem. There are, in any large organization, a great number of differing views, about what represents an opportunity or a threat. Opportunities tend to break down into three groups: the 'obvious opportunity', the 'grey area', and the 'obviously not an opportunity'. This is illustrated in Figure 5.3.

Some opportunities are so obvious that if we were to conduct a census of the company, everyone would agree it is an opportunity. Likewise there are some things that everyone in the company would agree are not an opportunity. Unfortunately, in the vast majority of

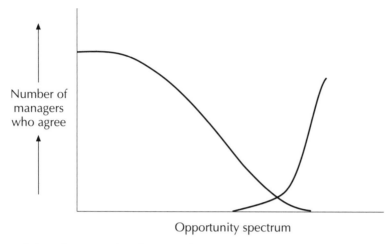

Figure 5.4a   Opportunity skew (positive).

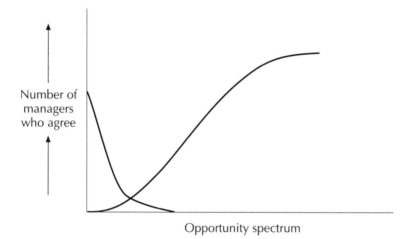

Figure 5.4b   Opportunity skew (negative).

situations there is some level of disagreement as to whether the information represents an opportunity or not. There are a number of
factors that contribute to this problem. The more entrepreneurial the
attitude is in the company, the more skewed the diagram is to the left
(see Figure 5.4a) and the more pessimistic the outlook, the more
skewed to the right (see Figure 5.4b).

For example, when providing sales leads to companies via the
STORM it is not uncommon to get contradictory views on whether
the lead is or is not an opportunity, depending on whom you speak to.

I am sure the same will be true in your company. The STORM meeting has to interpret the opportunity and learn to whom it is relevant and in what circumstances. GMAS distinguishes effectively in the grey area, in time, by using neuro-fuzzy logic modelling. Opportunities can be assessed, the number reduced to a manageable size, and the relevance of each prioritized by the computers. This prevents waiting for one door to close before you go looking for the next opportunity.

One of the most significant aspects of the STORM is its ability to identify paradigm shift. By monitoring emerging technology and by modelling the impacts of changes on the current paradigm, it is possible to identify threats posed before any new innovation has swept into the market. This allows time to develop competitive technology or even to acquire the new technology.

Two problems STORM does not solve overnight is a closed mind and an 'it will be alright' attitude. I have been amazed by the amount of intelligence required to change a manager's hard-held view and the tendency to underestimate the significance of some of the assumptions that are being relied on, especially when a paradigm shift is detected.

Let us look at the slow down in the computer industry in 2001 and the huge number of redundancies that have occurred as a result. As the spiral was developing, there were clear warning signs, but even when they were becoming blatantly obvious, the natural optimism of many considered it a temporary blip and thought that things would be 'all right' next quarter.

Red Herring, the high-tech industry magazine's survey of CEO's of the leading companies where they asked them when the recovery would come. Of the companies, 33 per cent said the third quarter of 2001, 33 per cent the first quarter of 2002 and 33 per cent the second quarter of 2002. What surprises me was that no one appeared to be saying the market might have changed forever. Time will tell who was right, but I suspect as you are reading this book the market will be quite different from its dot.com hyper-growth days and new paradigms are building in what was that market space.

Commission Research and Other Test Activities
In the real world things are not often clear-cut, usually information is vague or incomplete. There is therefore a need to commission research

to clarify information or verify assumptions. The STORM function prioritizes and commissions such research. The full spectrum of research techniques may need to be applied or just a simple test. What research is required and how best it should be done is determined in the STORM. In Chapter 5 we will discuss the processes and techniques that must be applied in order to generate irrefutable research. Any research must be able to answer questions quickly and accurately and, if possible, discreetly, so as not to alert competitors to your intentions.

Recommend Changes to Strategy, Operational or Tactics Plans

If a critical assumption upon which the strategy is based is compromised, it may necessitate a modification to the strategy or it may not. One of the most likely compromises is that the strategy assumes a growth rate based on sales. If the sales are not made, this has only one of two possible causes. The objectives are set too high and it is impossible to achieve the sales forecast or we have failed to perform at the operational or tactical level. If the fault lies at the operational or tactical level, the problem must be identified and new tactics applied in order to get the sales back on track. If the fault is at the strategic level, we have a more serious issue.

According to most literature sources in early 2001, the CRM market was forecast to grow at 40 per cent per annum. Many companies created CRM systems for niche markets on the basis that the sheer market growth would sustain them in their chosen niche. One such Scottish company was Coranta Corporation. Hailed as a rapid growth company in 2000, it fell into the hands of the liquidators in 2001 when the early growth could not be sustained. This was because the market had slowed but the company was still expanding as if the market was growing at the forecasted 40 per cent. Failure to make sales targets and the slump in IT stock should have given them enough warning of the impending downturn, which as a niche player would not allow them a large enough market to survive. When the market turns against such a company, it must cut back quickly or develop another strategy because to continue to follow the original strategy when its critical assumptions have been compromised can be a fatal mistake. The STORM alerts management to the need to rethink before it is too late.

Monitor Performance and Analyse Data

As you will now have gathered the STORM, and indeed GMAS as a whole, involves a great deal of dynamic forecasts, monitoring of performance, analysis of data and testing of assumption and scenarios. It may appear as if this is going to slow down the organization and that it is going to vanish under the weight of data, but this is where 'neuro-fuzzy' applications come into play. Neuro-fuzzy applications are fuzzy logic systems combined with neural net technology. These GMAS applications can process data that is not precise, learn from the results and then do better the next time it sees the same fuzzy pattern.

Fuzzy logic technology mimics the human decision-making process and allows computers to accept natural human language while neural nets imitate to some extent the way the brain learns. What is perhaps the biggest benefit is that, unlike traditional expert systems, which can only be operated using 'hard' data (true or false), fuzzy systems such as those in GMAS can work on terms like 'sometimes', 'almost', 'likely', 'pretty much' and deal with the uncertain nature of partial information or incomplete data. This is a tremendous advantage when dealing with uncertainty and gut feeling.

When some forecasts are met but others are not, this type of system is able to handle, more like the human brain, the uncertainties. A result of this is that it can deal with the more abstract issues such as 'almost reaching' budget rather than the they did or did not achieve of the typical computer software. This means that rather than issuing an alert because a number is 999.99 and not 1000, for example, the system accepts an 'almost' range, learned what short fall is significant and how likely it is to impact the company's critical assumptions.

No matter how well fuzzy logic applications dealt with data they could never be as good as an expert human. While fuzzy logic systems can handle large volumes of data and reduce it to a manageable size, humans are vital in the STORM interphase. They are the strongest link, but they are also the weakest. The STORM allows humans to do what they are good at: seeing patterns and linking information to form intelligence. They can put one and one together and generate 25. The breakthrough! Something computers cannot yet achieve. The human can deal with Faith, handle weightings better and deal with the first exposure situation better than any system. Let me explain. George Soros is said to have made $1 billion from a chance remark made by the then chief executive of Deutsche Bundesbank. During a speech, the CEO was asked what he thought about a single European currency, to which he said something along the lines of: 'I am all for a single European currency—I think we should call it the Deutschmark'. From this remark Soros concluded that the Bundesbank would not step in to support the Exchange Rate Mechanism (ERM) and he made a fortune when they did not do so and Britain was forced out of the ERM. No computer system could have drawn that conclusion from a single remark. Humans are therefore vital in a GMAS system and especially in the STORM.

Communicate

I define communications as the meeting of minds. One thing is to know, in a central location, what is happening and which scenarios are developing, but this is of little value unless it can be communicated to those who will be tasked with taking some kind of action. Therefore, Enterprise Neural Trails (ENTs) have to be developed so that who needs to be informed is known—not such an easy task in a large global company. The ENTs have to be built and kept current. This is a job that falls, in part, to the personnel function.

I am often surprised by the lack of current organizational charts in many of the large companies I have visited. Yes, they had charts at the senior levels, but they were rarely up to date and, as a consequence, did not truly reflect what was happening on the ground. Perhaps this is not surprising when you consider the staff movements in any sizeable organization in rapid growth or decline.

In rapid growth companies, staff recruitment can be carried out at a frantic pace and the staff roles and responsibilities seem to change almost daily. This mêlée is difficult to keep track of even for well-run personnel functions, who may know who they have employed and what they were originally employed to do, but have not managed to track the changing of staff duties after recruitment. Also, as priorities change, some functions become less important and get relegated to the organizational mist. I have found this quite often when I have tried to establish who was responsible for some function or another only to find on some occasions the task had grown into an empire, multiple people with no real authority, all passing papers to each other sometimes resulting in some tasks that would perhaps take one person one day to complete, becoming a full time job for four or five staff.

MMSI was once asked to establish an ENT for a UK government agency that was out-performing all other similar agencies in the UK for volume of public enquiries being dealt with. This was obviously a shining example of efficiency, you might think. Unfortunately, it was too good to be true. Each member of staff recorded the number of enquiries they dealt with individually; these were then added up at the end of the week by the office manager and recorded. To test the system I organized a mystery shop, an enquiry that could be tracked. To my surprise this one enquiry turned out to represent seven enquiries. How? Well, the person who answered the telephone and recorded the details of the enquiry recorded it (1), they then passed it on to a researcher to deal with (2) and as the researcher was too busy to deal with it that day they passed it on to a colleague (3). The colleague then consulted a supervisor about it (4), completed the work and passed it to the secretary (5) to return to me. Because the door had a monitor on it recording the number of people who entered the public area, which displayed brochures and had computers for self-help, they were also recording those visitors as enquirers. So, as the internal postman entered to pick up the envelope containing our reply they were re-corded as an enquiry (6) and again as they left (7). Thus, one telephone call generated a record of seven enquiries. No wonder this department out-performed the rest of the UK. Up until this point, this particular organization had been getting all requests for more staff approved immediately because of the huge volume of enquiries it was apparently dealing with, so the numbers had grown, managers' pay related to the number of staff and budget responsibilities, so that was also growing. They had built an empire by playing the reporting system.

Even today, there are in almost all organizations, the odd back-water that is doing a similar job to that government agency. It provides great statistics, but is not really performing a productive role and is at the same time consuming precious resources. The ENT networks do not allow these backwaters to build up. If the department cannot be linked on to an ENT then it is not serving the strategic goal. If the department is serving a strategic goal, the three Fs analysis of the information being received from the department soon separates Fact from Fiction.

If you think about it, had there been cutbacks in government agency budgets, it is hardly likely that they would have hit the flagship of productivity I described above. It is therefore imperative to have a meeting of minds to truly understand what is important. Keep these findings in mind when establishing an ENT, so that the operational reports that are being monitored provide clear, honest data thus ensuring they reflect more Fact than Fiction.

Action and Police Changes
In rapidly changing environments, and when multiple initiatives are running in an organization, what gets measured is what gets done. Therefore it is necessary that the actions required to be done are carried out and that the plan for change is vigorously policed. The STORM provides the feedback on the progress of change implementation. It surprises me how many initiatives in a company fizzle out before achieving their goals. The problem is that with so many priorities and heavy workloads, tasks with a strategic tag tend to get less attention and are often pushed off the agenda. Thus, the long-term adjustments needed do not get implemented quickly enough and the forecast situation that the plans aimed to avoid overtakes the organization. Unfortunately by then it is often too late to do anything but brush up your curriculum vitae.

Around the STORM is the core collection of GMAS modules. I will discuss each of them in turn.

Strategy

The strategy module is used in the preparation of the initial strategic plan and is responsible for keeping the plan continuously up to date. This includes all scenario planning and modelling functions.

The strategy and associated strategic plans, whether fed throughout the organization by Balanced Scorecard software or in a key performance indicator system, has to be monitored and particular attention paid to the associated critical assumptions. The way the plan is being implemented must be monitored against the staged milestones and the purpose spectrum that I mentioned in Chapter 2. The easiest way of ensuring that the strategy is kept in mind is by using some kind of dashboard or Balanced Scorecard system. Software products available to help in this area are discussed in greater depth in Appendix 1.

As is the case with operational plans, it is imperative to determine, if things are not going according to plan, whether the fault lies in the strategic thinking or in the execution of the plan.

Operational Action Plans

Strategy alone cannot do anything. It has to be effectively translated into operational plans and it is these that lead the company to the achievement of its mission. These plans must be as flexible as possible, but also be bound by the strategy. Therefore, the monitoring and testing of operational plans is a major source of data to the STORM. This information can be provided by STORM accessing reports produced by Customer Relationship Management, Enterprise Resource Planning or Balanced Scorecard software as well as other organization-based management information systems. This combined with ENT allows the quality of the data being derived from these systems to be assured.

While working on a strategic plan we had taken the consultancy day rates that the management team had mentioned as Fact. The team said the fees charged for a consultant were £600 pounds on average, but that they could increase the average to £900 by doing external work on fixed rate contracts, as they often could do the work in fewer days than the estimate. This, however, was usually linked to a tender request and they were more difficult to get, but the increased profit potential would more than cover the increased marketing cost.

I was about to use the figure given by the team in the business plan, but when I calculated the number of work-days available I found that they were already earning more than the stated average billable day rate of £600. In fact, they were earning more like £1200 per day already. This confused me, so I went to the finance director as I was sure he would be able to explain what was happening. Again I asked what the average daily rate was. After half an hour of explanation about the complexity of calculation and the different ways things were recorded, we sat down to calculate the average rate. An hour later we had a good estimate. Both the £600 and £900 were correct in that some jobs were quoted at a fixed rate and the number of days estimated did not always have to be done, so the effective day rate could be as high as £900 on those jobs, while the majority of work with long-standing clients was charged at less than £600 a day and *ad hoc* jobs were quoted at between £600 and £900 per day.

This company was somehow generating more days. I then went and talked to the actual consultants and discovered two important factors: staff worked late three days a week on average. This generated an extra day each week per billable staff member, but, more significantly, some consultants were able to do three jobs at the same time, effectively generating three days' income from one day's work. For example, some of the more routine work required tests to be run which took perhaps three hours, but after set-up the consultant was not doing anything until the test was complete, therefore they were working on other projects and some were running multiple tests for multiple clients. Each client knew that the consultants had to be present to ensure the test was run correctly and therefore did not question paying for their time. The management team had become detached from the operational environment and nature of the work that generated the income. This coupled with other income from a number of other sources being reported within the consultancy figures had given them quite a false impression about what actually was generating the largest income.

The management team had assumed it was the fixed price jobs, with their effective daily rate of £900, that was the source of the income, while they were unaware that estimates of how long jobs would take to do had become detached from reality.

We had missed that by focusing on certain types of lower paid work, which could be done simultaneously, they could increase the income while the strategy, about to be adopted, of aiming for the fixed-price work at £900 per day would result in them moving away from the most profitable work. Furthermore, the fixed-price work was difficult to get, difficult to do and difficult to satisfy the client with, while the routine work that could generate three times the £600 per day, or £1800 per consultant, was easier to get, easier to do and easier to satisfy the client with. They were in danger of making a 'Fiction thought Fact' or type 2 error. This would have resulted in, had they chosen to concentrate on the fixed-price contracts, them wasting market expenditure, generating less income and increasing bid costs. This would create two problems which most businesses would find difficult to escape from, of rising cost and falling income. The greatest benefit in GMAS is gained from a combination of operational intelligence and market intelligence. Therefore both operations and strategy need to interact and be developed together. In the defence of myself and the management team, the consultancy aspect of this business accounted for less than 5 per cent of their sales so it was less visible to them and correspondingly less time was spent looking at it, but it was none-theless an important source of income and profit.

Does getting it right in the first place matter in GMAS? Suppose that with a GMAS system we made a 'Fiction thought Fact' error. What would have happened? The assumptions on billable days and day rates would have been recorded and a critical assumption mon-itored. As the strategy was deployed two things would have happened. Both sales and profits would have started to fall. This would have triggered a STORM meeting to discuss why. The sales plan would have been analysed for failures in execution, the Real-Time Critical Assumptions would be looked at and testing undertaken. This inves-tigation would have revealed the 'Fiction thought Fact' error, the strategy team would be reconvened, the new information explained and the strategy would have been modified.

Compare this to an 'always right strategy' model. The strategy would have been hard wired, and failure to achieve the goals would have resulted in more marketing expenditure, or perhaps the replace-ment of an operational manager. There would be no record of the critical assumptions upon which management had made the decision to go for the fixed-price market. Therefore, it would have been un-likely that any challenge to the strategy would have been made and the strategy would have been continued until things got so bad that either operational managers would have simply ignored the strategy or man-agement would have been forced to admit it got it wrong. Both are bad for the company.

Strategy is an output from a process and is only as good as the inputs upon which it is based. Therefore, senior managers are the facilitators and communicators of the strategy and not its protectors. The strategy protects itself by working. If operational managers ignore the strategy to achieve the targets, the company is directionless and drifting. The marketing messages will be conflicting with the operational reality, marketing positioning the organization in one way while operations is delivering something else, often developing other sales channels at a complete tangent to the company's goals and public statements. Before long the operational reality becomes known and the credibility of the senior management is lost. GMAS prevents this by recording the critical assumptions and has an open mind as to whether they are Fact, Faith or Fiction—it instead modifies its opinion as the plan is executed and the results become known.

Staff

Just as significant as the operational plans being aligned with the strategy and vice versa, are staff being involved in the on-going planning process. This means that all your staff should have 'strategy influencer' added to their job description, because their opinions and the information they provide, will influence strategic thinking.

This does not create an organization that simply becomes completely opportunistic, but it does give the organization the option to be flexible if it so chooses. By being aware of the options, the organization can choose to take those bringing it closer to its goal and ignore those which do not.

Having those Real Options substantially increases the company's market value.

Having spherical vision and being confronted by multiple opportunities means that managers have to make more decisions more often and live with the consequences, right or wrong. The prize for this is global marketing advantage and you cannot achieve this without knowing what the opportunities are and having the ability to capitalize on those that speed you towards your goal. GMAS will strengthen the strategy if it is leading to the achievement of the mission, but will replace it if it is failing to lead to success.

Key Result Areas and Key Performance Indicators

Each of the staff must know where they fit into the organization and the achievement of the mission. The traditional way, based on performance management models, is the Key Performance Indicators (KPI) and/or Key Result-Areas (KRA) models.

A KRA is where an individual needs to focus attention and where success will build with co-worker's success to achieve the organizations objectives and associated mission. These KRAs are broken down to KPI, which are in effect 'SMART Objectives' as these performance standards should be Specific, Measurable, Achievable, Realistic-results-oriented and Time encapsulated. Dale Carnegie® Training provides very good training courses to help you phrase a KPI. They suggest you start the sentence that encapsulates the KPI with: 'My job, in this area, will have been satisfactorily performed when …'. I suggest shortening this to: 'My job will have been satisfactorily performed when …'.

Let me give you a hypothetical example of a KRA and a few related KPI for a quality control manager.

Mission Element: To produce products that don't come back for customers that do come back.

Related KRA: To manage the quality function and ensure we provide products that don't come back for customers that do.

Single element KPI: My job will have been satisfactorily performed when the monthly total of RMAs (Returned Material Authorization) has dropped to less than 1 per cent of dispatches.

Please note that there would usually be several KRAs related to achieving the mission element and for each KRA there would be several KPIs.

There are a number of ways of linking the KRAs to the business strategy ranging from Balanced Scorecard software to Dale Carnegie's® paper-based KRA system, to simple systems provided by Knowledge Point that are available in most software stores. Whichever method you choose, the important point is to keep it current and I recommend monthly KRA meetings to provide the evidence of KPI being met or being on route to being met. The KPIs must be monitored, as they are critical to the achievement of the company's mission and act as a leading indicator of emerging problems.

The thought of reviewing the performance of all members of staff on a monthly basis may sound excessive, but they are our most expensive and valuable assets and KRA systems maintain the asset at peak performance. Automated reporting and KPI measured from secondary sources means that there is no need for this to become a huge time intensive exercise or to become too subjective. Imagine the alternative: if things are not well, waiting twelve months for an appraisal could kill the company. Just think how much damage can be done by a 'malfunctioning employee' in twelve months, and with no record of performance in many, especially European, countries poor performers can be extremely expensive to remove. If objectives are not being met because you have the wrong people, just like having the wrong equipment, the company will suffer and in the end this failure to manage all the assets in achieving the mission will bring the company to a crisis point.

As the strategy changes or is modified as a result of market reality then the KRA and KPI change also. Whichever method you adopt for the management of KRA and KPI, you have to ensure it is flexible and easy to refocus and that no backwaters are allowed to develop.

Enterprise Neuron Trails

The ENTs run throughout the organization and follow the KRA and KPI trails. They provide the rapid response to market stimulation and are inclusive of all staff in the organization. The personnel department should maintain the ENT system. (I assume they know who joins and leaves the organization). The reason I mention this is because I know of one major international firm which had gone through the instant dismissal process, that is cards and keys handed over and a security escort off the premises. When we were building an ENT system in the department in which that employee worked, one year later, we noticed he was still being paid. This was even more incredible when it turned out he was by then working for a competitor. It is very easy, especially in companies experiencing rapid change, to lose track of who is actually doing what and for critical things to be dropped in favour of less onerous or 'nice-to-do' activities. Most organizations have procedures to stop this kind of thing, but are they current and does everyone know about them? Whose fault was it that the company was still paying an employee who had left over a year before—the manager, personnel or the system? Given that the company had been acquired in the interim, was it the previous manager, personnel department or systems? As takeovers and mergers get larger, just keeping track of who is doing what vital job is going to become increasingly complex. Without a live ENT system how can we ensure that the senior management can be confident that everyone in the organization is working to achieve the mission and that, as changes may be required in the strategy, backwaters where resources are being squandered are not being formed within the company?

Real-Time Critical Assumptions

By now it should be crystal clear that GMAS monitors the critical assumptions made in the business as a whole and specifically in the strategic planning process. It should also be clear that these critical assumptions have different priorities and that some are so important that they must be tested immediately, while others are nonetheless critical but probability theory or a strong Faith permits them to be monitored or tested only if time permits.

Critical assumptions have to be expressed and gathered with care. Resources are required to be spent to monitor them in real time so we really want to be sure that we have distilled them down to a concentrate that can be manageably monitored preferably in real time. While monitoring critical assumptions in real time is important, it is equally important to only report them at the right time. If every market fluctuation or analyst's off-the-cuff comment is taken as Fact then STORM meetings would be triggered daily in any sizeable organization. To avoid this, a technique from quality assurance has been borrowed. Frank Price back in 1984, published a book entitled *Right First Time* and brought statistical process control to my attention. We want to call a meeting when a critical assumption has really been challenged, but not when it is a result of our research only suggesting a problem. The risk of making the wrong decision is increased by inadequate knowledge, therefore the more irrefutable the data the more knowledge and, hence, better market intelligence we can gather. In order for the right decisions to be made, reporting every research-discovered anomaly is not going to be useful, but reporting too late is equally of no use. Therefore, we need to set some kind of boundary which if the real-time data exceeds it triggers a STORM.

In quality assurance, this is achieved by employing statistical process control where an action and warning limit is set. These boundaries of tolerance prevent false alarms being caused by background noise, but trigger a warning (calling a STORM meeting) and action required (where the probability of the critical assumption having been compromised is very high and action is required). In a similar way, critical assumptions being monitored in real time have boundaries that must be exceeded for a STORM meeting to be called and limits where a compromise of a critical assumption is almost a Fact.

Where there are multiple leading indicators, fuzzy logic allows a combination of indicators approaching a predefined limit to trigger a STORM meeting and in some cases to not call a meeting even when one of the indicators exceeds its limits while the others remain well within the expected range.

The following Real-Time mnemonic has been generated to help define a critical assumption.

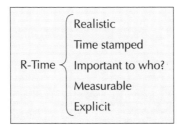

Realistic

Is the critical assumption realistic? Some things could be critical: for example, 'an atomic bomb could be dropped on our Glasgow office'. Yes, this would have a critical impact on our business success, but it has such a low probability and there are so many other factors that would then come into play that it is not realistic to log this as a critical assumption. While 'The market will continue to grow at the same rate of 40 per cent for the next three years' can be a realistic critical assumption. (I wrote the above before the events of September 11th. Terrorist threats are now considered in our Critical Assumptions and scenarios.)

Time-stamped

Critical assumptions have a life time as well as having an associated time frame. In the example given above, the 40 per cent growth has been framed within three years. After three years, the 'sell by date' of this critical assumption will have been reached, and will need to be replaced. Many critical assumptions have review dates that provide a point in time that requires the assumptions to be verified or measured.

If my critical assumption is related to business confidence in Scotland then I would measure this monthly, when the results of the Bank of Scotland's monthly economic report is issued. This report gives the NTC Research results from the Bank-sponsored survey of Scottish business. The 'review date' in this case is set by the publication date of the reports. This helps in the monitoring of the critical assumption and ensures a review will occur so that trends can be monitored.

I should perhaps explain what leading and lagging indicators are. A leading indicator is an indication of a market condition that predicts the condition to come. A lagging indicator is a measure that tells of the current condition. Thus, a profits warning is a leading indicator and published accounts are a lagging indicator of company performance.

Important to Whom?

By linking the critical assumptions to KRA and KPI, we know how the organization will be affected by this critical assumption and who may be in a position to provide leading indicators of this assumption's validity or potential compromise.

If our sales representatives talk to our customers and those of our competitors each day, they may be the first to know of a competitor price change or new product release. Hence it is imperative that market intelligence is quickly distributed to those who can capitalize upon it. Each critical assumption should be linked to the ENT system so that a corporate knowledge base can be effectively established and operated.

Measurable

Critical assumptions have to be measurable in some way. Using fuzzy logic has increased the measurability of many critical assumptions, but it is imperative that they can be measured. The measurement approach can, in some cases, be extremely difficult to identify and the more complicated the measurement specifications, the more difficult and unreliable monitoring becomes. This is a clear case where the KISS principle applies: Keep It Short and Simple.

Explicit

The critical assumption must be explicit because if it is not easy to understand and cannot easily be interpreted, it will be misunderstood and misinterpreted, making it impossible to monitor the true critical assumption. This is easy to say, but quite difficult to pull off in practice. Because many of the critical assumptions are derived in creative sessions during the strategic planning process, they are derived with a specific perspective in mind. Even when reread by their creator at a later date, they can be interpreted differently. Similarly, several senior members of the management team can read them differently upon reflection. This ambiguity has to be eliminated and the critical assumptions phrased so that a researcher knows exactly what they mean and can therefore derive the most effective methods of testing or monitoring.

Monitoring

As with testing, there is a wide variety of critical assumptions and action plans to be monitored. There are two types of monitoring: internal and external. Internal monitoring can be done via a Balanced Scorecard type system or Enterprise Resource Planning system and this means that it can be done in a very complex manner or in a simple way using weekly reports. The complexity is greatly reduced when you are quite clear what is important to monitor.

External monitoring can utilize tools such as almost fully automated fuzzy-logic-based systems to search Internet-based news feeds and web-based customer research through to simply scanning through the *Financial Times* each day. Some of the most common monitoring sources are shown in Figure 5.2 on p. 61. These include the following:

Press

Press Monitoring covers 80–90 per cent of press publications relevant to the specific sector your company operates within. These can be categorized into four groups:

1   The financial press such as *Financial Times*, *Wall Street Journal*, the *Australian Financial Review* and *Handelsblatt*. These are a rich source of business news, stock analysis and expert opinion.

2   National newspapers such as *USA Today*, *The Times*, *The Australian*, the *Japan Times* and *Die Welt*. These contain good local country coverage and are especially relevant when you are targeting consumer markets.

3   Local, citywide or regional newspapers such as *New York Times*, *Chicago Tribune*, *Houston Chronicle*, and *The Scotsman*, are important as many global companies have their headquarters within the area. They provide a good deal of local information that can be significant and cover local news in-depth. In addition, these publications tend to know about planning applications well before the national newspapers. They can also be good barometers of local feeling towards a project. For example, the local Silicon Valley and San Jose *Business Journal* indicated support for a new power plant to be built in the city even when covering local pollution concerns. This allowed the IPP (Independent Power Producer) to judge the mood and successfully negotiate the legislative and political barriers.

4   Weekly publications such as *Business Week*, *Time*, *Newsweek* and *The Economist* can be monitored weekly as they contain an in depth analysis of industry sectors and countries.

Press monitoring is a rich source of information, but you have to bear in mind that it is not always accurate and the growth in PR and investigative journalism can produce a confusing picture. Having written on many occasions for the press as well as having given comments over the phone to journalists myself, I am fully aware of just how information can be massaged. I am old enough and wise enough to no longer get upset by being misquoted, but when monitoring the press, it is important to be careful about getting corroborative evidence and also to bear in mind that volume of coverage does not mean the source is necessarily more authoritative. A leading member and chairman of a major political party and senior member of the Scottish legal profession was, some may say, entrapped by a local newspaper with a prostitute. Stories abounded about this person and his desire to be spanked with a slipper. Because of his status, the press had a field-day and the stories got wilder and wilder. This resulted in him being forced to resign.

Several months later when things had quietened down, he sued the newspapers concerned and received a substantial out-of-court settlement because the majority of what had been reported was pure fiction and each of the papers that carried the story found themselves having to pay considerable sums in compensation.

Scandals aside, the quality press tend to make more effort to authenticate stories than the tabloids and the information is reasonably reliable—especially in comparison with Internet newsletters.

Journals and Periodicals

Trade journals and periodicals are a vital source of news and information concerning the industry sector they represent. These journals contain detailed articles, expert commentary and report trends very accurately. Journals are widely read and the information they contain is known to most in the industry and, as these publications are often monthly, the news they report can be old. The Internet versions are more up to date and can be a valuable source to the agile company who can act on the information quickly. They are usually fairly authoritative and outside their 'advertorials' (articles that an advertiser is paying for) and the 'article for advertising' (the inclusion of a news article given to an advertiser) they can provide genuine insight. The better journals tend to have few advertorials, and where they are present, they are clearly marked as such.

Before you get the impression that I am condemning advertorials as not containing 'real' information, I am not: they can be a good source of competitor information, as often the PR agency is quite unaware of how sensitive some information they print can be. The company forced to disclose information to keep investors happy, quite often discloses its future plans in enough detail for the fast competitor to get to market first or to leapfrog the innovation or the promotional campaign that will inevitably follow.

Let me give you two examples of how information can be utilized with leapfrog promotion. A brewer in Britain went to press with how their beer was now the best selling German beer in the UK, only to have their huge spend nullified by a competitor who, using the same style of advert, simply stated: 'You have tried "A", the best selling German Beer in Britain, NOW try "B", the best-selling German beer in Germany'. One year later they were not only the best-selling

German beer in Germany but they had also become the best-selling German beer in Britain.

In the same industry, an innovation of creating a can that could hold 33 per cent extra had been a winner at the peak selling period of Christmas for one brewery. In their enthusiasm, and feeling that the competition would not be able to adjust their production systems, they announced their intention to the trade of repeating the very successful promotion, only to find that they could not sell their stock because the competitors had flooded the distribution chain by offering very large bulk discounts. Although the retailers knew they would be able to sell the 33 per cent extra cans easier, they had no room for it nor did they want to be left with the other brands so chose not to stock it. The 33 per cent extra promotion had been effectively countered by their main competitors. Had the brewery not been so confident as to announce its intention, perhaps the competitors would not have acted so quickly to flood the distribution channels.

Web Monitoring

As the name suggests, web monitoring involves the gathering of news articles and competitive information by using the Internet. For almost all industries, this can prove to be the most popular and productive source of information relevant to a company. The sites used can be categorized as:

- *Company sites* These sites can be used to obtain information regarding competitors and companies within a particular industry sector.

- *Newsletter sites* Various market research and web portals cover news dedicated to a particular industry or many industry sectors. These sites are a rich and productive source of latest news and information.

- *Third party, expert and consultant sites* These sites cover views, insights, commentary from analysts, organizations and companies and even case studies that can all provide valuable insight.

- *Government sites* Legislation and new regulations affect all companies equally within any sector. These sites contain federal or ministerial departments, governing bodies and regulators. The freedom of information legislation has made information more accessible. For example, on the US Navy website, presentations by vendors are often posted. While working for one company in the telecommunications industry we were able to see the entire presentation their competitors had made. This outlined their selling proposition and key benefits, all of which made it very easy for our client to design presentations that would match or better the competitors key selling propositions while introducing new areas that effectively outflanked the competitor winning our client business with the US Navy.

The main advantage of web monitoring is that it can be done in real time. Information on company and newsletter sites is often constantly updated and is of high quantity.

The main disadvantage of web monitoring is the overwhelming amount of information that can be found. All news releases concerning a particular industry may not be important and therefore the vital news has to be filtered and sifted. There are, however, various software packages on the market that can carry out the filtering and producing information that is needed. The problem with this is that repeated articles can give these systems difficulty in recognizing that they have already retrieved the same article from another source. The huge volume of data means that there is also a requirement for considerable computer power.

Library

The role of the humble library should not be overlooked. Libraries like the National Library in Washington and the British Library in London contain copies of a vast array of publications that are often too expensive to be held even by the rare, well-funded, corporate libraries. Some libraries will also provide search and research services so that for a fixed monthly fee you can have information relevant to your critical assumptions gathered and reported to you.

The main disadvantage of using a library is the time involved in researching and obtaining the information. Public libraries may be free, but trained researchers are required if the knowledge they contain is to be harnessed effectively.

TV and Satellite News and Current Events
The number of channels dedicated to providing general news and current events, financial and market news on a global basis 24 hours a day every day, is growing. Channels such as CNN and Sky News cover world news as well as world business news and reviews. Reuters have a channel dedicated to providing up-to-date news online as well as on television. There are specialist channels such as Bloomberg and CNBC that only cover business and stock exchange news, company and industry reviews and interviews with CEOs. Put a CEO in front of a television camera and you never know what you will get. You can find them bragging about their strategy, plans and even tactics or acting like parrots delivering a very carefully crafted stream of well-rehearsed sound bites, but saying nothing.

Testing (Research)

As well as monitoring activities some critical assumptions and plans need to be tested. Testing is split into two. The red area (Urgent and Important) is where action is taken during the planning process while the strategy teams are still in place and this is frantic and exciting. Tests are devised and executed often within days; results are back quickly and are being used in the following planning meetings. There is a great deal of debate over the findings and plans are built upon the results.

Non-urgent (blue) items, although important, are logged for testing at some future date. The excitement of the planning phase over, they are timetabled for testing during the life of the plan or that may not be considered necessary as monitoring is deemed to be sufficient. This testing or marketing research often utilizes the full spectrum of research techniques that will be discussed in the next chapter.

Blue item testing is unfortunately one of the things that often falls behind schedule as managers often feel that the testing is not required, and I can sympathize with this view because most of the critical assumptions or ideas to be tested are important but not urgent and therefore why not test them tomorrow, instead of right now? Added to this are the high proportion of tests that confirm the assumption as true, and the smaller proportion that prove to be inconclusive or raise more questions than they answer. Where an assumption is compromised, then an alternative tactic can usually be devised.

The reality, however, is that blue items are still critical and if they are compromised they will impact the strategy or implementation of the strategy and this impact must be considered. Therefore, regardless of how easy these are to ignore and excuses found for not doing it, they must be tested. It is imperative that the test programme, is policed and that senior management back the test programme even when things appear to be going well. The sad fact is the better things are going, the less enthusiasm there is for investigating critical assumptions that might spoil the moment.

THE CLIENTS ROLE IN A STORM

The STORM meetings are required to be conducted weekly by the strategic planning team. Where consultants are being used, these meetings may not require the client to be present.

Clients may wish only to have a weekly report delivered to them, but if they do they must be prepared to be called in when a critical assumption looks like it is being compromised. This is because no matter how familiar a consultancy becomes with your industry, they will never manage to match your experience and understanding. Therefore accept, when using consultants, that you are in partnership with them—that you are *not* abdicating responsibility to them.

GMAS works by combining theory with sound experience, which you are most qualified to provide. Even if you are new to the company, the exposure to the STORM meetings will provide you with a fast track to industry knowledge that you will find hard to match in such a short period of time by any other means. However, planning involves making decisions in the light of market intelligence and having knowledge alone is not enough. Risks have to be considered and decisions made. This is where you will find consultants get rather shy. They can provide you with the options, but they cannot make decisions for you. You must make the decisions, as best you can, based on your judgement and experience.

It is therefore better if staff can be spared to at least observe at the weekly STORM meetings if consultants are used and even if you are running the system in-house, you should try to invite staff members to attend and contribute to the process. However, be warned, knowledge brings power and those who seek power often want to attend all these meetings and the STORM must not become involved in company politics. The STORM should be like the British Army—apolitical—and take the necessary steps to remain so.

The best people to involve in the STORM meetings are those with an existing depth of knowledge about the industry and especially the company. They should have experience in the company, have a positive attitude, and above all they should have an open mind.

Key Points

The STORM is a necessary activity that involves the strategic planning team in making decisions and providing the human interphase with the various data inputs. It effectively replaces the strategic planning cycle, providing smaller inputs to strategy, rather like an autopilot in an aircraft keeping the plane on course and avoiding the need for major control movements.

The majority of events result in no or only minor strategic changes being required while paradigm shift can be detected and exploited. The fundamental ability to investigate early variations from plan, allows errors in execution to be corrected while the synergy from combining operational, tactical and strategic intelligence provides robust and aligned strategic, operational and tactical plans. This generates a strategically aligned and focused organization that lives the strategy because it is relevant throughout the organization.

SUMMARY

- We looked deep into the heart of GMAS STORM and explored its role and function as well as dissecting its component parts: Strategy, Operational Planning, Staff, Monitoring, Testing and Real-Time Critical Assumptions.

- We investigated the grey areas in the interpretation of market intelligence and the need for both monitoring and testing of assumptions.

- Finally we showed that change in strategy was not going to be too frequent and that GMAS provides a powerful mechanism for ensuring faultless execution.

6

Irrefutable Research a Necessity

NEEDED INFORMATION ONLY

You will recall that the breakthrough marketing model limits the amount of research that we should conduct to 'needed information only'. After reading Chapter 4, and especially the sections on monitoring and testing, you might find this difficult to believe.

Testing the validity of the critical assumptions we have based our strategy upon is clearly needed information, as is the monitoring of the critical assumptions for indications of them becoming compromised. The research associated with the critical assumptions is wholly justified by our needed information only research policy.

Research initially gathered in the strategic planning process can also be required in the plans derived from the strategy, for example the financial, marketing, personnel, quality, facilities plans and their derivatives. Research is required in the case of a simple strategic marketing plan about the product, pricing, promotion and distribution plans and their derivatives, in the case of the promotional plan the media, public relations, sales promotion, sales plans and their derivatives, in the case of the sales promotion plans the exhibition, point of sales materials and their derivatives etc., all the way to the individual action plans of those who will actually do the work. All these steps require some research or at least access to the corporate knowledge base. Thus, when considering needed information, a thorough understanding of what information is essential at each stage of the cascade down to the individual's KPI, has to be considered so as to maximize each piece of research data gathered.

If we are going to gather only needed information and there are a multitude of places where information is required, we should endeavour not to reinvent the wheel too often or gather the same information twice.

The need for a corporate knowledge base is therefore obvious. It will reduce the learning time for new staff and general research required throughout the organization. If we gather the information in one exercise, in the full knowledge of who will be interested in using it or at least keeping track of the sources, we can conduct the research to provide only the needed information quickly, effectively and efficiently.

When specifying what is 'needed information' it is necessary to:

- Consider all the potential users within the organization

- Have a storage and, more importantly, a retrieval system in place to access the information collected

- Record the sources of information and when gathering information from respondents keep in mind you will most probably need to talk to them again.

Before gathering any information you must answer the following questions to be sure it is needed.

Why do we need this information?

The information and the marketing intelligence and knowledge that it will lead to must be critical or at least important to your organization. If data collected is simply 'nice to know' or routine, it should not be gathered.

I am constantly surprised by the number of research commissions that we get only to find that most of the information the clients think they need they in fact do not need or use. There are a number of studies conducted, you can probably think of some in your organization, which were set up for a very good reason but have since lost their relevance and no one has questioned the need to go on collecting the information. Whenever you see a report, ask yourself what is the importance and relevance of the information being presented. If you cannot use the information or turn it into market intelligence or knowledge, then something is wrong and you should be questioning why this information is being gathered, or at least given to you to read.

What will you do with the results?

There must be a use for the information being gathered. When reviewing questions on a questionnaire, I often come across the common error of double questions such as 'How happy were you with the new product and service provided?' where the respondent answers on a satisfaction scale. However, what does the answer mean and what will you do with the answers given? If a respondent is dissatisfied, where is the problem? Is the dissatisfaction with the product or the service provided? Who should we report this information to: service or product development or both? If the respondent was actually unhappy with the service but loved the product, how would we know? Will taking action on the strength of the results leave a department searching for a fault that does not exist? Ultimately, both you and I would probably commission further research to try to find out where the problem lies, with the service or the product. This could have been avoided by simply asking two questions and avoiding the 'double' question error.

Always consider how the research will be used. Mock up the answers and ask yourself 'Are these results going to provide the information I need to take action?' Only commission research that will generate 'actionable' data, that is, that you can act on the results you get.

What would we do if we did not have the data?

Can you get by without the research results or would you be taking an unnecessary or even unacceptable risk to do so?

Some organizations give customer satisfaction research only lip service, despite it now being part of the new ISO 9001 requirements. If you do not conduct customer satisfaction research, in the short term nothing much changes, and if you are very close to a small number of customers you will probably consider this research as not needed information because the customers' views are already known and re-inforced daily. You would be right in this circumstance, but if you have multiple customers served by third parties, then customer satis-faction research is vital to numerous parts of the organization.

The chances are that a variety of departments within the organ-ization are all trying to survey the same customers causing more harm than good. Therefore, by considering how the results will be used within the context of the whole organization, needed information can be gathered efficiently. But if you can get by with the research then consider doing so.

Who needs the information?

Listing all the staff that can benefit from this information is a first step in building the ENT that I mentioned in Chapter 5. Sticking with the customer satisfaction example, who would benefit in your organization from measuring customer satisfaction? I think you would be pushed to find someone who would not; especially if we consider the internal customers who receive internally provided support and services. In Cisco systems staff bonuses use a multiplier on individuals' and de-partments' internal or external customer satisfaction score. If facilities do not provide you with good service, you get to let them know and it will affect their bonuses if they don't improve. Therefore customer satisfaction scores are needed by all but the perspective is different throughout the organization. What service wants to know in customer satisfaction terms is quite different from what new product develop-ment wants to know. It is important to get a thorough view on what each perspective is going to be before commissioning customer satis-faction research.

Have we already got the information?

This may sound simplistic and obvious, but before commencing re-search make sure the information is not already being gathered within the company. We have been commissioned to do research before now only to find, as we start to talk to the staff, that the same or very similar information has already been gathered. On one occasion I was handed a report that had been completed by a student on placement and contained almost all the information the client required. And, in case you are wondering, I did let the client know and simply updated the work, which had been done to a very reasonable standard. Information is also gathered for other purposes and it is always better to ensure you at least know what has been gathered before. In one company we worked for, we estimated that they were spending $3 million a year on various research exercises and talking to their customers, most of which was duplication of effort. We recommended that as a first step, they find out who was commissioning research and that all research had to be cleared through a central research agency in one area of their business prior to commencement. By implementing this, research bills were cut from an estimated $3 million to $900 000! Seven different parts of the business were surveying the same customer group, asking almost the same questions, each one unaware of the others' activities. Each group charged the research to a different budget code making it impossible for the finance department to clearly identify true corporate research expenditure.

Have we diagnosed the knowledge requirement accurately?
I have been talking about customer satisfaction research, but why do we really want it? The obvious answer is because we want satisfied customers. However, if we apply the 'why test', first developed by children just after they learn to talk, we come across a different reason.

PARENT	Go to bed
CHILD	Why?
PARENT	Because you need your sleep.
CHILD	Why?
PARENT	Your body needs time to get refreshed for tomorrow.
CHILD	Why?
PARENT	Go To Bed NOW!

Just as it can be infuriating to parents, it is extremely powerful at getting to the root of the issue. Perhaps because of our early experiences, using the word we forget to ask it often enough when we have become adults.

QUESTION	Why do we want to know about customer satisfaction?
ANSWER	So we can provide better products and services.

QUESTION   Why?
ANSWER   Because we want loyal customers.
QUESTION   Why?
ANSWER   Because loyal customers will stay with us longer and
            make us more profit.

From the why test, it is clear that it is not customer satisfaction in itself that is important but how this impacts customer loyalty. There is an old saying that you have loyal customers right up until the time they buy from your competitor. This shows that it is not just loyalty, but what causes it to break down that is important. Chasing customer satisfaction without understanding its 'elasticity' is just getting a part of the needed information. Customer satisfaction must be viewed in the context of loyalty, competitors, cost to improve and break factors (what causes the loyalty to break down and at what point does it occur?).

If we look at a branded computer and compare it to a non-branded generic one, an owner of the branded computer, in choosing his or her next computer will be influenced, of course, by the experience with the current computer, but will also be influenced by many other factors. When other factors draw the brand-buying customer to buy the generic product, just how strong these factors have to be is the degree of 'loyalty elasticity'. At some point the factors will exceed the loyalty elasticity and loyalty will break down. Therefore, simply measuring customer satisfaction is not always enough. Loyalty and loyalty limits have also to be understood for customer satisfaction data to be actionable and for that action to effectively strengthen customer loyalty and improve its elasticity.

What format must the information be presented in to be most usable?

Gathering information in a non-usable form is a waste of time. I have heard of marketing departments commissioning benchmarking information with a view to publicizing their ranking only to find that the information they have gathered has restrictions on its distribution and use for marketing purposes is expressly forbidden.

The classic examples are what I call the 'single number reports'. These reports produce a single number, say, for customer satisfaction, and you are expected to do something if the customer satisfaction falls and you are presumed to have done something right if it rises. However, many managers do not truly understand statistics and those that do agree with British Victorian Prime Minister Benjamin Disraeli when he said, 'There are lies, dammed lies and statistics'. What is happening when the customer satisfaction score rises or falls depends on a number of factors other than the actual level of customer satisfaction. There are error margins in all research and when you see a single figure, you can be sure that it is wrong. There is always a margin of error to take into account. You will have observed that pollsters report their results as, for example, 78 per cent plus or minus 2 per cent. What they are saying is that the real number is somewhere between 76 per cent and 80 per cent. If the next result was 76 per cent $+/-$ 2 per cent would there be a difference? Well there may be, but that is not certain. Returning to the customer satisfaction example, one week's results showing customer satisfaction at 78 per cent and the next week's showing it at 76 per cent may mean nothing has changed. In order for the information to be useful, the needed information is not the customer satisfaction score alone, but the score plus the margin of error.

How reliable and valid must the information be?

Above I mentioned the margin of error, however, if you need to know something accurately this must be specified and be within the realms of reality. At board level it may be acceptable to review accounts to the nearest million, at department level to the nearest thousand, while individual projects may be to the nearest dollar, pound, euro or yen. All of these figures, one assumes, are reliable. The margins of error may then be in proportion to the scale being used. A margin of error equivalent to rounding to the nearest million may be acceptable at board level, while no error may be accepted in a petty cash report.

There are two important concepts to get across in any type of survey and these concepts are reliability and validity.

Reliability

Reliability is the consistency of the survey tool. If I conduct a survey by telephone month on month, I can produce reliable data just as I can

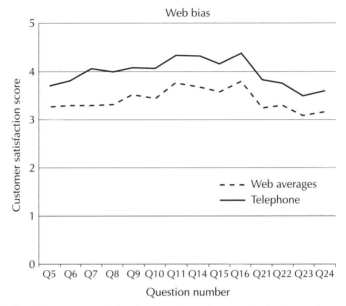

Figure 6.1   Customer satisfaction variance by method adopted.

if I survey by e-mail month on month. However, if I survey by e-mail one month and by telephone the next, even when both methods may be reliable on their own, I will have created an unreliable methodology. That is to say that the results would not be consistent month on month.

Validity
A valid survey tool is accurate in serving the purpose for which it is designed and provides correct information. The fact that a telephone customer satisfaction survey generated higher satisfaction scores than a web-based survey suggests that either method or indeed both may not be valid. However, they both become valid if the purpose is to monitor a trend, because both reflect the actual customer satisfaction reliably. Figure 6.1 which shows the same population's customer satisfaction being monitored by both telephone research and e-mail in a web-based survey (I have removed the margins of error for clarity).

Validity and Reliability

An interesting statement could be made at this point: if a survey is unreliable, it is invalid. Valid instruments are always reliable but reliable tools are not always valid. Testing my previous example, telephone and web-based research are both reliable, that is, they pro-duce consistent results. However, they do not produce the same answers, therefore one or both may not be valid. They both follow a very similar pattern and would appear to be correlated to each other and to the actual customer satisfaction. If the purpose is to map the trends in customer satisfaction, taken individually we find that they clearly do that. This suggests that they are valid instruments to moni-tor trends, if not the absolute customer satisfaction score. Therefore, as they are valid, they should be reliable—which they are.

Well, if you are still awake, the point is that you must be aware of the requirement for validity and reliability and, if you are pushed to choose, choose validity because a valid survey is always reliable. If you see unreliable surveys, be quite clear that the information they are providing is invalid. Like accounts, they can only be valid if they have been recorded in a consistent manner.

Publics Maps

Having taken on board the need to gather only needed information; the next question raised is to whom should we be talking? Publics maps chart the organization's external relationships and their exchange balance. They help focus on the most important relation-ships and what influences them. In addition, they consist of several layers of detail. At the top layer they map the main relationships, both influential and transactional, while at the more detailed level they will link to databases or industry directories. Using a package such as Ygnius or Idons for Thinking, you can build publics maps very quickly and interactively (see Appendix 1 for details of both packages). Figure 6.2 shows a publics map for a company in the power industry. Each of the arms can be hyperlinked to more pages of maps or to documents or websites. It is very easy using this software to generate publics maps. The level of detail required is a matter of judgement and will vary from organization to organization.

THE RESEARCH BRIEF

The research brief for monitoring and testing outlines the ways in which research is commissioned, recorded, gathered and reported.

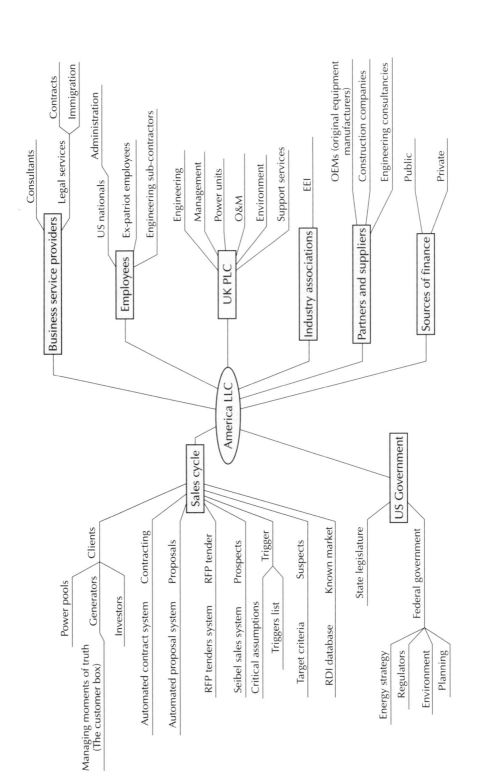

Figure 6.2 Example of first level publics—map power industry.

The results will only be as useful as the brief that is used to commission the research.

If you request that the rate of growth of the market be monitored you may be disappointed in the results because the researcher will not know whether you are referring to the rate of growth of the market as a whole (global), the national market, regional market or a specific segment of the market you are operating in. The growth element in a market may be for a new innovation only. For example, the software market may be expanding at 20 per cent per annum, but the niche that is causing the growth may be Internet-based applications and not the LAN (local area network) application segment that you are operating in. For this reason it is necessary to get the research brief right and to specify your critical assumptions in Real-Time format as I outlined in Chapter 5. In short, the more precise your research brief is, the more precise the results will be. Above all, the research brief must *not* be ambiguous.

Closed Domain Markets

With increasing storage capacity and processor speed improvements it is now almost possible to consider all markets in a closed domain context. That is to say, that we can identify all those who could possibly buy our products or services. I recently bought for $35, a four CD set containing the US and Canada phone book from CD USA. It has 104 million businesses and households listed including 16 million US businesses. Figure 6.3 shows the context of a closed domain market. The cuplike shape represents your company's market share and the other cup, the competitors. The market as a whole is bound and new suspects enter while others leave. The extent of your market share depends on how much of the market you can scoop into your cup, the size of the cup, the ability of your cup to retain customers as well as the number of free customers around.

As the data is usually available, it is gathered as the first stage of a typical GMAS sales module. A typical sales model is illustrated in Figure 6.4. Known market occupies the 12 o'clock position and to its right is a group known as 'suspects'. These are companies who you know will benefit from your product or service, but they may not know this themselves. Next to this group is a category called

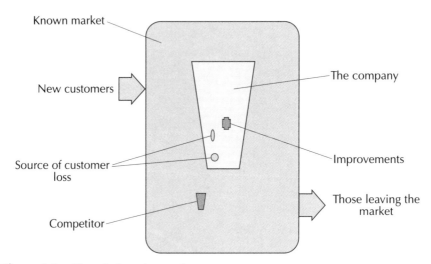

Figure 6.3 Closed domain market.

'trigger'. Triggers are events internal or external to the suspect or known market, which cause the companies affected to seek the kind of service you are providing.

Monitoring activities and testing research are very effective at identifying active triggers in your market and thus generating sales leads. Where you have a suspect subjected to an active trigger you have created the next group, 'prospects'. A prospect is a company that has identified a need for your type of service and you have the product

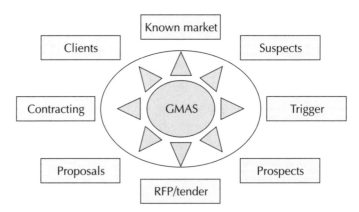

Figure 6.4 The GMAS business-to-business sales process model.

Figure 6.5 Screen shot of clients—Intranet showing edited highlights of panel findings.

or service to satisfy to your mutual profit. The remainder of the stages in Figure 6.4 refer to turning the prospect into a customer and there are further GMAS modules that can be utilized to turn a customer into a repeat customer. These are described in Chapter 10.

GMAS Panels

Having a closed domain market means that GMAS panels can be built. A GMAS panel is a group of the 'known market' members or influencers that are willing to take part in future research. This is built during the strategic planning process or during monitoring or testing research simply by asking those who participate if they would be willing to take part in future research. This group can be formalized into an expert panel or advisory group. The group meet regularly and are asked to consider some of the questions generated by the STORM or during scenario planning. The group is video recorded and edited highlights of the meeting is produced on a CNN style news bulletin which is available over the company intranet or for presentations to the groups within the company that the ENT suggests will be interested. Figure 6.5 is a screen shot illustration of an intranet bulletin.

The rapid and wide access to the actual panel members' views provides irrefutable accuracy. There is no 'interpretation' error or bias as it is their words almost live. I remember one client, for whom GMAS unfortunately predicted their imminent downfall and they chose to ignore the warnings.

Picture the scene: we were to present the panel results to a group of over 50 senior managers from this specific division who had to travel into Dallas Fort Worth airport from all over the US, Asia Pacific and Europe. The conference was at the airport and I was the item on the agenda just before lunch on the first day. I showed the videos of this company's major customers. Each had been interviewed individually and consented to having their message broadcast. One after another they described the way they were being treated and what they thought was good and bad about this company. As I turned off the video there was nothing but silence and absolute shock on the faces of the audience. They were speechless, they had no idea what the customer actually felt, they had, of course, read the market reports, but until they actually saw the customers and the intensity of their feelings, they had not realized the seriousness of the situation.

The rest of the conference was spent developing ways of addressing the issues raised. The mood was sombre and I think these managers were honestly frightened by what they heard. Just over a year later the company was in serious trouble with thousands of jobs being lost worldwide. The manager who had commissioned the research unfortunately could not get the attention of the very senior managers, who did not have time to watch the videos or visit the Intranet site we had built. Embittered, he resigned and went off to a start-up company.

This experience highlighted three significant challenges with GMAS research and its ability to generate irrefutable knowledge. You may not want to know the truth. It may appear too difficult to do anything about the problems. Others, especially in a blame culture, may not be willing to listen; after all they may have been responsible for the problems. The truth is, companies do not get into such a mess unless there are multiple mistakes and they are covered up. They remind me of deferred taxation—you can put off the day you have to pay your taxes, but in the end you always have to pay them.

A, perhaps regrettable, by-product of GMAS is that it uncovers all the skeletons in the cupboard. Perhaps this is why it has outstanding success with new companies, IPOs (Initial Public Offerings), MBIs (Market Buy-Ins), demergers or where new management is introduced or when the crises hits, because there are no skeletons in the cupboard or if there have been any they have already come out.

I remember a film where a man was granted a wish. His wish was that he could see the future. It ended with him plucking out his own eyes. GMAS does not give you a perfect vision of the future, nothing can, but it does provide a better insight into what the future holds than you may be willing to accept.

GMAS Research Pools
Research pools are usually built up during the strategic planning research by simply asking those who take part in research if they would be willing to take part in future research. Alternatively, they are built up from transactional research activities, again simply by asking respondents from transactional research studies if they would be willing to participate in future research, how frequently and by what mechanism (telephone, e-mail, website, fax, panel, focus group, personal interview etc.).

Thus, a pool is built up which, if you undertake regular transactional research, can be kept current. This pool has major benefits when answers are required to questions raised during a STORM where a survey has to be commissioned and reported within days. This is only possible by using research pools. I find the best customer pools are produced by organizations that do regular transactions research but for wider audiences. Omnibus type studies can serve the same purpose, and several of the major research companies have permanent industry-sector-based research pools to which you can buy access.

The main benefits from the pools are the lead-time in commissioning research, response rates are very high, and by profiling pool membership, representative samples of the population you are interested in can be constructed. I almost forgot—they are also substantially less costly than traditional research.

There are also some drawbacks, but these are mainly based on the nature of the sample. Because members are willing to participate in research, the pool population may be in some material way, different from those who are not willing to participate. This has happened in election opinion polling where those not willing to take part in the poll

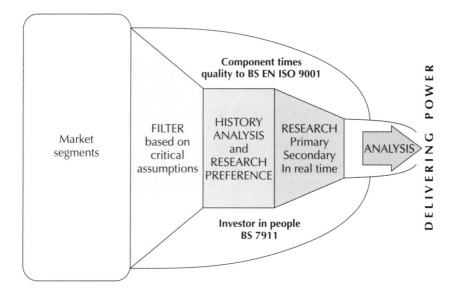

Figure 6.6   GMAS research engine.

held a strong political view and chose to express it only at the ballot box. This happened in the UK in the run up to the 1992 General Election when John Major (the Conservative Party leader and incumbent Prime Minister) was elected while the opinion polls predicted a Labour landslide.

GMAS Research Engine
Figure 6.6 shows the GMAS research engine. The engine uses transactional data to generate market intelligence in the following way: The known market is defined and then filtered based on the critical assumptions. Samples are drawn in this group and they are screened against the research history file and customer research preferencing systems. Research is then conducted to the quality assurance standards of BS EN ISO 9001, and BS 7911. The results are then analysed, verified and reported.

WHAT IS IRREFUTABLE

I have already mentioned the concept of irrefutable research. What I mean is that research that is valid and free from bias is irrefutable. The concept can be summed up using the formula $M = R + B$ What we measure (M) is equal to the real answer (R) plus the bias (B). There is always bias of some kind or another, e.g. interviewer, question design and sample. Irrefutable research aims to eliminate as much bias as possible therefore reflecting better the true result. While bias cannot totally be eliminated, it is possible to detect errors and, as they can be detected, they can be retrospectively allowed for or removed.

In the early GMAS trials, I found that the general quality of the research available on the market at that time was so poor that it was making GMAS ineffective. In order to overcome this, we designed our own research centre, and recruited and trained our own research team, with native speakers of 15 different languages. This allowed us to produce research to the required standard and get as close to irrefutable as possible. Quality assurance initiatives in the industry have gone some way to improving the general quality of research and the agency's membership of a professional body can be a safer choice when deciding on a research provider. Do not get me wrong; the quality is fine for most purposes but simply not always good enough for GMAS where you are using the results to manage your strategic alignment with the reality of the market environment.

Quality Assurance

Quality assurance in research is paramount and to get close to irrefutable research results you need to ensure your research provider at least meets, if not exceeds, the following four quality standards or their equivalents. BS EN ISO 9001, BS 7911, MRQSA and IIP. MMSI plc is registered/accredited to all four and these should be considered the starting point for achievement of irrefutable research.

BS EN ISO 9001

This is the international quality assurance standard. What is covered by the quality standard is specified in the scope of registration. For example, MMSI plc is quality assured to BS EN ISO 9001 'for the provision of market research and consultancy services'. It is wise to check that the scope of registration is appropriate to the type of work you require the partner or contractor to perform.

BS 7911
This is the British quality standard for organizations conducting market research and sets the minimum standard for quality control and research design and execution. BS7911 was established in 1998.

MRQSA
This is the quality assurance standard of the UK's Market Research Society and outlines the procedures that must be followed as a minimum to ensure quality in research outputs.

IIP Investors in People
The Investors in People standard is a quality standard for staff. It provides a framework that organizations use to help them improve performance. Organizations that meet the standard have to show that they are committed to developing their people; that they have clear goals, their investment in people directly helps them meet these goals; they understand the impact that this investment has on staff performance. I believe that at the end of the day, it is the quality of the research staff that makes the difference. Well-trained, motivated staff with a high level of integrity is essential in providing irrefutable research data.

Codes of Conduct
As well as quality assurance there are codes of conduct for most of the professions that conduct research, for example the codes of conduct of the Market Research Society and the Chartered Institute of Marketing, the Management Consultants Association. It goes without saying that these codes must be strictly adhered to.

ACCESS TO INFORMATION

As important as the conduct of the research, is the access to the research results and analysis. Flooding people with information is counterproductive, while depriving them of it is equally bad. Have you ever been at a meeting where you have been annoyed at not being informed about something, only to be told that it was in such and such a report that you routinely get?

Humans are animals that have survived by noticing differences in their environment. We can somehow block out the norm. Perhaps our

ancestors survived by noticing a movement in the bushes or an un-
familiar outline in the grass. This ability means that we tend to ignore,
or not notice, our 'familiar' environment after a while.

While working on projects in the hotel industry, I was often
amazed that I could see so many things wrong but those who worked
there day to day could not. A classic example would be a worn carpet.
Yes, they had noticed it, but after a while they did not and no action
was taken, meanwhile the image it was projecting to the guests was
costing the hotel money.

The art is to ensure that the right people get the right information
at the right time. This of course is much easier said than done. Routine reports tend to get ignored if they are not completely relevant
while e-mail contains so much internally created junk that managers
tend to ignore it too. The ENT network ensures that managers should
be interested in a piece of market intelligence they are given access to.
However, having access is not enough; they need access at the right
time, or when something has changed, not when everything is normal
or as predicted. Currently some managers have to see the 'as predicted' result for fear that if they do not get the information things
are going wrong. Perhaps this is because in many organizations when
things start to go wrong you notice it by the lack of information being
provided. 'No news is *not* always good news.'

As ENTs are established, there is a change in information flows
and more trust in information can be established. However, this is a
two-way process. Where there is no feedback on the relevance of
information or on how it is being used, the ENT system will tend to
default to sending too much information.

Information needs have to be divided into three colours very like
Critical Assumptions. Information or market intelligence coded red is
both urgent and of importance to the recipient (sales are falling below
estimate). Blue is important but not urgent (sales on target) and green
is information that the individuals must have the ability to access when
they choose to. Green presents the most challenge in that it is difficult
to predict what information an individual may require. For this reason
web accessible knowledge bases are the most suitable utilizing advanced search engines. In this way staff find what they are looking
for, and with practice and a little training with a very organized and
strongly policed filing policy, a knowledge base can be made to work.

Please do not underestimate the policing required because the knowledge tree created is only as strong as its weakest branches.

Knowledge Security

When you create a GMAS or any other knowledge base for your organization the issue of security will be raised. This has to be addressed because for a knowledge base to be effective it must give access to its knowledge. The more restrictions placed on the access, the less effective the knowledge base becomes but the lower the risk of unauthorized use. Information has to be classified into categories relating to its sensitivity. Clearly, financial information in a plc must remain classified until such time as the public announcement is made to avoid the potential for insider trading among other things.

The UK's Department of Trade and Industry recommends information is categorized into three levels: SEC 1, SEC 2 and SEC 3.

SEC 1 Information that is private but not highly confidential. The majority of information (I estimate 60 per cent) in a company knowledge base falls into this category.

SEC 2 Information that could cause significant harm if disclosed. This will be about 30 per cent of the information and include all market intelligence.

SEC 3 Information that would cause very serious damage if disclosed. This is very small—probably less than 10 per cent.

Who gets access to what is a matter for debate but a policy is required that balances the risks of giving access to information with the loss of opportunity that results from restricting access.

Web or Intranet Access

Knowledge access is one of those 24-7 things. It should be available when and wherever staff members need to have access. Therefore, the only practical solution is a secure web-access-based system.

Dynamic Reporting

The GMAS provides reporting systems using a system developed by MMSI called Dynamic Reporting. This system allows research results to be delivered securely and dynamically, so that users can request whichever survey, the period they want to look at and have the results generated in real time. From the broadest results overview, respondents can drill down to find out who gave a particular response to a particular question, at a particular time. The purpose of Dynamic Reporting is that it gives authorized users access to research being gathered in real time at the right time in the right format for the users purpose.

Competitive Intelligence Acquisition (CIA)

Fredrick the Great wrote: 'It is pardonable to be defeated, but never to be surprised'. I enjoyed playing with the anagrams for this section, but there is a serious message about the moral and ethical limits to marketing intelligence and its acquisition for strategic planning.

RECONNAISSANCE

Arthur Wellesley, the first Duke of Wellington said 'Time spent in reconnaissance is seldom wasted', and this is also true of the collection of market and Competitive Intelligence.

The Principles of CIA
Competitive Intelligence is the process of acquiring data in GMAS testing or monitoring, sorting and processing it and then determining what is useful and what is not. This is done in the STORM. Once the useful information has been extracted, it can be applied to provide a marketing advantage for your company.

What does CIA do?
Professor Bernard Jaworski of the University of Arizona reports that Competitive Intelligence leads to:

1 Increased quality.
2 Improved strategic planning.
3 Superior knowledge of the market.

What else can CIA do?
It provides the ability to:

1 Effectively identify and anticipate changes in the marketplace.

2   Predict competitor actions.
3   Learn in advance about political, legislative or regulatory changes that affect your business.
4   Benchmark and improve your organization's business practices.
5   Implement management systems and processes.
6   Provide a competitive advantage.

Why do organizations increasingly require CIA?

1   The pace of business is increasing and the time available to make decisions is reducing.
2   Data overload is making it increasingly difficult for managers to find the time to analyse data, let alone extract useful information and apply it to the company's advantage.
3   Increased global competition means that competitors arise from anywhere.
4   Existing competitors are becoming more aggressive.
5   Political changes have a faster and more forceful impact than they once did.
6   Rapid technological change and the increased dangers of competitor breakthroughs can produce paradigm shift and destroy your market in a very short space of time.

Why don't more organizations use CIA?

Regular reasons that are given for not employing CIA include:
1   We already 'know the market' (I hope they are right!).
2   Nothing important happens outside our company as we 'lead the world' (as did the American automotive industry until the Japanese taught them an expensive lesson).
3   Competitive Intelligence is 'spying' (a misconception caused by confusion between gathering Competitive Intelligence and industrial espionage: one of which is legal and ethical, while the other is illegal and unethical).
4   Competitive Intelligence is 'too costly' (if you think it is expensive, then count the cost of ignorance).
5   It has been tried before and it does not work (only recently has the technology to undertake effective CIA been available and GMAS to turn it into actionable knowledge).

Marketing Intelligence

The gathering of competitive marketing intelligence can be divided into six levels:

MI 1 Gathering secondary research on markets or competitors.

MI 2 Gathering primary research on markets or competitors.

MI 3 Undertaking private or public benchmarking with markets or competitors.

MI 4 Active intelligence gathering.

MI 5 Defence against industrial espionage.

The Legal and Ethical Line

MI 6 Offensive intelligence gathering, including infiltration and other forms of industrial espionage, which are best left to various state security services.

Marketing Management Services International plc offers a service from MI 1 to MI 4. We do not undertake work that would be classified as MI 5 or MI 6.

MI 1 This is standard practice in almost all firms performed when you look at the competitive market position as reported by third parties.

MI 2 Most firms gather information during surveys to determine how their products or services compare to those of competitors, GMAS companies do much more focused research.

MI 3 Many companies participate in the 'benchmarking' exercise. For example, almost all the major oil firms participate in IT Systems benchmarking activities for mutual benefit and to reduce IT costs across the industry. MI 3 is very effective at taking costs out of the supply chain and in remodelling or reengineering business processes and it is normally mutually beneficial to all those that participate.

MI 4 This is active intelligence gathering such as visiting a competitor and noting their prices or mystery shopping involving competitors' outlets.

In the telecommunications industry, Bell Atlantic and AT&T are both cited in recent literature as using active intelligence gathering.

For example, Bell Atlantic physically monitors their competitors' mobile phone coverage while AT&T maintains a database of in-house experience/expertise that is utilized to provide added insight into research gathering.

MI 5   These are the steps you take to defend your company from industrial espionage. This can include such things as sweeping board-rooms for bugs, having scramblers on telephone lines and most importantly, the defence of your computer systems from hackers. In one particular week I was amazed to find that we had had almost 10 000 attempts to penetrate our system. Our IT manager told me this kind of activity was unfortunately becoming more and more common.

MI6   Well, rather like its namesake Military Intelligence 6, this is the involvement in covert operations. Watergate is a prime example of this but there are many more. Companies who undertake this type of activity are breaking the laws of most countries in the world. However, we have been a victim of this and perhaps you have been, too. We once took on a trainee consultant, who was quite excellent and whizzed through our training programme getting some of the top marks. This chap came in early, worked late and always wanted to do extra work. He kept great notes and copies of everything, building a port-folio, as he explained, 'to help him do his job better'. One day my secretary came to me and showed me a letter that she had found in the waste paper basket. The document was a half written note to a com-petitor of ours thanking him for lunch and confirming that he would have the rest of the information he wanted by Friday. On checking the computer access records this chap had been systematically looking through all our knowledge base and copying files. I called him in and he resigned, but even then tried to leave with some of our files which were only all returned after a threat of prosecution was made. I contacted the police but they really did not want to know. We had been losing jobs to unknown competitors, which turned out to have been on many occasions the competitor this chap was obviously work-ing for. No wonder he was so good! The damage was considerable and could have been fatal for the company had it not been detected.

I subsequently found out this company had another great scam. It owned a temp agency, supplying secretaries, etc. and debriefing the temporary staff after each assignment. In this way it was able to identify the consultancy services it should promote and to whom in what company; knowing the politics and the problems was worth a lot to this organization.

I would like to tell you of this company's downfall, but life is not like that, they have been very successful and their business expands each year.

Having irrefutable research is key to being successful in the market and the methods of collecting the data, its accuracy, reliability and above all validity are paramount.

SUMMARY

- We reviewed the need for and methods of obtaining irrefutable research and looked at the essential elements in commissioning research of this nature.

- We talked about reliability and validity and concluded that valid research is always reliable, but not all reliable research is valid.

- We explored research options and closed markets as well as the quality standards of BS EN ISO 9001, BS7911 MRQSA and IIP and their role in research.

- Finally, we examined data security and marketing intelligence and separated the ethical from the unethical.

7

How to Use, Modify and Build GMAS Modules

THE GMAS MODULES

GMAS has been designed in an open modular format so that each part of the process of running and managing a business can be documented into the GMAS format. If the rules in the design are followed, GMAS modules can be built up over time and the whole organization can be integrated into the GMAS way of thinking, at a pace that works. Rather like the GMAS sales modules where suspects and the known market require an active trigger to buy, departments and managers require a trigger to be active for them to buy into the GMAS concept. Getting involved in designing a module is a very good way of introducing the concept and at the same time improving the operational parts of the business.

Figure 7.1 shows a typical GMAS cluster of modules. The software in use here is IDONS and each of the modules hyperlinks to the detail or to the appropriate package.

MODULES

As well as the core GMAS modules of STORM, Right-Time research, Monitoring, Real-Time Critical Assumptions, Strategy, Operations and Staff, there is a host of other GMAS modules related to best practice in strategy, implementation and research. These have

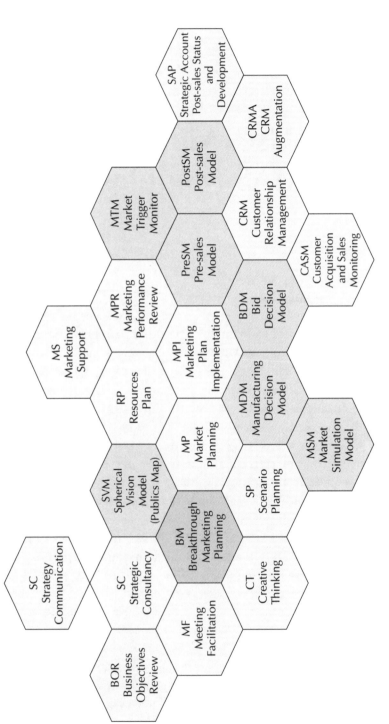

Figure 7.1 Typical GMAS cluster.

grown initially, out of the investigation of compromised critical assumptions, where the strategy was considered sound but somehow the tactical execution was flawed. In many cases the organization was following a process that had worked in the past, or that was well documented in practice-based literature, yet it was nonetheless failing to deliver in this particular instance. This investigation raised the question of what works in which circumstances.

The potential range of modules is as wide as the potential business activities you have to undertake in the strategic and operational management of your organization. It is hoped that GMAS modules that provide mutual benefit to many organizations can be benchmarked. The GMAS modules outline what works, on what occasion it works and why it works. However, before considering this, there are several things that need to be taken into account.

CONSIDERATION OF THE PUBLICS

One of the principles of breakthrough marketing is that the solutions are unique: no two companies are identical, rather like fingerprints or DNA. However, just because you have a unique fingerprint or DNA, does not mean that you do everything differently from everyone else. What you have to be aware of is that not everything is appropriate for everyone, some people's DNA may make them highly susceptible to cancer in later life if they smoke. Likewise, in companies, some forms of best practice work well in one organization but are not portable to another.

Care must be taken in adopting practice from other organizations experiences, and systems that claim to contain 'The best practice' are in my view flawed, because best practice changes depending on your firm's alignment, market conditions and your publics, among other factors. GMAS provides 'best practice', but also states under which conditions and in which environments this 'best practice' will have the highest probability of working. There is no one universally applicable best practice but the nearer companies are to a common alignment, the better a single best practice will fit them.

Because best practice may work on one day and not on another because of competitor, economic or environmental changes, reliability issues are addressed in a GMAS module. In addition, the variations that need to be tackled to ensure that the best practice is uniquely modified to perform as best practice for your organization, are also included.

The publics for the module have to be clearly defined and the relationships the module addresses well understood. This ensures that there is enough focus to make the module fit within the 80/20 rule that I will discuss below.

SYSTEMS THEORY 80/20

I am often made aware of why some things will not work and I am never short of the example of where a system will not work in this or that circumstance. Likewise, I am continuously bombarded by sales literature claiming that one system or another will work 100 per cent. The reality of systems is that if they can be made to handle 80 per cent of the situations you will face, they can be regarded as perfect. If you try to build them to handle 100 per cent of possibilities, you get into a circle of diminishing returns.

I am reminded of the old quality story: what level of quality is good enough—99 per cent, 99.9 per cent or even 6 Sigma 99.9997 per cent? Don't ask me why it ends with a seven; ask Peter Pande *et al.*, the authors of *The Six Sigma Way* (2000). If we accepted only 99.9 per cent quality, thousands of babies would slip from the nurses' grip each day in our maternity wards; a jumbo jet would crash each day; the list goes on and on. If this is true at 99.9 per cent quality, how can I call a system that has a reliability level of 80 per cent, good?

If we took all the things that go into getting an airliner from A to B, we would find systems for almost everything, but no one system handles the whole process from start to finish. There are just too many variables and trying to build the system that could handle every eventuality would be too complicated. There are systems to fly the plane, load the passengers, book slots with air traffic control, etc., each one, if taken individually, may be to six sigma quality but nonetheless, they will not be able to handle 100 per cent of eventualities.

Building GMAS to the Pareto Principle (80/20 rule) allows for the design to get started. I feel an untracked source of system failure, perhaps the single most common cause of failure in any system is that it never gets built because in design, the innovators are trying to make their systems handle everything and simply give up when they find they cannot handle every eventuality their creative minds can imagine. In GMAS first deployments we assume the 20 per cent of non-standard events will need to be handled by our most adaptable but expensive tools: a human being.

Business systems such as GMAS should be capable of handling the 80 per cent of routine events to more than 6 Sigma quality, if it is appropriate and justified. However, trying to develop a system that can handle everything is just not practical. No system, known to me at least, can handle every eventuality and this is because of the unique aspect of some events: there may be very low probability of occurrence and no effective method of predicting the occurrence. The GMAS modules are designed, in the first instance to be effective in 80 per cent of circumstances the remaining 20 per cent will require alterations to the module to be made to fit requirements, or require human intervention if it is an automated process.

SCALE AND GROWTH

Scalability is very important in GMAS systems, as the whole idea of having a system is to ensure that your business is scalable and can grow faster and/or be more flexible. Any restrictions in the size of the system should be clearly shown. I should also add that GMAS has a lot of manual processes and procedures that do not involve computers but are know-how based explaining the optimum way of undertaking an operational activity. If the strategy involves rapid growth, systems have to be appropriately scalable.

Growth is essential but growth does not necessarily refer to size. A company can grow its knowledge, expertise, financial security, etc., but one thing is for sure, growth is essential if decline is to be avoided.

THE ABCD OF A GMAS MODULE

GMAS modules are designed with the following questions in mind:

A—Advantages

What advantages will this module bring the organization? These advantages should be quantified as far as possible. For example, successfully acquiring other companies and integrating them faultlessly can increase a company's rate of growth.

B—Best Practice

While I have argued that there is no one best practice there are known best practices or at least case studies available in most subject areas from designing a strategy to writing a company manual. Just because your organization is unique does not mean that everything needs to be original. Use as much as you can from others' experience. Just remember, you have to consider your uniqueness and particular environment before you apply the knowledge acquired.

When we start a new consultancy assignment, the first place we look is the library. I have been surprised how few times we have not been able to find something similar in the literature, a case study or even a book addressing the very challenges we are considering.

One of our trainee consultants was helping design a strategy for a theatre and I asked her if she had found any books on the subject. She told me this was a unique theatre and therefore she had not bothered looking. I spent 2 minutes 37 seconds on the Internet and had found among other texts, Philip Kotler's work *Standing Room Only*. She was just about to reinvent the wheel, but it is much better to start from the most up-to-date theory and practice and develop from there, I tactfully suggested. Be unique in the final solution but make all reasonable efforts never to reinvent things.

On one assignment where we were looking at the marketing strategy of a city, my starting point was to give the client team a summary of a book on the subject. In this way, we all started from a base of the existing 'best practice' or at least one person's view of best practice. This saved hours of work, allowing us to develop a breakthrough strategy that delivered for the city.

C—Checklists

Having identified case studies and what examples of best practice you can find, the next step is to borrow or build your own checklist. I have found that studying several best practice models provides the material for you to build a robust and detailed checklist. This checklist is used in the same way pilots use their checklists as an aid to ensuring that all the steps in a process are undertaken, in the correct sequence and that nothing gets missed. A GMAS module has to be the same. Ensure that all the steps required are listed and the optimum sequence is determined. This reduces the chances of missing something.

As with flying, there are two basic types of checklist that can be used: the generic checklist and the specific (aircraft type) checklist. The checklist you derive from the literature and or primary research is the generic checklist. Not many pilots would be willing to fly an aircraft with a generic checklist. They would want to have the specific checklist for the type of aircraft they are flying. That is because, as the old flying saying goes: 'There are old pilots and there are bold pilots but there are no old bold pilots'. For example, you have to know the correct take-off speed, stall speed and landing speed for your aircraft, therefore a specific checklist is needed. This is where the uniqueness comes in as the generic checklists have to be tailored to be applicable to your organization. Failure to provide this tailoring will result in you stalling and crashing to the ground.

While the specific checklist is needed for safe aircraft operation you will not be surprised to know that much of the generic checklist is the same as the specific, but the critical parts are different. This is the secret of GMAS best practice and module design: identifying and tailoring the critical parts to ensure the system works in your organization.

D—Date Stamp/Revision Date

Like Real-Time Critical Assumptions, every GMAS module has a sell by date. This date is when the module needs to be revised or at least reviewed to determine if it is still effective and likely to remain so. Nothing lasts forever and GMAS modules are no different. As I have said before, what is considered to be best practice one day may not be so the next. In strategic planning and operational planning what is effective changes over time and what is possible also changes over time. Therefore, if we had not reviewed our ideas of what is best practice, we may still be carrying out practices that are no longer appropriate.

Ten years ago, when the Internet was in its infancy, the idea of going for funding, with nothing more than a good idea for an Internet business and lots of enthusiasm, to a Venture Capitalist would not result in a very long or successful meeting. However, had you done the same thing five years ago, you would have stood a very high chance of walking out of their office with a cheque in your hand. Today, we would be back to the same scenario as ten years ago. Clearly the opportunity window came and went. Therefore, a GMAS module designed to ensure success in approaching Venture Capitalists would be in at least revision number three by now.

GMAS WOW

The acronym WOW is used for a further set of questions that must be answered if a GMAS module you design is to be an effective tool in your organization.

W—When does it work?

There is an almost childlike belief that when something works in one situation it will work in another. It is necessary to determine when best practice works and when similar practices have failed. Let us look at mergers and acquisitions. Why is it that some companies like Cisco systems (see the example below) are able to acquire companies with relative ease and integrate them almost faultlessly not once or twice but many times each year, while some of their emulators have met with failure and reduction of shareholder value?

The detective work required has to be as thorough as any masters or doctorate dissertation. The case studies, best practice suggestions checklists and primary research must all be employed to fully understand what is happening. When a merger is successful the conditions can be determined by careful examination. With the painstaking precision of a forensic scientist, you have to study the scene. Next, the elements that appear to make it successful should be separated and the actions isolated. By cross-referencing to other successful mergers, you can start to build the generic checklist. It should be noted that there is a lot more study required to build a specific checklist that will have a high probability of working in your particular organization.

I should now perhaps mention it is sometimes difficult to separate the three F's (Fact, Faith and Fiction) in the merger stories you will read in the press and trade journals. I remember reading one that sounded great until I realized it was the same one we had been brought in to fix.

O—On what does it work?

When I say 'on what does it work?' I mean what are the McKinsey's 7-S characteristics of the organization that the best practice example has been drawn from? By doing this we develop a set of best practice models that are known to have worked in at least one specific structure. The nearer the profile of the company to that where the practice is successful, the higher the probability of obtaining similar success.

In the example of the merger, each of the companies involved need to be assessed to determine which profiles are more likely to succeed. There is no real surprise here that the closer the company gets to the 7-S characteristics, the less problematic the merger. Hence, in mature industries where companies are similar they can be merged relatively easily and with little risk. At other stages where no model has been evolved, integration challenges are larger.

W—Why does it work?

You will remember this question: WHY? WHY? WHY? This is a drill down question. You have to establish without any shadow of a doubt why the particular examples you are studying worked. There are never perfect answers unfortunately, but you have to develop your GMAS theory for testing. By developing a theory, listing the critical assumptions and then testing and/or monitoring implementation you will be able to refine the why? and develop the specific checklist.

RESEARCH

From the 'ABCD–WOW' you will have gathered that there is a sub-stantial amount of research involved in producing a GMAS module. However, the research does not end there. Like all GMAS modules, it should be tested and its performance monitored against expectation. Deviances from expectation should be explored and corrected by improving implementation or by redesigning the module.

INTEGRATING WHAT YOU HAVE ALREADY DEVELOPED

A short cut to developing GMAS modules is to take previous research work or your own successful systems and document them in the GMAS format. This provides a formula for gathering corporate knowledge into useful modules that can then be made available on your company's knowledge base.

By adopting the GMAS approach, successful operations and tac-tical deployments along with strategic planning and management tools can be documented and recalled when required. Provided the firm's 7-S structure remains similar, you will have removed one of the variables from the process and reduced the risk of failure.

Internally developed GMAS modules will enhance the company by providing a consistent format that considers the factors that need to be tailored for successful deployment of the module in another part of the company or market served. This makes the corporate knowledge base even more valuable and flexible.

PROJECT PLANNING

Like any project, the development of a GMAS module will take time, effort and resources. The typical development time for a GMAS module is three months and will involve a team of three people: two full-time and one in a supervisory capacity. Well, when I say super-visory, perhaps I mean 'devil's advocate' role. It is essential to chal-lenge thinking and ensure research quality if the module is going to have any chance of working, but remember do not to try to allow for every eventuality, the most common 80 per cent of eventualities is OK to start with.

The planning process involves the following steps:

- Review of existing knowledge.

- Identification of research candidates potentially exhibiting best practice.

- Screening using primary research of these candidates to determine the three F's of their claims of best practice.

- Conduct primary research around the case studies aimed at determining:
  The 7-S of the organizations involved
  The publics involved and the balance of their relationships
  The market, social, organizational, economic, political or relevant environment.

- Formulation of the generic checklists.

- Examination of your own organization to determine the fit.

- Tailoring of the generic checklist to the specific checklist.

- Documenting the rational and drawing out the critical assumptions made.

- Testing and or monitoring programme developed and assigned.

- Pilot of module.

- Launch the module.

- Date stamp for review.

Each of these stages will take more or less time depending on the size and nature of each module being developed. Critical factors identified in the process can be added to the general GMAS monitoring to detect indicators that show that the module's usefulness in its existing form, is ending. Never persist in using a module when indicators are suggesting that the critical assumptions it is based upon, are becoming compromised before first investigating the consequences of the compromise in the STORM.

ABCD–WOW OF MERGERS AND ACQUISITIONS

I propose to take you through how we developed the GMAS Mergers and Acquisitions Module.

As with all modules, the first questions have to be: What value is there in developing this module and what will it provide for the company? By studying the literature, these are established. There is no shortage of literature on the subject of mergers and acquisitions and no shortage of professional expertise and their associated guides and tip sheets. From this literature, associated advantages and disadvantages can be gleaned.

A—Advantages

The advantages to an organization in getting its mergers and acquisitions right are many, but the main drivers are considered to be: enhanced business or brand value, the acquisition of talent, a route to globalization, improved customer relations, acquisition of intellectual property or some other technical enhancement. There are, as with all things, some dangers including: management difficulties, management distraction from the core business of satisfying customers, danger of decreased shareholder value, lack of cohesion and perhaps the over-stretching of systems.

B—Best Practice

From the literature it is possible to construct a list of prospective companies that have been referred to as demonstrating excellence, and it is even possible to draw out the elements that will make up best practice. This again can provide both a list of reasons that lead to success and a list of reasons that generate failure.

By now the complexity of the module will have grown. Mergers and Acquisitions will now be divided into stages: exploration and selection, investigation and acquisition, merger implementation and evaluation. This may have generated an equal number of prospective models of best practice for each stage.

At this time primary research is required. The companies that have been highlighted as models of best practice have to be interviewed to determine if they truly exhibit best practice or merely have good PR departments. This exercise will reduce substantially the number of examples and will require you to define 'successful'. As we are not designing these modules to be of purely academic merit but as practical tools, we switch to detective mode and now really investigate the very best, consistent examples. When you do this and if you have been successful in cutting through the PR jungle, you will find that a few companies stand out, some of which will be more like your own company than others. These are the ones, which if they have the same or similar strategic objectives for merger, are the case studies you need to dissect.

In our investigation out of the many examples, the most consistently successful and most acquisitive company we found was Cisco Systems Inc. It was here that our dissection began. We investigated all the reported interviews with Cisco's CEO and senior managers for anything they had said about acquisitions and mergers. It was very obvious that Cisco had a well-oiled, highly experienced team and associated systems in place that were used to acquire companies and integrate them in to Cisco, winning over the hearts and minds of the workforce in the acquired company.

It was obvious Cisco was using acquisitions to acquire intellectual property, technical expertise and talent. In interviews with senior mangers it became clear that acquisition was, despite being done so well and so often (60+ acquisitions at my last count), the third activity in a cycle.

The first phase determined if they could do the particular activity in-house. If they could not, they determined if they could poach the expertise and then do it in-house (second activity). Only if they could not do either did they consider the third and final step of acquisition.

The size of Cisco's acquisitions, not their worth, but their physical size, was extremely interesting. The stage of its product development of the acquired company and the market potential of the new innovation was also of interest. Cisco would have to be capable of securing a sizeable market share of a developing innovation's market.

From this in-depth study along with others, it was relatively easy to establish the criteria that would make a merger work. However, like all qualitative research, it allowed the identification of the factors, but not of their relative importance. Because Cisco had made so many acquisitions, in studying each one the relative importance could be established to a reasonable degree of accuracy. It is, I must admit, relatively rare to find a company making so many acquisitions at a time when the market remained at a fairly constant level of growth. It is due to this that there were less variables to contend with and that there was less need for fuzzy logic models to determine optimization of groups of imprecise measures. Hence, a best practice model could be developed easily and the circumstances and objectives, management systems and even integration formula could be determined with a high degree of confidence.

By comparing the many failed mergers that were going on at the same time, it was possible to model other company's failures against Cisco's successes and determine where the mergers had their root cause of failure. To my surprise the majority were firmly at the very first stage. The mergers were doomed, because the strategy chosen was erroneous. Because of this, no amount of integration expertise or consultancy would have been able to save them or make them work effectively.

C—Checklist

Having determined the criteria for successes, a checklist was drawn up. The checklist produced, when based on a single example, should be specific to that particular environment and 7-S structure. If your company's 7-S model or the marketing environment differs significantly from that experienced by Cisco, their successful formula will need to be modified and tested to take account of your marketing environment and 7-S structure before a specific checklist can be reliably utilized within your company.

D—Date Stamp

Cisco was operating in a very rapid growth market with lots of highly innovative start-ups being funded by venture capitalists, while its own growth rate was close to 100 per cent per annum, resulting in it having the funds to acquire or invest in almost anything that showed promise. Clearly, if any of the variables change then the module has to be reevaluated in this new light to ensure that there is no change in the factors that made the practice work so successfully for CISCO Systems.

W—When

When does it work? Here are a few of the criteria that must be present: the merger has more probability of success; the closer the alignment is in both shared vision and culture. There must be clarity on all sides as to how the synergy between the two parties will be gained. For example, Cisco bringing scalability and reach to a partner bringing innovation and know-how.

O—On What

Again to illustrate, it would appear the companies both must be in the same broad field of expertise. Size does matter. The size of the company to be acquired must be small enough to be digested by the acquirer.

W—Why

Taking each of the criteria outlined above: Cisco has realized that it cannot develop tools fast enough, nor are innovations particularly easy in a large company. In addition, they cannot be sure where the next breakthrough will come from. Therefore, they have a clear strategic need to acquire companies. Acquisition is given the management attention, the resources and the specialist provisions it requires. I estimate that for every one company Cisco has acquired, it has probably rejected acquiring equally if not more prospective firms because they did not meet all the requirements to ensure a successful merger. The last thing a company that is experiencing meteoric growth needs is indigestion caused by a bad acquisition. Therefore, careful selection has played a pivotal role in Cisco's success.

I hope this has given you a flavour for building GMAS modules of your own and you can pick up the generic version of the acquisitions and mergers module on the collaborative website.

HELP IN BUILDING THE 'COLLABORATIVE'

The GMAS 'Collaborative' (see Chapter 11) will provide a forum that will help you develop and test your modules. The website will provide examples and a section where you can find prospective collaborators willing to develop a particular module for a particular application.

As well as collaboration in building it is hoped that benchmarking forums can be established to provide optimum ways of undertaking fairly generic activities that can drive costs out of the supply chain. Each member of the benchmarking group can therefore derive competitive advantage from the collaboration.

Dissemination of Ideas and Research

The collaboration will also act as a communications centre for organizations wishing to sell, exchange or gift their modules, or thoughts on modules. It is hoped that modules will be developed and the generic versions made available for others to build their specific applications upon. In this way each deployment of GMAS modules will be unique to the company in question, but there will be a pool of generic modules that companies can use to tailor to their specific requirements.

It is hoped that this will provide synergy and all those who participate will receive more than they invest in the collaborative.

The following modules have been developed or are in the process of being developed:

A&M	Acquisitions and Merger
ABC	Activity Based Costing
ART	*Ad hoc* Research Trigger
AVM	Analyst View Maker
BDM	Bid Decision Model
BM	Benchmarking
Bmark	Breakthrough Marketing Planning
BORE	Business Objective Review and Evaluation
BP	Breakthrough Planning
BSC	Balanced Scorecard
BSDC	Balanced Scorecard Data Collection
CA	Compensation Alignment
CAM	Critical Assumption Monitoring
CARP	Cause Analysis and Rectification Programme
CASM	Customer Acquisition and Sales Monitoring
CoAn	Conjoint Analysis
CPR	Customer Problem Resolution
CRM	Customer Relationship Management System Deployment

CRMA	Customer Relationship Management Augmentation
CSM	Customer Satisfaction Monitoring
CU	Customer Audit
ENT	Enterprise Neuron Trails
eGO	Exploiting Global Opportunities Centre
ERP	Enterprise Resource Planning Integration
ERPA	Enterprise Resource Planning Augmentation
FG	Focus Groups
ICR	Internal Communications Review
ICSM	Internal Customer Satisfaction Monitoring
KB	Knowledge Base
KPS	Key Performance Systems 'KPA/KPI'
LT	Loyalty Tracking
MCC	Management Control Centre
MDI	Marketing Data Integration
MDM	Manufacturing Decision Model
MF	Meeting Facilitation
MI 1	Market Intelligence
MI 2	Market Intelligence
MI 3	Market Intelligence
MI 4	Market Intelligence
MI 5	Market Intelligence
Mind Map	Mind Map Interface to Knowledge Base
MM	Market Monitoring
MP	Marketing Planning
MPI	Marketing Plan Implementation
MPR	Marketing Performance Review
MS	Marketing Support
MSBM	Matched Spectrum Benchmarking
MSM	Market Simulation Model
MTM	Market Trigger Monitor
MYS	Mystery Shopping
O&A	Organizational Alignment
OBE	Out of Box Experience
OPS	Open Reporting
PACE	Post-Acquisition Communications Evaluation
PostSM	Post-Sales Model
PreSM	Pre-sales Model

PRUP	Primary Research Update Programme
Pub Map	Publics Map
QFCIA	Quality Failure Customer Impact Analysis
QR	Quality Reporting
RO	Real Options
RPDM	Research Pool Development and Monitor
RPS	Recognizing Paradigm Shift
S Com	Strategy Communication
S Plan	Strategic Planning
S Pro	Sales Promotion
SAP	Strategic Account Post-sales Status and Development
SC	Strategic Consultancy
SP	Scenario Planning
SRUP	Secondary Research Update Programme
STORM	Strategic Tactical Operational Review Meeting
SVM	Spherical Vision Model
TR	Transactional Research
VOCAL	Voice of the Customer Appearing Live
VS	VAR Status
WAVE	Real-time WAVE study
WM	Web monitoring

Chapters 8, 9 and 10 discuss these modules in more detail.

SUMMARY

- We have discovered how to use, modify and build GMAS modules and investigate the ABCD–WOW concept in GMAS module design. Special attention was paid to the importance of the environment and the acceptance that 'best practice' must be tailored and modified to fit the market and your company's unique profile.

- In addition, we established that considerable research is required to provide a useful GMAS module, but also that there is probably the basis for many modules already in your own company.

8

Strategic Planning Modules

The principal objective of GMAS is to ensure that the strategic planning in your organization is aligned with the operational planning and that synergy is derived from the market intelligence being generated for and by both processes. There are therefore a number of modules that are focused around the strategic planning process and its on-going control and maintenance.

CLUSTER 1   STRATEGIC PLANNING

The modules listed below are relevant in the strategic planning process.

ABC	Activity Based Costing
BORE	Business Objective Review and Evaluation
BP	Breakthrough Planning
BSC	Balanced Scorecard
CAM	Critical Assumption Monitoring
ENT	Enterprise Neuron Trails
ERP	Enterprise Resource Planning Integration
KPS	Key Performance Systems (KPI/KRA)
MCC	Management Control Centre
MF	Management Facilitation
Mind Map	Mind Map Interface to Knowledge Base
MSM	Market Simulation Model

O&A	Organizational Alignment
Pub Map	Publics Map
RO	Real Options
S Com	Strategy Communication
S Plan	Strategy Planning
SC	Strategic Consultancy
SP	Scenario Planning
STORM	Strategic Tactical Operational Review Meeting
SVM	Spherical Vision Model

As you will no doubt notice, there are more modules in this list than there are illustrated in Figure 8.1. This is because not all modules will be relevant to your particular style of strategic planning nor will your organization necessarily require to use all the available models where you have substitution systems in place such as Balanced Scorecard software or ERP systems.

MERGING STRATEGY AND TACTICAL OPERATIONAL PLANNING

A goal of GMAS is to achieve the synergies that are accrued when both strategic and operational intelligence are brought together. This involves aligning strategic planning with operational planning and this can lead to blurring of the strategic planning-operational planning divide. In the longer term, when the planning cycles have been replaced with an 'right time model' this is not a concern, nor is it during the initial 'traditional strategic planning'exercise that kicks off the GMAS process. Where it becomes an issue is in the implementation of the initial strategy where the old model gives way to the GMAS model. Some managers will want access to everything all the time like children let loose in a sweet shop. The position of being able to influence strategy can be abused if the responsibilities and obligations integral to this empowerment are not equally well communicated.

The other major problem to arise after the initial euphoria of empowerment has passed is fear. Fear is something we had not allowed for in some GMAS deployments and this resulted in the

Figure 8.1   Strategic planning model cluster.

initiative being sunk. When GMAS starts to determine the most applicable best practice it has the unfortunate by-product of alerting senior managers to the reality of the ability of their subordinates. Where a member of staff has been getting away with poor performance and bad management, this is detected and the gap between current performance and appropriate best practice can be alarming. A manager faced with having their 'real' performance known has only two choices: To admit their mistakes, learn and move up a gear or two, to make things happen for the better, or, they can bury the initiative before too much comes out. Regrettably, more managers choose the latter option rather than the former.

Of course, I hear you say, their performance will eventually be uncovered without GMAS. Well, here again I beg to differ. I know more than a few managers who are running very large successful companies who have lurched from one disaster to another throughout their careers and always somehow managed to survive; always coming out of each company they destroy smelling of roses. As Jeffrey Archer the novelist, a fundraiser, a former deputy chairman of the Conservative Party, a member of the House of Lords, and now in prison showed, you can rise very high before the past catches up with you.

In business, some failures have been very highly rewarded, e.g. Procter & Gamble's former CEO Durk Jager got $9.5 million after a mere 9 months at the head of P&G with stock down 50 per cent costing P&G shareholders some $70 million. While *Business Week* estimates that Mattel Inc. have to sell 600 000 Barbie dolls each year to pay the $1.2 million annual pension of their former CEO Jill Bared as part of her $50 million severance package. *Business Week* also supplied a list of severance packages payed to former CEOs: Bank One $10.3 million, Coca-Cola $25.5 million, Walt Disney $38.8 million, and Conesco $49.3 million. While in the UK Railtrack has been severely criticized for similar payoffs to its executives at a time when the company is experiencing major problems, before its collapse.

It is therefore fair to say that not all managers will welcome a GMAS deployment. The secret of good management systems is the ability to take ordinary people and support them in producing extraordinary results. GMAS supports ordinary managers, the ones who are usually left behind to pick up the pieces after the meteor has passed through, and provide them with the tools to deliver extraordinary performance and be justly recognized.

Breakthrough Planning

Breakthrough Planning comprises the seven principles of breakthrough thinking applied to marketing problem solution. As I mentioned previously, breakthrough *thinking* principles were developed by Gerald Nadler, of the University of Southern California and Shozo Hibino, of Chukyo University in Japan.

Breakthrough Planning is about the provision of marketing solutions that don't just match the competition but blow them away. In most wars the availability of a breakthrough weapon was what achieved the victory as often as the strategy, for example the long bow, the tank or the atom bomb.

The seven principles:

- Uniqueness

- Purposes

- Solution after next

- Systems

- Needed information collection

- People design

- Betterment timeline

Uniqueness

Every business and marketing problem is unique regardless of any apparent similarities. As such, each requires an initial approach that dwells on its unique contextual needs. Solutions from elsewhere should only be used if the context shows that it is appropriate. Copying others rarely provides a breakthrough.

Purposes

Unless you are sure and can agree on the purpose, little progress can be made in finding a lasting solution to the marketing challenge. Purposes can be viewed as a spectrum focusing on the part that can be achieved while leading on to a greater purpose can be determined by continually using the question of why? This process allows clear focus on the real purpose and strips away the non-essential, which so often slows up project completion or confuses priorities.

Solution After Next

By accepting purpose as a spectrum, whatever we do to solve the current challenge will affect the future and should be considered a stepping-stone rather than a barrier. Consideration to the future solutions and innovations is achieved easiest by working backwards from the future purpose. For example, building a flexible production line to ease future model modifications may be a better solution than building a rigged production system. Although in the short term costs may be less in the rigged system, knowing our future purposes will help us make better decisions today that may work out better in the longer term.

Systems

Any marketing solution will affect the rest of the organization and its effects should be calculated and implications assessed. Sometimes the less obvious implications are often the most critical, so ample time should be given to exploring the consequences of implementing any solutions that are derived.

When building a system around your solution, it should be your aim to deskill 80 per cent of the associated tasks and make them routine. Only when a system is in place delivering consistent results can quality improvements be effectively introduced. The remaining 20 per cent deals with the non-standard solutions, and very few systems can predict the demands this 20 per cent makes. Therefore, the cost benefit analysis of building a system capable of handling 100 per cent of situations often does not warrant its introduction, at least in the early development stages.

Needed Information Collection

We live in the information age—data is not in short supply. The problem is effectively mining the right information from the vast assortments of information that are available today. Clear purposes make the gathering of information much easier, as only information which will help achieve the focused purpose, should be gathered. There is a real danger today of information overload, which can be almost as dangerous as not gathering data at all.

People Design

All those who are involved in the success of the implementation of a marketing solution should have been given the opportunity to contribute to the solutions being proposed. Only when those involved in the implementation have 'bought into the solution' will the solution be effective. Many projects have failed because of sabotage, which has resulted from the actions of those who felt a solution was being forced upon them and of which they felt no part.

Betterment Timeline

Nothing lasts forever and no system will last forever. Therefore, solutions should be regularly reviewed in the light of the focused purposes and these review dates should be built into the system. A process of continual improvement should be introduced and policed as the future achievement of purposes means building systems that will grow and adapt to the changing market environment while remaining focused on the purpose for which they were designed.

This set of rules allows planning to be more effective and can be adapted to most planning situations with quite remarkable positive affects.

The Japanese New Product Introduction Model

The Japanese model used to introduce new products takes about the same total time as in the traditional Western models with much the same issues arising. The difference is that in the Japanese process there is much more consultation, discussion and scenario testing. In all, about 80 per cent of the time is spent in this planning phase hidden from the glare of the open market compared to 20 per cent of the time spent in planning in the typical Western model.

In the Japanese model the remaining 20 per cent of the time will be spent dealing with the inevitable problems that arise in the early introductory phase of a new product introduction (80 per cent planning, 20 per cent fire-fighting). This compares to the typical Western model where spending only 20 per cent of the time on planning results in the need to spend planning and 80 per cent of the time in unscheduled fire-fighting. High profile fire-fighting in full view of the public can damage the company image and consumer confidence in the product.

GMAS supports the Japanese model and maintains 80 per cent of any process should be completed prior to full market exposure, thus minimizing the fire-fighting that is required to ensure a successful launch. Giving weight to the old adage of the five Ps : Poor Planning Pretty Poor Performance OR Pre-Planning leads to Pretty Pukka Performance.

Take the time to plan and implementation goes faster with fewer problems.

Applying the Breakthrough Planning Model

1 Identify as many purposes for the assignment as possible.
2 Expand the purposes from those small in scope to those with the largest scope, placing them in a hierarchy, then, most importantly, select the focus purpose. Be 'SMART' about this, i.e. state the purpose as you would an objective. That is, be **S**—specific, make it **M**—measurable, **A**—achievable, **R**—realistic and **T**—timed.

3 Generate as many solutions after next until you see the achievement of the focused purpose. Each solution should be 'SMART', then group these alternative options.

4 Design systems that will be capable of handling 80 per cent of things (the regular conditions). Do not try to build systems to accommodate everything, it is impossible. What you can not design in initially will determine your solution after next target.

5 Involve those who will be responsible for implementing the solution in designing the solution. Take full account of their input and solve problems that they perceive may ensue from the solution models proposed.

6 Gather only the information you need to develop the systems and ensure their successful implementation.

7 Develop the recommended marketing solution that stays close to the target, but consider how the 20 per cent of irregular conditions will be handled.

8 Detail the recommended solution and pilot it, if possible.

9 Design the project plan including installation and transitions between the steps to achievement of the purpose.

10 Implement the plan, project, manage and trouble shoot.

11 Set dates for betterment to attain larger purposes and parts of the target or to redesign the target.

Breakthrough planning is an extremely useful tool in determining strategy and in preparation of revolutionary plans. It allows for great creativity, but focuses the energy of the team towards a clear purpose. It will be responsible for more breakthroughs than almost any other single theory, if applied. It is what marketing has lacked in recent years. As a problem solver, it will allow clearer thinking, allow more effective solutions to be found, and more efficient implementations of those solutions, with less unforeseen problems arising.

THE CORE STRATEGY MODULES

The core strategy modules are based around the preparation of the strategic plan and provide the inputs to the strategic planning process.

These include: the STORM as discussed in Chapter 3, breakthrough planning, scenario planning, etc. as illustrated in Figure 8.1.

For the purposes of explaining the various models illustrated above I will assume you have no preconceived process for the initial strategy planning exercise.

In the pre-strategy meeting phase, strategic consultants would perform a BORE, a review and evaluation of the business objectives. An SVM (an internal as well as external publics map) would then be created along with an organizational alignment review. This organizational alignment review uses the 7-S model to determine the alignment of the organization and its principal parts. This phase would be concluded by an initial breakthrough planning meeting. This meeting would provide the list of needed information and allow the MSM (Market Simulation Model) to be built using the information subsequently gathered. Further meetings would be facilitated to enhance the MSM and to look at the most probable scenarios facing the company.

The strategic consultants and facilitators along with the senior management of your organization would then go through a formal strategic planning exercise utilizing the scenario planning and market models as required to play with ideas and possibilities. If a Balanced Scorecard or Enterprise Resource Planning model is being utilized, as illustrated in Figure 8.1, the strategy would be developed in line with the BSC format and information extracted for ERP configuration. During the whole exercise, the facilitators would be gathering the critical assumptions and these would be programmed into the STORM format. During this phase the initial drafts of the ENT would be prepared and the strategy communications exercise commenced. This would involve a corporate wide view on the strategic issues as well as expert opinion and market comment.

On the conclusion of the strategic planning exercise, the strategy communications process would take effect and the control of strategy would pass to the Management Control Centre (MCC), where the STORM, monitoring, testing are carried out. The MCC team consists of the corporate strategists and representatives from all the main operational divisions. This is the physical manifestation of the STORM module.

The MCC taking over the responsibility of maintaining the currency of the strategy, does not indicate abdication of responsibility for maintaining a successful strategy, it merely ensures that all information is focused into one physical space. From that location management can access the expertise required to provide market intelligence at the right time and ensure the right people are getting access to it and using the knowledge. While at MMSI plc's headquarters in Glasgow there are example MCC's layouts, in practice the activities are carried out in various locations around the company and the MCC may simply be a secure area within the Intranet where access to all the information pertaining to the strategy and its monitoring and control can be found.

When established in the MCC and the STORM is working as previously described, it takes a little time to get used to the variance in information being derived and the whole process of 'trimming' (adjusting the weightings in order to control the number of STORM meetings being triggered). As the system beds in, it may take as long as three years before it has been fully established and is operating at maximum efficiency. To install the initial system may take as little as three months, but to diffuse throughout the organization and to link to current as well as legacy systems can take a considerable amount of time. This is not to mention the resistance to change that will be strongest from your organization's weakest links and from the less than optimised functions. This noise must not be permitted to distract implementation timetables or hijack the initiative.

RIGHT-TIME STRATEGY

Having established the MCC, ENT and STORM, right-time strategy is operational, but before you will be able to determine whether all is well internally, right-time planning will have to be instigated within the company.

I should at this stage differentiate budgeting, as a form of planning from implementation planning. Many firms still consider a plan to be a budget. In GMAS thinking, the budget is determined from what can be achieved, not from some historic record including a percentage of what was achieved. The first step in a GMAS plan is to determine, in the light of the marketing intelligence, what we are capable of achieving and taking a view on the risks involved. From this view, very much determined by the company's propensity towards risk and Real Options, the money is allocated to make it happen. As GMAS monitors the success or failure in execution, leading indicators alert the company to the way the plan is developing in relation to the projected scenario. If all is well, the money continues to be spent and the objectives are achieved, if the indications are not favourable then the budget can be pulled or the implementation plan modified.

When trust is built up in the effectiveness of GMAS at separating the three F's, then more and more the fuzzy logic systems can be allowed to develop and automate the processes. In the first stage, however, it is better not to use fuzzy logic models, as until the human interfaces are able to get it reasonably right, the computer models will not be able to function well. This is because they need to have the input in the first instance from the 'expert', but once established, the neuro-fuzzy models are capable of learning so long as feedback is provided. I mention this because getting feedback is like drawing teeth; it can be extremely difficult, especially when things are going well. Market intelligence is good but without feedback it may not be read as well as other information supplied and the source not given a higher credibility weighting so that in future it may be downgraded when other less reliable sources contradict it.

It is therefore necessary in all the GMAS modules to first understand fully how they work before attempting to automate the system. Before the recent developments in fuzzy logic all this would have been impossible. If fuzzy logic can keep our cars on the road when driven recklessly, it is not surprising that the same technology is capable of keeping our companies on track.

DECISION SUPPORT ROLE

I have mentioned fuzzy logic and by now you will have realized that it plays a role in GMAS systems primarily because it is able to handle the natural words that we use and understand and convert them into a form a computer can handle. Having translated the words, fuzzy logic can then feedback to us the same fuzzy words which we complex humans can find easier to understand than '76.78 per cent of respondents said yes'.

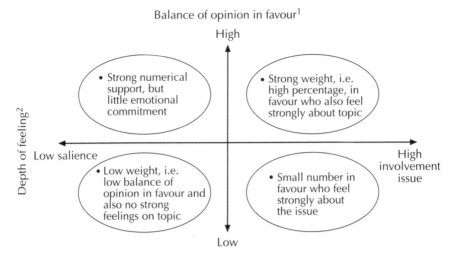

Balance of opinion in favour[1]

[1] Balance of opinion: this provides a 'quantitative' assessment of how many individuals favour one option rather than another. (In a quantitative survey this would be statistically based and with a qualitative study based on 'counts' taken as part of the content analysis of transcripts, and so on.)

[2] Depth of feeling: an insight into the intensity of feeling that people experience on this topic. (This could be based on a qualitative assessment of verbatim comments and/or on quantitative structured attitude questioning.)

Originally published in Smith, D. and Decter, A. (2001). Whenever I hear the word 'paradigm' I reach for my gun: how to stop talking and start walking, *International Journal of Market Research* 43(3), pp. 321–40.

Figure 8.2 Weight of evidence.

David Smith and Andy Dexter (2001), in the *International Journal of Marketing Research*, explore the problems faced by traditional research methods and especially the complex issue of how to turn data into market intelligence. They use the three evidence matrices to illustrate the issues: weight of evidence, power of evidence and direction of evidence. The first matrix, Figure 8.2, shows the weight of evidence as measured on the axis of depth of feeling and balance of opinion in favour. Figure 8.3, Power of evidence, is a matrix with as its axes, implicit prior knowledge and explicit data. The last matrix Figure 8.4, shows direction of evidence and has its axes Internal Consistency and External support. These three matrices can be modelled using fuzzy logic even with the scale as: very high, high, medium, low and very low. This allows a table to be created combining all three factors.

In a non-fuzzy logic, a traditional expert system to work out all the

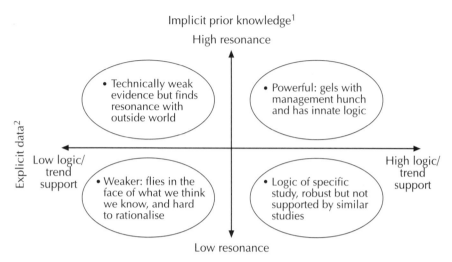

Implicit prior knowledge[1]

High resonance

- Technically weak evidence but finds resonance with outside world

- Powerful: gels with management hunch and has innate logic

Explicit data[2]

Low logic/ trend support

High logic/ trend support

- Weaker: flies in the face of what we think we know, and hard to rationalise

- Logic of specific study, robust but not supported by similar studies

Low resonance

[1] Implicit: this tells us where our piece of data fits into the wider context of what we already know about this topic, after taking into account existing management 'prior knowledge'.

[2] Explicit: this refers to what we know about this particular 'genre' of data. For example, are these data of a type whereby one single, free-standing observation leads us relentlessly to a logical conclusion, or are they the type of data that only make sense when fitted into a time series and/or evaluated against a benchmark?

Originally published in Smith, D. and Decter, A. (2001). Whenever I hear the word 'paradigm' I reach for my gun: how to stop talking and start walking, *International Journal of Market Research*, 43(3), pp. 321–40.

Figure 8.3   Power of evidence.

rules to handle this type of uncertainty would be a factor of the number of variables and the intervals. In this case, there are two variables per matrix and three matrices. Therefore there are six variables each with five intervals (very high, high, medium, low and very low) and hence 6^5 options or combinations (7776 possible combinations). This can be simplified as above by selection from each quadrant on each matrix. Thus, because we have three matrix and four intervals, this provides 3^4 or 81 combinations. While 81 combinations are manageable by a traditional expert system, that is, you can define each of the 'if-then' statements, 7776 are not. However, any system of any complexity is beyond the traditional expert system's capability and changes to the coding would be a nightmare, as the system would only have a limited ability to learn from its successes and failures.

Fuzzy logic algorithms on the other hand, translate natural language into an algorithm using a mathematical model. This allows even

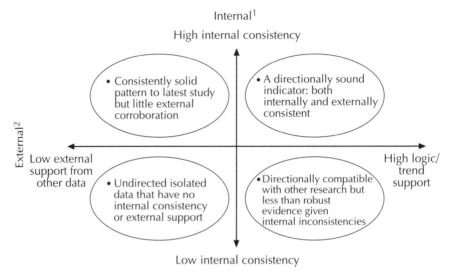

Internal[1]

High internal consistency

- Consistently solid pattern to latest study but little external corroboration

- A directionally sound indicator: both internally and externally consistent

External[2]

Low external support from other data

High logic/ trend support

- Undirected isolated data that have no internal consistency or external support

- Directionally compatible with other research but less than robust evidence given internal inconsistencies

Low internal consistency

[1] Internal consistency: there is the question of whether the data are high or low in terms of their internal directional consistency. Do different parts of the dataset come together to reinforce the consistency of the story?

[2] External consistency: there is the issue of the external consistency of data – where do the data sit in regard to being supported (or not) by other external evidence.

Originally published in Smith, D. and Decter, A. (2001). Whenever I hear the word 'paradigm' I reach for my gun: how to stop talking and start walking, *International Journal of Market Research*, 43(3), pp. 321–40.

Figure 8.4   Direction of evidence.

the most complex decisions to be modelled using only a few rule sets. This is what makes fuzzy logic such an exciting solution to complex human decision problems and in the handling of issues such as the weight, power and direction of evidence associated with both qualitative and quantitative research results.

What is even more interesting in the work by Constantin Von Altrock (1997), is the suggesting and application of neural network theory to fuzzy logic to produce systems capable of learning from their experiences. In this way a module that can be built to handle the initial 80 per cent of situations and will learn how to do better itself.

There have been over 32 000 articles written on fuzzy logic, but relatively few on its applications in management theory. I hope this book will stimulate more work in this area.

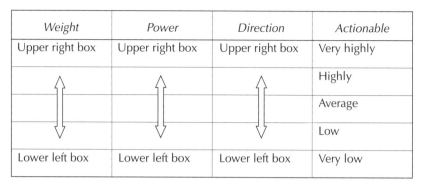

Weight	Power	Direction	Actionable
Upper right box	Upper right box	Upper right box	Very highly
			Highly
			Average
			Low
Lower left box	Lower left box	Lower left box	Very low

Figure 8.5 Fuzzy logic decision table rule window.

RIGHT-TIME PLANNING

In GMAS, the planning cycle is eliminated and strategic planning is undertaken when it needs to be. This, like most 'on call' type activities, usually happens when you are busy. A natural law states that there are no strategic assumptions compromised when you are quiet but the moment you get really busy, they are compromised left, right and centre.

The reality and potential weakness of strategic systems is that they are very seldom truly urgent. The need for strategy change tends to be gradual rather than revolutionary. The weight, power and direction of evidence for strategic change gradually build. Even in paradigm shift situations, the market does not switch overnight. There is plenty of time to take the necessary action.

This time to act is relative, of course. It takes time to realign systems and change KPIs etc., and the sooner the change requirement is known, the better the prospects are of capitalizing on the change. The danger lies in waiting too long to act. The changes can be very gradual and the temptation is to explain them away for too long by which time the weight, power and direction of evidence is so strong that the rest of the market has already moved and your company pays the price of being late into a market. Even worse, but still a possibility, is that the company has not enough time left to act and is caught high and dry as the tide turns.

Right time is therefore as soon as practical after the critical assumption compromise is detected or is highly likely to be compromised. A few days delay will not change much, but a few months will. Time scale to action should therefore be measured in days and weeks, not months or quarters.

In the operations areas, clearly time to act is correspondingly less if the business units are to take advantage of emerging opportunities or are to avoid competitive threats. Here the action can be required in hours or days instead of weeks.

CRITICAL ASSUMPTION RECORDING

I have talked rather a lot about these Real-Time Critical Assumptions and the databases that are required to record and monitor them. Their importance is not fixed, however, and as time passes some become redundant as their importance to the organization dwindles while others, which were relatively unimportant six months ago, can become paramount today. As the strategic plan unfolds and the future becomes the present and then the past three Fs are being separated all the time, the relative weighting of the remaining assumptions must be adjusted accordingly. As new, unforeseen events unfold the STORM generates new assumptions and these must be added to the database.

The whole critical assumptions module is alive and dynamic. If the critical assumptions are not changing, then the system is dead.

INTEGRATION WITH OTHER MANAGEMENT INITIATIVES

It is rare in any company, almost regardless of size, for there to be only one initiative in progress at any one time. With this in mind, you will have to consider GMAS in the light of these other innovations. Currently there are three major initiatives that tailor very nicely with GMAS. These are ERP, CRM and BSC. If you are deploying an Enterprise Resource Planning system, Customer Relationship Management system or a Balanced Scorecard system, then GMAS can be added with little disruption to the deployment programmes of these systems. In fact, GMAS will help in many ways to define how much flexibility you will need to allow for in each of these systems. Clearly, the earlier that you are in the process, the better the synergy and returns that are enjoyed by deploying them together.

SCENARIO PLANNING

Scenario planning has become more and more important in the strategic planning process since one of its leading exponents Arie de Geus, published his book '*The Living Company*'. This GMAS module utilizes Idon's software (see Appendix 1) and the concepts discussed in Miriam Galt *et al.*'s (1998) book Idon Scenario Thinking. By combining Idon's software and methodology with GMAS business intelligence, the power of the scenarios is enhanced and you will be spellbound by the creative thinking that is forthcoming and by what fun scenario planning can be. That is not to say it should be taken lightly, however, as it is a very powerful tool at dealing with uncertainty.

The fundamental benefit of scenario planning is that as situations change decisions can be made extremely quickly as the outcome modelling has already been done for the majority of stages. This model also helps strategists record and monitor strategic implementation, assessing the success of various scenarios for future reference.

The scenario planning module takes a very pragmatic view of the future by distilling it down into a series of 'what if' options and then classifies these by the probability of occurrence. Then taking the two extremes of 'happens' or 'does not happen' from this and the subsequent trees of events, it is possible to derive the best and worst scenarios. Having strategies to cope with both extremes allows the actual position to be addressed effectively, whatever comes to pass.

The Idon scenario impact matrix is then used to derive the decision options and differentiated competences and to develop robust options for taking the appropriate action. The derivation of the differentiated competences effectively produces the unique proposition that will be required to be successful given any particular scenario.

This Idon modelling ensures that actions that are essential continue to be carried out, actions that we may have to take in the short term are dropped at the appropriate time, and actions we will have to prepare to commit to are developed. In addition, we are alerted to the possible impact, both favourable and unfavourable, of the actions we are considering. All this allows the identification of the future core competences and the capabilities required under the various scenarios. Thus, competitive advantage can be gained and maintained even in an uncertain future.

Idon software also provides priority modelling, option mapping, goal navigation modelling, process modelling, system thinking, dilemma modelling and creative modelling methods. Thus, providing a platform for a complete range of scenario and strategic modelling exercises. All of this software has a role to play in developing strategic direction and clarifying your organization's senior management's thinking.

The advantage of the software-based system is that various stages in the thinking process can be saved and a track record is obtained. In this way, when a critical assumption is compromised and a review of strategy is required, the exact steps utilized by the strategy team in the previous scenario planning process can be retraced. This allows the team to pick up from the point at which the compromised critical assumption was used. This saves considerable time and allows managers to very quickly retrace the logic root they were following during the strategic planning session.

This ability to fit back into the active mindset of the previous strategy session has two advantages: it can expose other, less obvious, errors in the previous logic followed and it ensures that the strategy correction is not out of context in the wider strategy picture. If the original mindset is not reestablished, it is remarkably easy for the strategy team to go off at a tangent in seeking a solution to the emerging issue. If this is allowed to occur, the resultant modification will be out of tune with the rest of the corporate strategy and long-term mission. A quick run through of the series of models previously derived (a storyboard) has an almost Neuro Linguistic Programming (NLP) effect of bringing the participants minds back into the previous mindset. This is essential for a consistent approach to strategy planning where there has been a time interval or even personnel changes.

Where there have been personnel changes, I have found that, while the new participant may not wholly share the views of the original strategy team, they should at least understand how the view was derived and the logic that was followed. This allows their questions to be answered quickly and for them to agree the logic of the old model or to highlight errors that, in context, others can agree were wrong or can convince the newcomer of their validity.

The ability to save various visuals of the strategy development, at important points in the development process, is one of the fastest ways of reminding the strategy team how they got to the original strategy. A similar technique is employed in advertising where, after an initial long advert has been broadcast, it is possible to have the audience recall the whole advert just by showing highlights in subsequent much shorter advertising or promotions. Strategy model capture is a fast recall mechanism for strategic planners which does not delay the initial strategic process.

MARKET SIMULATION MODELLING

Using various marketing modelling tools, this system models the markets you are operating within. This includes the standard market models such as: Ansoff Matrix, Boston Matrix, Directional Policy Matrix, Income/Profit Gap Analysis, Market Share Analysis, Perceptual Mapping, Risk Analysis, Strengths and Weakness Analysis and Market Mapping.

This visual right-time system allows a clear and accurate picture to be presented of your market. It is extremely valuable in simulation exercises where the effects of various scenarios can be modelled in terms of market perception, income gaps, etc. This helps by enhancing the image of the future scenario and shows what issues are likely to be generated from the impact on the market.

These models are useful in day-to-day operations and can be linked to real-time market data such as that produced by omnibus or panel research. This overtime provides a lapsed photography type model of the market as it grows and develops. These can be represented on websites and you can look back using our Dynamic Reporting module to see how the market has changed over the time of study you are interested in. As well as the dynamic market simulations and models, we are developing internal models that map the internal alignment of the organization and a similar dynamic model for this purpose will be available soon. These models will allow you to see how the internal environment is moving and will enable you to compare this to the environment required by the strategy.

Both the internal and external mapping requires access to market intelligence and are only as real as the data provided. In some cases where the data is very difficult to acquire or is simply not available, these models and simulations are subject to the three Fs. The more unreliable or infrequent the data, the more they tend to move away from Fact and towards Faith and ultimately Fiction. These models are excellent when you have invested in rich data, but can be misleading where the investment in quality data has not been made.

CONCLUSION

Strategy is dynamic and must respond to the realities of the environment and market and should not be considered fixed. It is as alive as the rest of the organization and should not be brought out every five years, dusted down and then reassigned to the cupboard. Strategy is immensely valuable when combined with operational and tactical planning and will ensure that you achieve your mission regardless of what the world or your competitors throw at you.

SUMMARY

- We looked at the synergy attributable to merging strategic and tactical planning and explored the core strategic planning modules.

- The issues of evidence and its weight, power and direction were explored. Also, we looked at the role fuzzy logic can play in providing decision support.

- The concept of 'right-time' was explored further as well as the need to integrate the various business initiatives and how GMAS can accommodate these.

9

How to Use Testing and Monitoring Modules

The following modules are utilized in the area of testing and monitoring. They are clustered around quality, customer satisfaction and internal systems. The line between monitoring and testing is most easily imagined when you think of monitoring as a continuous activity while testing as a single occurrence. Both involve research in one form or another, monitoring relying heavily on secondary research and continuous primary research such as benchmarking and transactional customer satisfaction.

ART	*Ad hoc* Research Trigger
BM	Benchmarking
BORE	Business Objective Review and Evaluation
BSDC	Balanced Scorecard Data Collection
CAL	Compensation Alignment
CAM	Critical Assumption Monitoring
CARP	Cause Analysis and Rectification Programme
CASM	Customer Acquisition and Sales Monitoring
CoAn	Conjoint Analysis
CRMA	Customer Relationship Management Augmentation
CSM	Customer Satisfaction Monitoring
CU	Customer Audit
ERPA	Enterprise Resource Planning Augmentation
FG	Focus Groups

ICR	Internal Communications Review
ICSM	Internal Customer Satisfaction Monitoring
LT	Loyalty Tracking
MDI	Marketing Data Integration
MDM	Manufacturing Decision Model
MI 1	Market Intelligence
MI 2	Market Intelligence
MI 3	Market Intelligence
MI 4	Market Intelligence
MM	Market Monitoring
MPR	Marketing Performance Review
MSBM	Matched Spectrum Benchmarking
MTM	Market Trigger Monitor
MYS	Mystery Shopping
OBE	Out of Box Experience
PRUP	Primary Research Update Programme
QFCIA	Quality Failure Customer Impact Analysis
QR	Quality Reporting
RPDM	Research Pool Development and Monitor
RPS	Recognizing Paradigm Shift
SRUP	Secondary Research Update Programme
TR	Transaction Research
VOCAL	Voice of the Customer Appearing Live
VS	VAR Status
WAVE	Real-time WAVE study
WM	Web monitoring

The list of modules is always growing. For the latest list visit the collaborative website at www.ridingthestorm.net.

RESEARCH AND GLOBAL MARKETING ADVANTAGE

Producing irrefutable research and achieving global marketing advantage are inextricably fused. Global marketing advantage requires global knowledge based on global marketing intelligence, which in turn requires irrefutable information and data.

The world is moving faster and faster. Yesterday's sacred cows are today's jokes, rapid response is king, change is continuous and doing the unexpected is an advantage. The world is an uncertain, indecisive, fuzzy place where nothing appears to be constant for long. Views, beliefs and trends are changing faster than ever before and keeping pace is a challenge to even the most generously funded research departments. Keeping pace on a global scale is even more of a challenge.

Among all this apparent chaos there are, however, many constants that we often forget about: emotions are the same the world over. Feelings such as happiness or sadness, in their most basic sense, are the same regardless of cultural or geographical differences. What makes us happy or sad may differ, but the emotion still feels the same to the individual. As Homo sapiens we all have recognizable traits, which persist regardless of environment, culture, creed or colour. Whether you are for or against globalization, the reality is that it has occurred to some extent in every country in the world. To gain global marketing advantage does not mean that we have to become a global village, what it means is that we can provide a service on a global scale that will dominate the markets in which we choose to offer our product or service.

The understanding of basic human behaviour is the key to understanding business relationships. All business is done with and for the benefit of a person or persons. Therefore, regardless of its channel complexity in the end it is simply one human bartering with another for mutual gain. Culture, language, country, etc., are layers added over generations, but these cannot fundamentally change the genetics of the human being.

Global research has to strip everything away and understand each layer so that it can develop the model in order to allow for culture, language and country. By understanding these constituents and their impact on basic human behaviour, we can quickly appreciate and can start to quantify regional variations. For example, if I were to ask a European, an American and an Asian to complete a satisfaction score for a similar service, they would show geographical variance. Let me be more specific. On a worldwide survey, a level of service was defined and met. We asked those who had pegged the service at the same scores, to rate their satisfaction on a scale of one to ten where 10 was completely satisfied and 1 dissatisfied. What we discovered was a cultural variation between scores, as all the other variables, as far as possible, were constant, for example: same jobs, responsibilities, level of experience. In Asia, where compromise is an admired characteristic, scores tended around the middle range, there was reluctance from respondents to score high or low. In the USA there was a tendency to score very high or very low, while in Europe not too high and not too low was the norm. This allowed a weighting to be applied to satisfaction scores that would make them globally compatible. This is one of the largest challenges to global research compatibility. By centralizing research using only natives to carry out the research, you can minimize the impact of geographic differences, but care has to be taken when comparing data obtained from different geographical zones and sources.

DEATH AND DECAY AVOIDANCE

Most of the monitoring work in GMAS is done to avoid death and decay. I previously mentioned the product life cycle and the many chasms that can be found in it. Each chasm can be predicted and leading indicators can pinpoint the cliff's edge. This is done by providing a continuous monitor rather like passive radar which can detect the approach of a craft without revealing its own location, instead of testing research which is more like active radar that emits a signal and measures the return echo.

By ensuring that the natural danger zones in product life cycles are successfully navigated, and knowing that each stage can be profitably managed, the product life cycle provides little fear for organizations using GMAS.

Paradigm shift is the cause of many premature deaths of leading organizations, but it needn't mean death and decay; it can be detected. Two options are: like Cisco Systems have done, you buy into the external sources of paradigm shift as *your* research and development department, or alternatively, you simply purchase and sink or bury the new innovations to prolong the life of existing products. Atlas Copco delayed launching an oil-free compressor for 10 years in the 1980s in order to ensure that they were able to squeeze every penny from their older technology. By detecting the emerging challenge to your existing

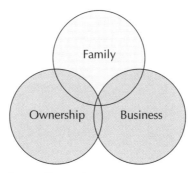

Figure 9.1   Family business dimensions.

paradigm, you have flexible options on the actions open to you. In this way, paradigm shift can become an opportunity, rather than a threat. Real Option analysis values these options.

Continuous development can be easily managed by listening to the needs and desires of your customers and prospective customers. This should enable a company to extend its product life cycle by continuously introducing new 'must have' features.

Having the knowledge to avoid death and decay is one thing, but having the resources to do something about it can be quite another. There are several factors that come into play here, not least of which, is your company's risk-aversion level.

One type of company that offers valuable lessons in survival are the family-run businesses which appears to survive bad times better than their non-family business counterparts. Some lessons can be gained from their structure and methods of avoiding death. In bad times, family businesses are able to perform much better than public companies. The pride, history, sacrifice and sheer will to survive allows the former to have much more resilience to adverse market conditions. Figure 9.1 shows the three dimensions of a family-run business: family business, and ownership. The ability of the family to emphasize and call on the three elements appears to be both their weakness as well as their great strength. They are able to suspend dividends and profit or reduce wages (more likely increase the hours worked for the same income). Guilt can also be a powerful coercive force, especially when delivered by your mother: 'I don't really mind if you are too busy to help out, I'll manage somehow...'. By effectively swinging the firm between the three elements, family businesses can survive, where other companies would fail. To give you some idea of how much this factor has affected the natural selection of businesses in the UK, let me point out that 75 per cent of businesses are family run.

In terms of survival, the family businesses abilities to mix family, business and ownership is powerful and something that non-family businesses find difficult to establish with their respective stakeholders.

Lessons from the Recession
Business Week August 2001 proposed six lessons from the slow down.

1 Good information required good judgement.
2 Stay flexible.
3 Know your customers customers.
4 Look beyond a backlog in orders.
5 Planning goes only so far.
6 Don't just sell them serve them.

They could have been written with GMAS in mind because:

1 The three F model helps you make better judgements supported by fuzzy logic systems.
2 Strategy remains flexible to change in market reality.
3 There is a lot of emphasis on knowing your customer and the publics maps help identify and track customers.
4 Forecasts are treated within the three F concept.
5 One view is not enough, multiple views are required and testing as well as monitoring of critical assumptions. Scenario planning comes to the fore.
6 Service is more important to stop consumers buying boxes (co-modity) therefore it plays a vital role in a companies portfolio.

QUALITY CLUSTER

There are a cluster of monitoring and testing modules based around quality control and systems; these are shown in Figure 9.2. The modules featured are: CARP, Customer Analysis and Rectification Programme; CPR, Customer Problem Resolution; QR, Quality Reporting

Figure 9.2 Quality cluster.

and QFCIA, Quality Failure Customer Impact Analysis. I will now explain their purpose and how they operate in a little more detail.

CARP Customer Analysis and Rectification Programme

This is a module that was called 'post mortem' but our customers found this title a little too morbid. I thought it captured the essence of the process rather well. However, as the saying goes: 'He who pays the piper, calls the tune', and it is now affectionately referred to as the 'CARP'. It involves a team of experts from the client meeting with a team from your organization to identify and rectify the root cause of a fault. It is not about blame, but is about providing the customers with an outlet to allow them to voice their dissatisfaction and then working with your team to generate solutions so that the same mistake does not get repeated again. The event is filmed and the tapes used to present to other experts that were absent in order to allow them to provide input as required. An action agenda for improvements is then drawn up and implemented.

The benefits from this type of exercise are many but two worth noting are, first, you tend to get a fix quickly and, second, it has a positive impact on the customers who now feel that they have invested in the solution. These two effects produce measurably higher customer satisfaction scores and, in limited repurchase research, indications of higher account retention and increasing spend.

This is typical of GMAS modules in that by evolving from considered best practice and being tailored for the company, the impact is enhanced and benefits are gained not just for quality, but also for account management and sales.

QR Quality Reporting

This module pulls together the various quality failure reports from around the organization, including refunds, penalties paid, late deliveries, return material authorizations (RMAs), and spoiled stock and to provide a corporate wide view on cost of quality. This helps pinpoint the areas where large savings would reward attention or where investment payback would be most immediate.

Understanding the cost of quality is essential if you are introducing an Activity Based Costing (ABC) initiative, as only by knowing the costs can a justification be made for the increased cost of data collection associated with an ABC system. Therefore, a QR is a basic requirement of any organization contemplating ABC, for the monitoring of the returns being achieved from ABC, and to identify the optimum ABC investment.

QFCIA Quality Failure Customer Impact Analysis

Quality failure that costs the company money is of course important, but so is the identification of the impact of quality failures on your customer's business. This allows areas where a customer would be willing to pay more for increased reliability to be identified and Service Level Agreements (SLAs) risk to be better understood. This is especially important where there are liquidated damages clauses.

CUSTOMER SATISFACTION AND LOYALTY CLUSTER

There are a host of modules clustered around customer satisfaction as shown in Figure 9.3. Here are the details of some of them.

Transactional Research

The Transactional Research module, you will recall, is a good source of research pool participants who provide very reliable, highly

Figure 9.3   Customer satisfaction cluster.

responsive, tailored respondents. Respondents are used to confirm assumptions for a whole spectrum of *ad hoc* research activities. The Transactional Research module provides a pulse for the organization and monitors its relationships with its customers. Keeping a track on the Customer Satisfaction Index (CSI), a measure of loyalty derived from customer satisfaction scores, intention to recommend and intention to repurchase is essential. These are a vital indicator of both potential problems ahead and of your organization's position in relation to the competition. Transactional research is equally effective whether you are selling a power station or a computer service contract. Knowing when things are going wrong is the first step in identifying a solution.

CoAn Conjoint Analysis

When *ad hoc* groups are derived from transactional research pools, it is possible to measure the elasticity of their loyalty by using conjoint analysis. This quick and highly effective methodology allows customers with a known CSI to have the rationale behind their loyalty investigated and the limits of their loyalty explored. Thus, providing the marketing function with such information as to what competitive factors, if present, would cause loyalty to breakdown. Keep in mind we are working with systems that cover 80 per cent of eventualities as

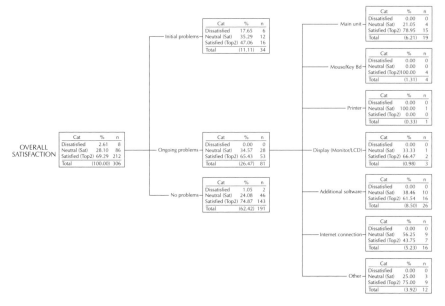

Figure 9.4   Computer manufacturing decision tree model.

these can predict the limits in the majority of cases given the same trade-offs.

MDM Manufacturing Decision Model

Although not shown in the cluster, this module is showing great promise. Figure 9.4 shows a screen shot of the module. Those of you familiar with fish bone and decision trees models will see the similarities. Based on the results of detailed post-launch customer satisfaction research, a model is built of the new product within days of its launch. This model is expressed in a tree format. Staff on the production line can then model the impact of a quality fault on end-customer satisfaction.

Let me give you an example. Imagine you are a computer manufacturer and the model is monitoring customer impact of manufacturing defects. Like all good manufacturers you are running on a 'just-in-time' basis, when your games disks do not arrive for inclusion with your computer. What do you do? You could put a note in each box and ask the purchaser to call the help line, allowing you to mail out the games disk later. In taking this course of action, you would incur the cost of the leaflet, telephone line charges, operators, increased demand on call centres, cost of postage, etc. Alternatively, do you stop production, (a very expensive option)? Or third, keep producing, set the computers aside and hope the disks arrive soon? This option involves rework and late deliveries. If a store does not have your brand, they are very good at switching customers to other brands they do have in stock. All in all, this is apparently a no-win situation.

The MDM reveals that the impact of the first option hits customer satisfaction hard, especially through the main retail channels such as FNAC in France and PC World in the UK. You can imagine your year's bonus vanishing out of the window. But the MDM will also show some channels have no negative impact from this type of failure. Simply by redirecting an assignment from one channel to another will allow you to ship without the games disk and have no impact on customer satisfaction. Many of the same models get shipped through various channels and not all channels are sensitive to the same quality issues to the same extent. Some channels supplying computers for SOHO (Small office and Home Office) install their own preconfigured software. Therefore, having a games disk or even any software at all is of no consequence to this group of Value Added Resellers (VARs). Hence by reassigning computers destined to this group of VARs to FNAC and PC World and shipping the current production run to the VARs there is no appreciable impact on customer satisfaction and major costly exercises are avoided.

The MDM lets manufacturing and channel managers work smarter because they can understand the consequences of their actions on their customers and simulate faults. This further allows management to pinpoint exactly where quality improvements are going to have the biggest impact on customer satisfaction. This eliminates the rather futile and inappropriate corporate wide goal of improving quality by 1 per cent across the board. It would be more appropriate to look at the areas where if they were improved, they increase the value of the product to the customer. What may be needed is 5 per cent improvement in delivery times instead of a 1 per cent increase in quality across the board or in areas where the customer is already satisfied. Identifying individual areas that are of special importance to the customer will yield a greater increase in satisfaction overall.

When I first used this example, the computer manufacturer I told quickly informed me that it could never happen on their production line. Only a year or so later they confessed that shortly after their statement, a similar thing happened at one of their main European plants.

MSBM MATCHED SPECTRUM BENCHMARKING

This module stands traditional benchmarking on its head and was developed in response to a problem encountered by Sun Systems Inc., in California.

Sitting with a leading light in the company, enjoying the weather, outside the original JAVA café (where the Java language was born, or so I was told), I heard of the problems that had been encountered by Sun when they had decided to take a closer look at some benchmarking results they had been getting and using to drive quality initiatives. It was clear they were not looking at like for like. I had been visiting companies around the valley, Oracle, Compaq, Silicon Graphics, Hewlett-Packard, etc., and they all had the same problem with their benchmark provider. Were they comparing peers with peers? Unfortunately, the answer was no. Sun's computer systems were being compared to Hewlett-Packard printers, high-end systems with PCs etc. In short, the research company had lost the plot. At the time, we had a benchmarking product that I thought could solve the problem in the traditional way by simply ensuring that we were comparing like with like. However, when we delved more deeply it became clear that like with like would be very difficult to find.

GMAS accepts that every company is unique, but like every unique chemical compound, it is made up of fundamental elements each of which produce a unique spectrum. Each part of a company—like a complex chemical compound—would contain identifiable telltale peaks in a spectroscopic examination. By building a picture of the company's unique spectrum, it would be possible to identify common elements between companies. Should these be perfectly compatible, benchmarking would be reliable and valid.

We set out to build a company spectrum. We achieved this by considering each of the prospective market segments that were apparent in the markets being served. In this way, high-end computers sold in small numbers with high levels of support and maintenance would be at the far left of the range, while PCs sold to the home market were at the extreme right of the spectrum. All the remaining markets featured somewhere in between.

In this way, all the major computer suppliers were classified and a spectrum established. In keeping with GMAS philosophy, this spectrum would be dynamic as firms acquired others or entered or exited various markets. Gathering benchmark data at a specific point (element) allowed a near-perfect comparison to be made and the benchmarking data derived was relevant to all the participants buying into that element. This ensured that benchmarking was not being distorted by product or service elements from other parts of the spectrum.

MTM MARKET TRIGGER MONITOR

In previous chapters I have mentioned the importance of a trigger being active in sales. A trigger is defined as an event that has caused a company to realize a need for a product or service. These triggers come from three sources: environment, competition, and/or originated by your marketing. The MTM monitors competitors and the environment for triggers. It is obviously much easier to sell to someone who has identified a need for your product or service than it is convince a sceptical buyer of its merits.

In Scotland there was a quite clever advertisement for double glazing (those reading in the Scandinavian countries will realize that Scotland has not yet got around to considering triple glazing). They simply used a very short main media advertisement that simply said, 'Don't sign until you've seen Living Design'. They were very happy to let other manufacturers sell the benefits of double glazing to a sceptical public, simply playing on the buyers' scepticism to get them to call after they had been convinced of the need. Because they saved in salesforce costs, Living Design could offer a better price and match or exceed their competitors' quality.

The MTM finds the events in the environment that are likely to act as a trigger to your suspects or to the target markets and allows the focusing of your sales effort to where it will have the highest probability of being successful.

In the same way, it can also help focus promotions to the best point in the sales process where you can capture sales generated at competitors' expense.

PRUP AND SRUP PRIMARY AND SECONDARY RESEARCH UPDATE

The PRUP and SRUP are simply events triggered by a diary action to ensure that you keep the primary and secondary research used in the strategy or operational plans up to date. It sounds simple, but it is rarely done in practice. In the case of secondary research used in the initial strategic planning process, it may have been several months old. Some of the assumptions will inevitably be based on the most recently available secondary research, which should be monitored to ensure that any subsequent issues do not contradict or significantly change a view that was the basis of decisions made during the strategic planning process. The SRUP ensures that all secondary research used in the planning process is updated and compared to that used in the initial planning process and that any compromises are reported via the STORM.

The PRUP is very similar, but renews the primary research instead of secondary, within a suitable time frame.

BORE BUSINESS OBJECTIVES REVIEW AND EVALUATION

A BORE it may be, but it is a necessary activity nonetheless. This audit-like exercise examines all the business objectives and ensures that they are SMART: Specific Measurable, Achievable, Realistic and Time framed. The business objectives are then compared to the strategic goal, vision or mission in order to evaluate if they are compatible and will be effective at achieving the steps required to realize the company's vision.

The objectives are both compared internally with historic performance and achievements as well as externally, in comparison to the observed best performance. The BORE ensures we do the right things and indicates how the right things should be done.

BSDC BALANCED SCORECARD DATA COLLECTION

In the Balanced Scorecard models there is a need to be fed with information. GMAS is particularly good at monitoring assumptions and providing information. Balanced Scorecards are only as good as the data provided and GMAS data is the very best (even if I say so myself). By using BSDC we provide data directly to the software you are using to administer your Balanced Scorecard. The area where this is particularly true is in that of the supply of customer information, which can be unreliable if internally gathered. I remember once being very angry with the airline Sabena. I was en route to a meeting in Munich and I was on the early flight out of Glasgow with a change of plane in Brussels. As the departure time slipped past and I could see no crew in the aircraft, I was concerned that I would not make the connecting flight. I asked what the problem was and was told not to worry, as I would make my connection. The crew were out of flying time and arrived more than an hour after the departure time. I was by this time very concerned and said to the ground staff that if I was going to miss the connection the next one would make me late for my meeting. As it was Friday, the people I would be meeting would not be happy to stay on into the evening. I was reassured and told, now by the cabin crew, that the flight would be waiting for us. On arrival in Brussels, it was no real surprise that the flight to Munich had left on schedule. I noticed that Lufthansa had a flight and if I got that I would make my meeting, so I asked at the Sabena helpdesk if they could transfer me to the Lufthansa flight, only to be told that the flight was full, and they could do nothing.

I settled down to wait and thought about where I would stay in Munich. Just before calling Munich I decided to wander over to Lufthansa desk and see if they had an earlier flight than my Sabena one, only to be told that they did and that the flight was now boarding and was far from full. I returned to the Sabena desk to be told that I was on the later flight and that was that! I ran back to the Lufthansa desk as the flight left. I was extremely angry and so, I went back to the Sabena desk and asked to speak to the supervisor as I had a complaint to make. I was rather abruptly told she was not available and given a customer complaint form and told I could get a voucher for a coffee by joining a growing queue at the next set of counters. I completed the questionnaire and handed it to the lady at the desk. As I was standing in the queue for the voucher I watched the lady read and then bin my complaint form.

I went ballistic and this time demanded to speak to the manager. After half an hour or so, she arrived. I explained the story; she simply blamed the staff at Glasgow and said her staff member had accidentally discarded the form, but she would deal with it. At no point was I offered any kind of apology. I have never heard from Sabena and I have never flown with them since.

Why am I telling you this story? Well it is very unlikely, in my mind, that Sabena's management ever heard of the problem and perhaps the other poor service events being experienced by their customers.

When I look back, I was frequently put up at Sabena's hotel in Brussels when travelling back from Munich—especially on Sundays. This usually made me late on Monday morning, but I had accepted it as one of those occupational hazards of being a frequent flyer. This final experience cost Sabena my business and who knows how many others. The internal reporting system, from my observation, had problems and was unreliable, as I mentioned earlier, if research is unreliable it cannot be valid. Therefore, if you want to know what your customers are really thinking before its too late, get in the professionals. Your ability to react is only as good as your knowledge of the problem.

CRMA CUSTOMER RELATIONSHIP MANAGEMENT AUGMENTATION

The Customer Relationship Management Systems (CRMs) require to be populated with data and kept current. The CRM systems utilize such features as a 'sales pipeline', a graphic representation of your sales process and how well your organization is doing at each stage.

The GMAS's CRMA module provides data inputs directly into your chosen CRM system. It ensures that press information and web monitoring information is available so that the sales team always know the latest developments in the organization they are preparing to sell to.

This provides sales teams with a reason to contact the customer or prospective client without trying to sell them anything. Instead, they can call to congratulate the company on their good fortune. This provides the detail that ensures your organization 'cares about the client or customer' and is after all, what CRM is all about. If you do not know what is happening to your customer and you only contact them with sales offers, they quickly classify you as a vendor and not a true business partner.

All CRM systems tend to have limited access to the news and current events impacting your customers, while they contain good internal contact information and histories. Without CRMA you are not optimizing your CRM investment.

CSM CUSTOMER SATISFACTION MONITORING

The new ISO 9000 quality assurance standard being introduced now, for implementation before 2003, requires quality assured companies to undertake customer satisfaction research. This requirement, which is no bad thing, means that many more companies than ever before will desire to contact their customers and get feedback on how well they are performing. While this is very positive, there is the high probability that the same customers will be targeted by various parts of the organization to satisfy their quality assurance requirements. This will place a great burden on customers who will very quickly stop cooperating with research requests if they are bombarded with questionnaires from the same organization. As more research is conducted, customers will become increasingly difficult to talk to and reluctant to complete questionnaires, which can be time consuming and not considered worth while if they do not result in tangible improvements in the service being received by the customer. If the customer takes the time to tell you on several occasions about a weakness in your product or service and you do not respond, they will stop telling you and perhaps take their business elsewhere.

It is therefore necessary to ensure that research involving customers is minimized, that the information gathered is utilized and that the respondents get feedback about what has happened as a result of their contribution. Furthermore, in order to ensure that respondents will continue to complete your research when the background noise of other companies surveys grows, you will have to ensure that the respondents are given the opportunity to choose the means and frequency of research which suits them best.

Even more of an issue will be the ability for customers to opt out of taking part in research. If a customer does not want to take part in research and advises you of the fact, you will be damaging your company's image and reputation by continuing to subject that person to requests to take part in research studies. In many countries new legislation is being introduced to protect the consumer and this may be extended to contact for research purposes if we do not become more considerate of the wishes of our customers.

The CSM module set ensures that a coordinated approach to contacting customers is taken throughout the organization. It brings together the various customer databases that exist within the organization and provides a preferencing service for the internal data ensuring that if a customer has told one department that they do not wish to be involved in research, this information is available across the company. The CSM captures a history of customer involvement in research and their preferences for methodology and frequency. Ensuring that if a customer is willing, for example, to answer two questionnaires a year that is all they will be asked to complete, but those two questionnaires will be the most important in ensuring loyalty and understanding of the issues needing to be addressed.

The system also ensures that each participant is kept informed about what has happened as a result of the overall research programme in which they have participated.

CU CUSTOMER AUDIT

The GMAS customer Audit module is used to maximize the potential of each customer account. It provides a measure of share of customer and potential of customer. Many companies know how much of their product they sell to a customer, but do not know the potential or how much business goes to competitors. By undertaking a customer audit each customer account can be maximized, SMART objectives set and their full potential realized. The module uses a mixture of research and industry estimates to determine each account's potential and identifies the competitors and estimates shares and future as well as current potential. In this way, your customer base can be segmented and sales efforts targeted where there will be the most potential within the existing customer base.

This module links with the Strategic Account Post-sales Status and Development implementation module to ensure that the audits results are translated into an effective sales programme.

WAVE REAL-TIME WAVE STUDY

A WAVE study is a view across the entire market. It compares your company's performance with others in exactly the same segment. It utilizes Matched Spectrum Benchmarking techniques but is not done in collaboration with any other organizations.

It is therefore necessary to capture competitor's customers and trace their experience against your own customers' experiences. In the most common format, the respondents tracked were in the first instance considering your offering but opted for a competitor's product. In this way the loyalty of competitors' customers can be directly compared to your own customers in real time and over the entire life cycle of the product to repurchase and beyond. This provides valuable information about what events impacts loyalty and the critical stages in the customer relationship where loyalty ties are established and reinforced.

INTEGRATION OF MODULES

Each of the modules described are designed to be compatible with the others in the GMAS range and to interface with open object-oriented systems. Bespoke designed systems and non-open systems involve integration which may or may not be justified in terms of benefits gained. The most common integrations are with ERP, CRM, BSC and Creative Thinking (CT) software. Some of the suppliers of which have kindly contributed to this book by each providing descriptions of their products (see Appendix 1).

As I have said, many human interventions are required in GMAS and it is perhaps three to five years away from being an almost completely automated system. The reality is that data is not always compatible and there is the need to, if not rekey, at least verify that the data has been successfully transferred. The biggest issue comes from inconsistent data input into the other systems. Let me explain: operators in France enter the telephone number, but do not log the country code. Telephone numbers in the UK have a local dialling code as well as a national dialling code: which was given and which recorded? Zip codes go at the end of an address in the UK, but before the name of the city in Spain. All these small differences along with a thousand others can cause interesting data compatibility issues when the data is combined. These are, of course, true of all multicountry systems and, despite the hype, most IT managers will admit to having had their fair share of data compatibility issues. In GMAS systems, we accept there will be some issues to be straightened out. Perhaps at first, as much as 20 per cent so there is a human presence required until all the little wrinkles have been ironed out.

BUYING IN GMAS SERVICES

Not all the modules need to be run in-house, and although each GMAS module will conform to the uniqueness of each user organization, there is information that can be most economically collected by a group of users. The process of turning this information into market intelligence and knowledge, however, should be an in-house or privately provided service.

Modules such as web monitoring, press monitoring, broadcast news monitoring, etc., can be subscribed to as 80 per cent of the information you require will be similar to that required by any other company operating in the same sector: 20 per cent will not be—it will be unique to your organization and will enable you to derive your specific marketing advantage. The point is, why pay to have the system 100 per cent tailored when you can get 80 per cent off the shelf?

Regardless of whether you choose to subscribe to one of these services that provide everything in-house, monitoring and research modules are the essential ingredients in keeping your strategy on track. Like your garden, your strategy will become wild if it is not looked after. GMAS systems are only as good as the investment you are willing to make in tending them, by providing vital feedback and in using their produce. A garden which is beautifully tended and which produces beautiful strawberries year after year is wasted if the strawberries are never eaten.

SUMMARY

- We reviewed a range of GMAS testing and monitoring modules and how they are applied.

- In addition, we looked at death and decay avoidance in modules.

- Finally, we examined the integration of modules and the need to maintain modules in peak condition.

10

How to Use Implementation Modules

There is a variety of implementation modules that has been derived over the years as a result of the need to understand operational activity and ensure that it is performed sufficiently well to enable the strategy to be fulfilled.

The list below itemizes the range currently available or in development. There is obviously no limit to potential implementation modules as they are effectively the unique best practice for organizations. As such, they cover all aspects of your business and are almost the operational manuals for each of the activities that are vital to your organization's success. Similar to quality systems which are used properly, these modules are dynamic and change to reflect what works. In line with the changing market, and like all GMAS modules, they come in a generic form which has to be tailored to the specifics of your organization and marketing environment.

Modules may not be appropriate in every environment. Because the models are built using the 'needed information only' principle, if there was no need in the design to consider, for example, acquisitions in a declining market (which is not the case at the moment), the model would not necessarily have even a generic outline for acquisitions in a declining market as this was not appropriate for the purpose behind the module design.

Where the model has not been designed for the specific environment you are interested in, it may be no more use than a good book on the subject. Alternatively, it may contain all the answers you require and only need testing in order to adapt to your environment and tailor to your organization.

Individual modules can be used on their own where a company has a specific issue they need to address. The same is true of monitoring and testing modules: they can be used independently of adopting a corporate wide GMAS. In most GMAS deployments today, with the exception of those in start-ups, privatizations, MBOs, deregulations, or MBIs, they have all first involved the adoption of one or more of the monitoring, testing or implementation modules.

In one global company, the first module was a research module—FG. This was added to by CASM, CAM, CU, CSM, QFCIA, and then implementation modules such as AVM, BCS, CARP, CPR and the list grows. However, they do not utilize the STORM or strategy modules yet.

GMAS modules provide a pick-and-mix of solutions to research and operational planning issues. Perhaps there are areas in which you would like to develop a module or commission a module?

The current list of implementation modules is given below, but for the latest list, see our website at www.ridingthestorm.net.

A&M	Acquisitions and Mergers
ABC	Activity Based Costing
AVM	Analyst View Maker
BDM	Bid Decision Model
BSC	Balanced Scorecard
CA	Compensation Alignment
CAM	Critical Assumption Monitoring
CARP	Cause Analysis and Rectification Programme
CASM	Customer Acquisition and Sales Monitoring
CPR	Customer Problem Resolution
CRM	Customer Relationship Management System Deployment
CRMA	CRM Augmentation
CU	Customer Audit
eGO	Exploiting Global Opportunities Centre
ERP	Enterprise Resource Planning Integration
ICR	Internal Communications Review
ICSM	Internal Customer Satisfaction Monitoring

KB	Knowledge Base
KPS	Key Performance Systems 'KPA/KPI'
MCC	Management Control Centre
MDI	Marketing Data Integration
MDM	Manufacturing Decision Model
Mind Map	Mind Map Interface to Knowledge Base
MPI	Marketing Plan Implementation
MPR	Marketing Performance Review
MS	Marketing Support
PACE	Post-Acquisition Communications Evaluation
PostSM	Post-Sales Model
PreSM	Pre-Sales Model
S Pro	Sales Promotion
SAP	Strategic Account Post-Sales Status and Development

To give you a flavour of some implementation modules I will describe a few.

PreSM PRE-SALES MODEL

This module involves the sales cycle and ensures that the time of the sales team is spent pursuing prospects that have the highest probability of becoming clients.

This module is often run in or on a CRM system. Figure 10.1 shows the sales cycle and this module follows the scheme of known market, suspects, triggers, prospects, pre-proposals, proposals, contract and customer or client.

Suspects are defined as companies drawn from the known market that you know would benefit from your product or service but may not realize themselves that they would. With the cost of a salesforce being high, you should not devote its time to knocking on doors with this group where the probability of success may be as little as 10–20 per cent. In some industries, of course, this is what is done and the costs and structure make this a very attractive return, but where sales cycles are long or the customers are highly dispersed, this can be a very inefficient process as multiple visits may be required.

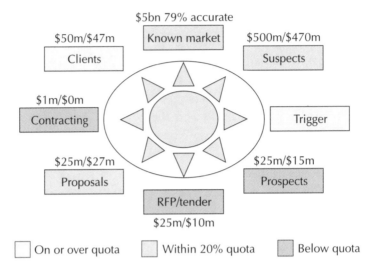

Figure 10.1   GMAS sales cycle.

Therefore, this group becomes the target for marketing promotions that flush out the prospects from the suspects. Prospects are
suspects with an active trigger; that is, a need to buy your or similar
products. Good marketing can alert suspects to this need and hence
they are targeted. Marketing to the known market would be wasteful
because response rates there can be as low as 1–3 per cent.

The PreSM module goes into the promotions that work in certain
circumstances with suspects and with over 300 to choose from, there is
little chance of not finding something appropriately different to your
specific market. The most appropriate promotions are selected by
entering the market conditions and characteristics of your suspect
group. Each promotion recommended is documented in terms of
what, why, where, when and how it works as well as being indicatively
costed. It also contains expected return and any caveats relating to its
use. Thus, this module provides all the tools required to effectively
manage the pre-sales process and see it through to the sale. There are
other modules that then develop the sale into a repurchase.

Figure 10.2 shows the pipeline that is used to ensure that marketing and sales efforts are applied at the right places in the cycle to
provide a more even delivery of projects. Like GMAS, Siebel has
its opponents in deployments because it directs sales effort to where
it is needed and not always where the sales people want to spend their

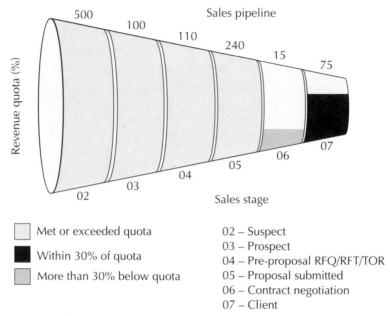

Figure 10.2   The acquisitions and mergers cluster.

day. Combined GMAS and Siebel sales provide the alignment of the marketing activities with the sales activities to ensure both work together; not independently or worse, against each other.

PUTTING THE SCIENCE BACK INTO MANAGEMENT SCIENCE

I do not want to open the debate about whether management is an art or a science, but what I do want to discuss is the application of science to management. The module I described above and the use of fuzzy logic-type applications allow many more tools to be made available to managers.

These applications range from marketing tools, like those described above, to production and personnel management systems. By increasingly being able to monitor outcomes from certain stimulation in known environments and limiting the application to similar environments, the ability to understand and predict outcomes increases. Similar to Neuro-Linguistic Programming (NLP), the range of responses from known stimulations can be calculated and we can build management systems that reduce the amount of uncertainty, and therefore risk, in the management of operations. The art in management is therefore better supported by the application of science.

IMPLEMENTATION MODULE CLUSTERS

Like the testing and monitoring modules, implementation modules can be clustered around themes or activities. The range that we have developed at MMSI plc has been done more by chance than by design as they have been based on the problems encountered in our customer base rather than an organized development process. As a result of this, we have developed the needed modules only. There are obvious gaps in the range and I am hoping others can step in to fill these gaps by adopting the ABCD–WOW approach and working with GMAS collaboration.

One interesting cluster has developed around acquisitions and mergers for the purpose of acquiring technological advantage and avoidance of paradigm shift. This cluster is illustrated in Figure 10.2. This group of implementation modules includes A&M, the core module for successful Acquisitions and Mergers; PACE, Post-Acquisition Communications Evaluation; AVM, Analyst View maker; RPS, Recognizing Paradigm Shift and eGO, Exploiting Global Opportunities.

I have already mentioned that the A&M and PACE modules are a means of ensuring that after the merger, communications have been established and that there is a feeling of the organization being 'one company' and that nothing unhelpful remains from the previous company. Below are a few of the other modules I would like to share with you.

AVM Analyst View Maker

In most large companies, a large percentage of very senior management's time is spent dealing with the City and in particular, the analysts. In the US this has necessitated the need for the COO (Chief Operating Officer) position because if the CEO spends most of the time with the investors and the rest of the time with the customers, who looks after the business? Similar to the family business, there are circles of conflict pulling on executives' time. Simplistically, these are: the business, the owners and self-interest. Self-interest, as you know, always takes the back seat. Where management's time is absorbed exclusively by one of these circles, someone needs to ensure a balance is achieved. The danger is that in separating the CEO and creating the COO, the very thing the owners/shareholders want to protect—the CEO's control—drifts from their grasp, and as a result, so too does the business. I, as you can tell, am not in favour of employing the management assistant model which to me appears to just create more work for everyone. Give someone a job, give them the authority and responsibility for seeing its done. If the job is too big, it should be divided instead of creating an assistant. If the COO's job is to be real, they have to have the authority to run the business and if they do, what does the CEO do? And what is the chairperson doing? Anyway, I digress. The point I am making is that in the real world, the CEO has to spend time wooing the investors, and we should help that process by designing a system that ensures that the investors get reliable access to the information they need in order to develop trust in the CEO. All this allows the CEO to do his or her job and that is to manage the company to its full potential and, therefore, to the shareholders benefit.

The AVM module influences analysts by understanding them as individuals within an organization. Thus, it allows the criteria they favour to be quickly brought to the fore and the reality explained in such as way as to reassure rather than alarm the individual analyst. Companies adopting this approach have consistently more favourable analyst reviews and recommendations even when they have faced dramatic sectorwide downturns.

Both the RPS and the eGO Centre are designed to exploit paradigm shift. A paradigm shift is fundamentally, a shift in the basic rationale upon which a market is based. For example, computer speed may be considered a rationale for purchasing a computer. If this rationale was replaced by design, this would mean that a shift in paradigm had occurred. The classic example of this is in the disk drive market with the move away from density in the days of mainframes, to size in the era of the portable and handheld computers.

If you can detect a paradigm shift, you may be in a position to do something about it. If you don't detect it or misdiagnose it, you can land up in trouble. Lucent Technologies' downfall over the last three years has been blamed on it missing a technology wave, as did IBM, and most of the other once colossal names that are now merely large companies.

The RPS module very effectively detects paradigm shift or the potential for paradigm shift. The unfortunate reality is that many products or services with the potential for paradigm shift die in their infancy. Over 70 per cent of patents are not commercialized and these lapsed or dormant patents can be extremely valuable. The Japanese patents office has hundreds of staff searching through worldwide patents and notifying companies and universities in Japan about technology that they may like to look at. The government is not alone in this and many of the larger Japanese companies have in-house patent check teams.

The fact that when innovation is combined with the right management team and investor group it can become a real winner is not lost on the Japanese government or industry.

The RPS module looks a lot wider than patents and is more focused on products and services that have survived their infancy. Detecting the paradigm allows you to take the action required to defend yourself or to exploit the innovation.

eGO CENTRE

The eGO Centre was developed after it became clear that large companies are not very good at exploiting discontinuous innovation. You just have to look at the computer industry and most of the big names have been born as a result of disaffected staff leaving to exploit their innovative idea that was spurned by their employer. For example, Tandem computers and its high reliability concept in computing for mission critical applications, Dell and its innovative distribution concept, Compaq Computers and the PC market, Hewlett-Packard and its printers.

The eGO (Exploiting Global Opportunities) Centre is an incubator and business planning centre for the development of spin out technology from large organizations. Rather than have your most talented staff leave and set up in competition, why not support them in leaving and help them build a scalable business that you can ensure survives its infancy. The businesses set-up are free from the parents' return on investment criteria, market positioning, channel policy, corporate legal department, investor relations and all the other killers of innovation. Free that is, with the exception of a golden share. This golden share allows the parent to choose, at an agreed time, to have first option on buying back the company. This option lapses if not utilized on the specified date so that other investors can maximize their return if the parent still cannot see the benefits in the innovation. In this way, staff are effectively seconded to the eGO Centre and the new innovation's development is planned. If it fails, they return to be more content with corporate life in the parent company. However, if they succeed, they will have taken market share away from not only their parent but in equal measure from their competitors. Hence, a new market leader is created if the parent exploits its options and its ability to scale is utilized. This ensures the future success of both the old and new company.

By utilizing other investors, more innovations can be developed and the more that survive, the more likely the parent is to survive and incorporate the new paradigm.

MIND MAP

Tony Buzan, in my opinion, is the father of mind mapping. In his book *Use Your Head*, he describes the process by which mind mapping can be used in teaching and learning. Mind mapping is also a very good format for both business planning and for GMAS control functions. There are now packages on the market that allows mind mapping to be both painless and fast even on a computer screen. Figure 10.3 shows a typical mind map.

A mind map is a very useful way of outlining a plan. Hyperlinks can then take the reader to subsequent levels of detail or plans. In this way an entire company's knowledge base can be accessed in quick time. Figure 10.3 shows the first level window to a set of windows offering more detail on the various topics. This format of business

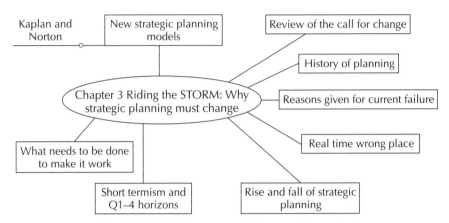

Figure 10.3   Mind Map, Riding the STORM.

planning is particularly relevant to small businesses where the elements of the strategic plan can be visually represented and you can drill down to the part of the plan you wish to see or be hyperlinked to websites or into sales and marketing systems.

With ERP investments ranging from $1 million to $50 million, the investment in simple tools to ensure you get your thinking down clearly at around $150 is money well spent.

BDM BID DECISION MODEL

One aspect of business that we have found in a number of companies is the lack of a consistent and considered approach to responding to tenders. In some companies they grasp at everything and can have atrocious success rates, while in others what they bid for depends on who is in the office that day and what mood they are in. Both of these approaches are not effective ways of running a business. Having developed a strategy, it is imperative that this is translated into a meaningful sales strategy and in the case of those companies who elicit or respond to tenders that this aspect of the business is quickly brought in line with the company's strategy. Just as the saying goes that 'we are what we eat', so a company becomes a provider of what contracts it wins. If the decision is not made to focus and a robust BDM not produced, then the day-to-day activities of winning business will not be aligned with the strategic vision.

The BDM was developed because of the number and strength of resistance in certain sectors to change—especially in traditional service and heavy engineering industries. The module provides a decision guide and criteria check that allows tender requests to be assessed against the strategic goals and maintains a firm focus on winning the strategically important accounts and not allowing them to be diluted by effort being wasted on less important bids.

The time and expense of producing a tender can be significant and the quality of the submission is only as good as the market intelligence surrounding it. When there are too many tenders being done and while there is a 'busy feeling', the organization is failing to achieve its full potential by not devoting enough attention to winning the key ones. It is better to have a quiet department which, when called into action, delivers rather than one that is run off its feet but provides marginal success. The BDM provides the market intelligence to make those bids that are strategically important, significantly more winnable.

IMPLEMENTATION SYSTEM REQUIREMENTS

There are five core requirements in getting the most out of GMAS. These are attitude, people, skills, software and hardware. The easiest to acquire are hardware and software. The most difficult are attitude, people and skills. Of the last five GMAS deployments, despite what we thought airtight restrictions on clients from poaching our staff, we have had GMAS teams poached.

The problem is that the interface between the systems and the research is the individuals in day-to-day contact with the client's managers. The client, after a very short time, grows to depend on the information and assistance obtained which they unfortunately perceive as emanating from the consultant they talk to daily. To be fair, as I hired the majority of the consultants and our training gave them the skills they required for the task, they were not generally poor performers. They were the best we could recruit and therefore, on the whole, a very worthwhile addition to the client's staff. It just makes

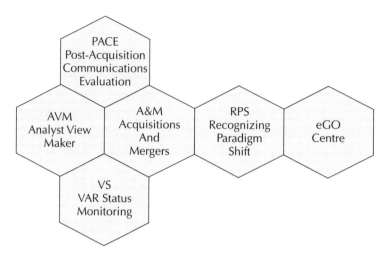

Figure 10.4   An example of an implementation module cluster.

me mad! To prevent this, MMSI now trains your staff as an option instead of using MMSI's staff and they can even get a university diploma in continuing and professional development in management consultancy as a by-product.

The people to run the GMAS systems can therefore be recruited, hired or you can have your own staff trained. The latter option is only applicable where the staff possess the right attitude and basic knowledge level.

As the software and hardware is readily available, problems arise usually with the IT staff who can find the systems far in advance of where the company is currently positioned. I have had examples of these mission critical systems being placed on highly suspect platforms or where the back-up arrangements fall far short of the minimum requirements. As a result, and as all new GMAS systems are designed to be secure and web-based, they can be hosted on MMSI plc servers, if the company's IT department is likely to hinder deployment. Your IT staff may have very logical and real reasons for this such as compatibility worries and non-standard configurations being required on some PCs, not to mention having to understand a strange, new system. However, working with the IT department and getting the necessary level of authority means that all things are possible in time.

You can see when starting with a clean sheet of paper in, for example, privatization, how GMAS can be installed quickly but equally how implementation into an established system can become a slow tedious process which can become bogged down. In one case, we waited six months for a project management tool to be bought and installed which would have cost $1000 but landed up being charged at $6000 because of the 'internal' charges etc. We now provide PCs with everything you need on them from day one. This supplies all the support required until the IT department catches up, which is remarkably quickly when they feel the need to.

TYPICAL THINGS TO CONSIDER ON MODULE DEPLOYMENT

A typical SAP project, according to the Aberdeen group, has its cost broken down as follows: 6 per cent training fees, 36 per cent consultancy fees, 20 per cent software licenses, 17 per cent Hardware Costs and 21 per cent in-house labour. Therefore, when deploying any system BSC, ERP, CRM or GMAS you will have to allow for each of these aspects of deployment.

SUMMARY

- We explored GMAS implementation modules and their role and function.

- The pot-pourri of modules ranged from Bid Decision Models to Recognizing Paradigm Shift and gave a flavour of the range and how they can be utilized.

- The chapter ended with a discussion on implementation requirements.

11

The GMAS Future

As you will have gathered, GMAS is still in the early phase of development and will require your serious consideration before it can, as Moore (1995) puts it 'cross the chasm'.

GMAS RESULTS

GMAS has had some promising early deployments, but like most initiatives in companies of any size, I cannot claim that GMAS was the only factor involved, or even that it played any significant part, but I like to think GMAS at least had a role in the following companies' successes.

Railway Maintenance Company
A full pilot of GMAS saw the company's sales grow from $35 million to $117 million in 18 months.

Government Agency Responsible for Inward Investment
Pilots of some of the modules helped the team bring 11 000 jobs to the city and attract investments of $252 million.

Professional Indemnity Insurance Provider
Pilots helped them recover their market position which resulted in achieving 85 per cent market share in the target market.

Utility
During the deregulation process, the company was able to retain 95 per cent of its market share in the highly competitive business-users market.

Computer Manufacturer
Estimated benefits are in the region of $25 million and have been achieved from deployment of the transactional research and manufacturing modules.

Telecoms Supplier
Impact of the CPR, CSM and CARP modules has had an estimated $50 million positive impact on one product division alone.

Share Price Impact where Companies Subsequently Merged or were Acquired

Tandem Computers' purchase by Compaq computers was announced on the NYSE on the 20 June 1997 at a price of $15. The transaction was valued at $3 billion. MMS commenced work with Tandem in 1992 when the share price was at $9.50. The share price had risen 60 per cent in the interim period.

Jarvis purchased Relayfast, a private limited company not quoted on the Stock Exchange, in 1997 for a consideration of £9.9 million. Relayfast had experienced an increase in value of almost 100 per cent since MMS's involvement in the original management buy-out of Relayfast Ltd from British Rail in 1996 for £5 million.

Gamut Technologies was founded in April 1994 with the explicit objective of addressing the needs of the corporate customer in CRM and the Internet. Gamut Technologies was subsequently purchased by Druid plc (itself subsequently purchased by FI Group) for a consideration of $15 million.

The purchase of Ascend Communications by Lucent Technologies was announced on the NYSE on 24 June 1999. The shares were valued at $103 in a transaction that created a merger worth $24 billion. Marketing Management Services commenced work with Ascend in 1998 when the share price sat at $47. This shows a share price rise of 120 per cent.

GMAS is still being developed and I am interested to hear

your views on the book and your experiences in deploying or building your own GMAS applications. Please let me know your successes and not yet successful experiences by e-mailing me on Gerald.Michaluk@ridingthestorm.net

THE FUTURE

As the speed of change approaches warp speed, the storms will get more intense and frequent. Adaptive, flexible, customer-focused strategy will not be a luxury: it will be a necessity in the 21st century.

Organizations adaptable enough to perform in whatever the market conditions will become the leaders in this new era, those with loyal investors, customers and staff will have an edge and those with the ability to ride each paradigm wave will reap rich rewards. Those who remain inflexible and glued to a fixed obsolete strategy no matter how well communicated throughout the organization, will perish.

'Optionality' will be the salient word of the strategic companies of the new era. They will have developed their own customized best practice that uniquely delivers to them the optimum performance, which others may observe but be unable to copy effectively. They will constantly change and adapt their systems to maximize and squeeze costs out of the supply chain and deliver higher and higher levels of customer value. The markets once considered a mass will increasingly fragment in the wealthy nations and be born in the developing nations. 'Legacy-free companies' that have the edge today will come under pressure from the 'amoeba companies' of the future who grow and divide and grow adapting to the markets. I will expand more on this theme in my next book.

The giant companies will have to adopt GMAS-like systems to defend themselves from paradigm change, which may come from sources other than market, such as governments driven by public opinion or fear.

THE LAST WORD

GMAS offers a structure in which strategic planning can be spread throughout the organization. It eliminates the need for the 'token' annual planning cycles and five-year strategic plans replacing them with a corporatewide understanding of the strategy and the factors behind it and a continuous process revealing Real Options in real time exploitable at the right time.

It makes strategy ordinary and vulnerable and therefore flexible and changeable when it needs to be. It provides the right managers with the right market intelligence at the right time. It tunes in on your market and the economic environmental realities and provides a means of monitoring and testing what is changing.

GMAS brings strategy and operations together and allows each to feed off the strengths of the other. It provides templates for providing your organization with your unique best practice that will deliver competitive benefit to your organization. It detects operational failures or strategic failures and provides means of correction.

In short, it is the corporate strategy equivalent of Viagra!

Appendix 1

THE THEORY OF GMAS AND SOFTWARE APPLICABLE TO IT

In this appendix there is a review of ABC, BSC, CRM, and ERP, as well as a list of some of the vendors whose products can be utilized in GMAS systems. I asked each of the companies to write something about their products. This is included here. The list is not exhaustive and I am not endorsing one product over another. Vendors that are GMAS certified can be found on the GMAS collaborative website at www.ridingthestorm.net.

ABC Activity Based Costing

Kaplan and Cooper (1998), in their book, *Cost and Effect*, describe the Activity Based Costing model (ABC) as 'an economic map of the organization's expenses and profitability based on organizational activities'. Activity Based Costing very basically measures activity costs based on the process driver and the resources consumed. All activities have a purpose: inputs and outputs, and ABC measures the activity and allocates costs to the outputs. It differs from traditional costing models in the level of detail and accuracy it provides. This detail and accuracy allows management to make process improvements to meet cost objectives and provides performance measures. It has the disadvantage in that it is more expensive than more traditional costing models and for this reason a trade-off is made between the cost of

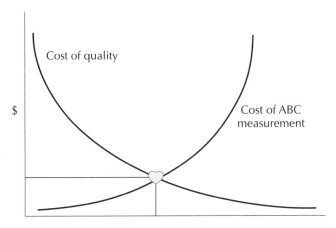

Figure A1.1   Cost of Quality to ABC cost.

accurate measurement and allocation of process costs and the savings to be made by reducing the cost of quality (see Figure A1.1).

Logic suggests that the optimum place for the ideal system is at the bottom-most point of the total cost curve. The pay-offs from even a simple ABC system can be spectacular, therefore the majority of systems should be self-financing (at least on paper) after a relatively small initial investment. The difficulty arises in defining the cost of the quality curve and therefore what investment in ABC is optimal.

ABM Activity Based Management

Activity Based Management (ABM) is the strategic management process that utilizes ABC data to reduce or eliminate costs while increasing customer value. While all this sounds new and exciting, I remember a group of students from the Asia Pacific region who were on an MSc course over 15 years ago who had a very similar philosophy. I remember feeling that several of their strategies were simply not being awarded the results they deserved in the computer market simulations because their ideas were smarter than those that the programs used to calculate market reaction, etc. Let me explain this further. This group would first ask what the market price was. Next, how elastic the market was. If the market was elastic (that is, a small change in price would increase demand) then they would calculate the price required to allow them to dominate the market. Following this, they would design a production process that would firstly allow them both flexibility, for incremental improvement and secondly would achieve the target price.

Had they known about the ABC model, they would have mastered the processes to be able to achieve the target price. The computers simply did not let them reduce costs by process improvement to the extent they required for their strategy to be effective because the program assumed only modest improvements could be made regardless of spend.

I hope these students went on to become multimillionaires despite the computer's limited understanding of how ABM could drive costs out of processes and provide customers with improved value.

By analysing and attributing costs to a process, ABC allows that process to be understood. Reengineering the process using a GMAS module permits the optimization of that process commensurate with the unique nature of your company and its markets.

BSC Balanced Scorecard

Balanced Scorecard (BSC) converts a company's operations and strategy into an inclusive list that supplies the structure for a tactical assessment and control system. The BSC supplies an organization with expertise, which it needs to guide potential triumph. It offers an organization's corporate level personnel with a complete structure that interprets its operations and strategy into a logical set of performance indicators. Organizations are in the middle of the information age, which has evolved from the industrial age. In the industrial age, financial methods had been used to measure the performance of an organization. In today's information age, traditional financial measures have become outdated as they provide information on historical events. A new set of indicators had to be created that would include stakeholder benefits, output, customer service indicators, the time spent in various business processes and usefulness of new product expansion. Therefore a comprehensive scorecard of performance measurements, the BSC was established.

Balanced Scorecard is for organizations that feel the need to link and bring their company in line with new strategies, a fair distance from the previous focus on reducing expenditure and low-price competition. The BSC model is arranged around four viewpoints, which are explained below.

The Financial View
The ultimate objective of this view is to 'improve shareholder value'. Improved shareholder value comes as a consequence of the offsetting of income growth against increased productivity within the company. The factors of income growth and productivity both consist of two main subsections. Within income growth, the contributing factors are the expansion of the market and the increasing of income from the present client base. The two factors that lead to increased productivity are increased efficiency and better use of current resources combined with large investments being replaced by gradual investments.

The Customer View
Kaplan and Norton describe this section as 'the heart of the strategy'. This area outlines the exact strategy for gaining new custom or for enlarging the current customers' division of business.

The Internal View
This view outlines the corporate processes and exact actions that company must perfect in order to maintain the customer view, which as has already been said is fundamental to the model.

Learning and Growth View
Kaplan and Norton outline the 'unquantifiable' resources that are necessary in order to allow the goals of organizational actions and client/company interaction to be carried out at increasingly sophisticated levels, to be achieved. There are three main sections to be considered within the learning and growth view. The first is that of strategic capabilities. This section encapsulates the knowledge and abilities demanded from the staff in order to maintain the strategy. The second section is that of 'strategic technologies' (Kaplan and Norton, 2001). This part is concerned with the technological requirements that are necessary to maintain the strategy. The third and final

area that contributes to the learning and growth view is that of the environment for the activity. Within this part the effect of shifts in the social atmosphere of the organization are taken into account as the optimum environment in which to maintain the strategy is examined.

ERP Enterprise Resource System

Enterprise Resource System (ERP) involves the consolidation of all units and operations across an organization into an individual computer application that can assist specific needs and enable contact within the organization as well the common use of data that is produced by the application.

The term 'enterprise resource planning' was created by the Gartner Group in the last decade of the 20th century to relate company software applications. They determined that these applications had to encompass combined elements for accounts, financial matters, sales and distribution, human resources, materials control and various corporate operations founded on systems used across the entire organization that established a means of communication in the company to its clients. This definition involves three fundamental components:

1   ERP applications are versatile in range, covering various functions including economic effects, proposals, purchasing, construction and personnel.
2   ERP applications are consolidated and involve data being entered into a certain operation thus altering data in all connected units is also transformed instantly.
3   ERP applications are composed of modules and are therefore applicable in any amalgamation of the modules.

Global ERP application companies including SAP-AG, Oracle, J.D. Edwards, PeopleSoft and Baan have a share of about three-quarters of the ERP market. At the moment, $24 million a year is being spent on enterprise applications, and a major fraction of that was on ERP systems.

An ERP system can be assembled in a number of ways including the deployment of software from a single supplier. In other circumstances, the company can install various components from a number of suppliers. Both methods have their own advantages. Using various modules can offer the best purposes for each module, but installing them can be particularly difficult due to certain boundaries that need to be created. A single supplier application may not have all the purposes required, but it can be simpler to install. Even though numerous global organizations have installed ERP applications, most of them have implemented them towards the end of the 1990s. Therefore, these applications are somewhat unknown, and there is a lack of information on hand relating to the installation, functionality or outcome. Therefore, knowledge on ERP is sometimes conflicting and distorted to fit particular opinions.

There are three major reasons why companies undertake ERP:

1   Consolidation of financial information
2   Homogenization of operations
3   Streamline human resources data

CRM Customer Relationship Management

Customer Relationship Management (CRM) is a system that gives a complete overview of the client/company exchange. It involves itself in every means of communication and exchange between the organization and the customer. A CRM programme is customized to effectively meet the needs of any individual organization's customer's requirements.

Individuals who experience a beneficial exchange with a business are commonly more faithful and lucrative. Taking into account that obtaining a new customer usually costs more than retaining a present one, investing in a process that keeps your customer has obvious benefits for the company. Sizeable organizations may expend vast sums of money on a CRM system. The most notable CRM providers include Siebel Systems, Oracle and IBM. The purpose of CRM is to tailor it to an actual organization's requirements, there therefore is no global description of CRM. The acronym CRM was initially applied by companies that produced and sold salesforce automation (SFA) software. These are robust pieces of software used by sales teams to control daily communications with clients. The sales teams log all they know about the client, note all communications, and describe the outcome of every meeting into the SFA software. In addition, they plan next activities to the sale, and the application notifies them when those actions should be carried out. These applications can connect to databases within businesses in order to draw out previous financial transactions, product utilization, remittance history, as well as additional knowledge that assists the sales team in maximizing its relationship with the client. These applications allow managers to assess what each member of the sales team is working on and how efficiently they are utilizing the applications.

The CRM technologies are important in the process, but they represent only a section of it. This technology encompasses:

- Databases.
- Strategies.
- Complex statistical analysis.
- Effective communication.
- Timely and widespread application.

The advantages that can be gained by employing a high-quality CRM system include:

1. Increased customer retention.
2. Improved levels of client loyalty.
3. Maximization of profit from present client base.
4. Increased company recognition.

Overlapping between the models:

- ABC and ERP.

There can be possible overlapping between an ABC and ERP models relating to costs assigned to activities.

The ABC model encompasses the concept of linking costs to resources that are used when completing a process. Similarly, an ERP system that combines all computer systems of a company into a single system also has financial data that includes revenues by customer, costs by department and costs by expense type. Non-financial data, such as resource driver and activity driver volumes can also be obtained from the ERP system on a timely basis.

However, using both an ERP and an ABC system together in a company can save valuable effort and time for a company. Using an ABC system on its own involves manual gathering and data input, which is much more time consuming. An ERP system can feed the ABC system with all the activity costs and information about the resources consumed.

- CRM and ERP.

The CRM can be seen as a system for transferring to one place information that otherwise would be dispersed in a big company. Information is gathered from a number of sources including call centres and websites, from networking with sales teams or via the clients' meetings with retailers. An ERP system also combines information from all departments including those that deal with customer contact. Just like a CRM system, an ERP system makes all data available to every department in a company.

- BSC and ABC.

A BSC model involves a multidimensional set of performance indicators that a company must fulfil in order to succeed. As described earlier BSC becomes the central organizing framework for important managerial processes such as individual and long-term goal setting, resource allocation, budgeting and planning, and strategic feedback and learning. This is similar to the seventh stage in ABC implementation where performance measures are established that support company objectives and move the organization in the direction that management desires.

Now that we have gone over the theory, you may find the following pages of this appendix useful as it contains the details of software that puts these theories into practice. Please note that the information on each product was contributed by the vendor concerned. Again, I would like to state that this list is by no means exhaustive and that I am not endorsing any of these products over any other—I am merely aiming to provide you with a starting point for your own investigations.

Software Vendor Contributions

COMSHARE: CLOSING THE GAP BETWEEN STRATEGY AND EXECUTION

To thrive in fast-moving, turbulent markets organizations need to be, above all, responsive. However, a recent survey* confirmed that 82 per cent of organizations are still accounting rather than strategy driven. The challenge clearly remains to marry bottom-up plans with the top-down strategic plan.

There has been a realization that the solution lies in implementing management planning and control (MPC). Management planning and control is much more than a set of processes for planning, budgeting, reporting and analysis. It synthesizes these once disparate processes into a single, ongoing system through which management can implement strategies better, strengthen decision making and make management more effective.

Management planning and control is both a way of thinking about the business, and a way of running the business. It involves continuous evaluation and adjustment of plans—setting the organization's goals and the strategies to attain them; providing organizational insight, communication and focus; monitoring against performance

---

*A survey conducted as part of a budgeting Webcast hosted by Comshare and *Business Finance* magazine revealed that only 13 per cent of delegates' organizations are driven by the strategic plan. An overwhelming 82 per cent confirmed that their organizations are accounting or operations driven.

goals, analysing alternatives, and taking corrective action to ensure that strategies are achieved.

Therefore, MPC is engaged not just 'once-a-year', but as an on-going process to make sure the company is on track with everything it wants to achieve.

Comshare MPC

Comshare was the first software solutions provider to unite all the aspects of financial planning, management and reporting into a single solution. Within a single application, Comshare MPC, information is continually cycled throughout the enterprise in a closed-loop process that provides ongoing feedback and promotes collaborative decision-making.

- Shared business rules, definitions, data and processes result in more efficient planning and reporting processes, less time spent on low-value activities and reduced implementation and maintenance costs.

- Built-in financial intelligence reduces implementation time and improves integrity. Comprehensive currency support allows organizations to plan, budget and report in multiple currencies, to evaluate the impact of currency fluctuations on performance and to provide fast, accurate public reporting.

- A central database using mainstream database technology ensures 'one version of the truth', eliminating the inefficient process of distributing and collecting spreadsheets or files. Changes, such as reorganizations, are fast, easy and immediately available to all users.

- Fully web-architected for data entry, reporting, analysis and administration users access the system through a web browser from any location. Administration and maintenance costs are reduced because software is loaded only once on the server.

- Also available as client/server—functionally identical both versions can be used individually or concurrently to suit customer requirements.

- Exception alerting warns users of 'out-of-guideline' plans, budgets and performance. Capitalizing on powerful analysis non-technical users quickly and easily investigate exceptions, create custom reports and analyses and gain greater insight into problems and opportunities.

Comshare MPC can be implemented in total or one application at a time. Comshare Planning is a strategic and top-down planning application that delivers powerful and flexible analysis; Comshare Budgeting combines budgeting, actual reporting, and forecasting; Comshare Financial Consolidation meets the needs of statutory and management reporting; Comshare Management Reporting broadly deploys enterprise-wide management information; and Comshare Production Reporting is a financially intelligent report writer.

Organizations who require specialized reporting and analysis use the Comshare Decision platform to develop custom BI applications such as performance measurement, sales and customer analysis and BI portals. These applications can fully integrate with Comshare MPC.

The company
Comshare has built long-term relationships with over 3000 customers ranging from medium-sized companies to large global organizations. Many of these are FT 1000 and Fortune 500 companies. Comshare MPC customers in the UK include Carpetright, Dutton Forshaw, ICI Paints and Smiths Industries.

For further information, please visit Comshare website at www.comshare.com.

CORVU RAPIDSCORECARD

Among the greatest challenges facing senior level executives today is effective strategy execution. According to *Fortune*, 'Less than 10 per cent of strategies effectively formulated are effectively executed'. Of course, aligning operational activities with strategic objectives and budgets in today's rapidly changing business climate is easier said than done. The real challenge is how to implement your performance management solution before the pace of change in the market renders your system obsolete. CorVu's RapidScorecard is a performance management vehicle that not only communicates, monitors and manages strategy execution, but also deploys in the speedy timeframe necessary to derive maximum value from your system.

Immediate Balanced Scorecard Solution

Following the Kaplan and Norton model, RapidScorecard provides an immediate automated Balanced Scorecard solution. Using your strategy, objectives, initiatives and measures, our consultants will design and rapidly deploy your customized performance management application. By delivering the application framework necessary for both departmental and enterprise deployments, RapidScorecard is your fastest path to an automated Balanced Scorecard solution.

Gain Strategic Insight

With RapidScorecard, you receive CorVu's flagship product, CorManage. Delivering native access to corporate information, CorManage provides powerful analysis options enabling users to develop intelligence about their historical performance while allowing users to gain insight into future opportunities. Additionally, CorManage provides the latest innovation in Balanced Scorecard automation. Using regression analysis of scorecard results, it statistically validates organization strategy models. Once a valid strategy has been formulated, users perform 'what-if' analysis to identify how performance improvements in one area of the organization impact, either positively or negatively, performance in another area. This knowledge empowers managers to more effectively allocate valuable time and resources to those activities that are most strategic—those that have the most impact on the desired outcome.

Key Features

- Web-based data capture.
- Intelligent update notification.
- Administrative control over user security and functions.
- Simple entry of 'soft' measures.

- Cascading scorecards.

- Support for unlimited companies, business units, departments.

- Unlimited Perspectives, Objectives, Initiatives, Metrics.

- Metrics can relate to multiple Objectives.

- Initiatives can relate to multiple Objectives.

- Objectives can relate to multiple Perspectives.

- Robust standard reporting options.

Performance Reports

RapidScorecard offers standard performance reports that allow users
to analyse performance by company, business unit and department.
Additionally, users can analyse performance by Balanced Scorecard
components such as Perspectives, Objectives and Owners. These reports may be linked to external Business Intelligence objects, which
allow users to delve further into the underlying detail, and thus, better
understand performance results. Through such analytic exercises
users are better able to bring their daily decisions in line with organizational strategy.

Alignment Reports

RapidScorecard also provides alignment reports, which are designed
to highlight how well activities are aligned with strategy. For example,
a key alignment report shows the relationship—or lack thereof—
between each Initiative and each Objective. When the organization
is engaged in an Initiative that has no relation to any Objective, it is
said to be 'out of alignment'. Other alignment reports highlight how
efficiently budgets have been allocated by Initiative and Objective.
These reports in particular enable companies to align their budgeting
and project management activities with their strategy.

Initiative Reports

Initiative reports are designed to keep users abreast of the status of all
Initiatives and their subordinate tasks. Users are able to identify

which Initiatives—or individuals—are ahead of (or behind) schedule. Ultimately, Initiative reports allow users to analyse how effectively they are accomplishing the activities, which will lead to successful attainment of their strategy.

Key Benefits of the Software
- Rapid implementation of an automated Balanced Scorecard solution.

- Extensible growth path for enterprise deployment.

- Align tactical initiatives with strategic objectives.

- Align budget allocation with strategic objectives.

- Monitor and manage performance at all corporate levels.

- Integrate Balanced Scorecard with analysis of detailed corporate data.

Users of RapidScorecard include Hilton Hotels, Credit Suisse, Société General, Robert Bosch, Promina Healthcare and London Underground's Infraco JNP.

For more information on CorVu's Business Performance Management solutions please visit www.corvu.com.

Other products include:

CorManage

CorManage creates a robust enterprise measurement model, which allows users to delineate key success factors, track performance against goals and perform comparative analysis with industry benchmarks. By clarifying what happened, CorManage enables organizations to understand performance results within the context of their strategic goals.

HYPERION PERFORMANCE MANAGEMENT

The foundation and methodology for advancing corporate performance and organizational effectiveness, Hyperion's solutions enable companies to measure corporate performance and organizational effectiveness. The software helps to integrate processes and value drivers, and provides the mechanism to model, measure and optimize resources, operations and individual behaviour. It empowers people at all levels within an organization to effectively act upon corporate strategy in efforts to measure performance, drive profitability and increase shareholder value.

Hyperion's performance management applications include Hyperion Performance Scorecard and Hyperion Business Modeling. These solutions help organizations become more strategy focused by addressing several challenges within one complete solution:

- Corporate Scorecarding.

- Customer and Product Profitability.

- Strategic and Operational Planning.

- Business Modeling.

- Industry Metrics and Benchmarking.

- Cost Management.

- Activity Based Management.

- Activity Based Budgeting and Planning.

- Economic Value Added (EVA®).

- Resource Optimization.

- Target Costing.

The Solution

Hyperion® Performance Scorecard is a powerful web-based business intelligence application that helps create strategy-focused organizations by communicating organizational strategy and fostering accountability. Additionally, Hyperion Performance Scorecard helps to integrate individual objectives, measures and rewards into organizational strategy—from each enterprise desktop through to the CEO—to help measure performance and drive profitability.

The unique flexibility in Hyperion Performance Scorecard allows an organization to design its own custom scorecard framework, or implement performance measurement frameworks including the Balanced Scorecard, Arthur Andersen's Value Dynamics®, Stern Stewart's EVA® Scorecard, The Baldridge Criteria, NQI and EFQM. Hyperion's application embeds 2600 different benchmark metrics for more than 80 discrete processes from Hackett Benchmarking & Research, a division of answer*think*. Hyperion Performance Scorecard also includes:

- *Benchmarking and best practices data.*

- *Web-enabled* Fast and easy enterprise deployment to engage a broader range of users. Web scorecards also provide employees continuous, real-time feedback on individual or group performance.

- *Creates focus and communicates strategy* Actions are easily traced to the business objectives and critical success factors that they serve.

- *Accountability* Actions can be mapped to critical business areas, groups and/or individuals to communicate accountability for performance achievement.

- *Performance* Report and monitor progress towards goal achievement.

- *Integration with Hyperion strategic analytic platform* Using the power of the Hyperion Essbase, for extended reporting, analysis, modelling and planning.

- *Integration with Hyperion financial applications* Supplements KPI reporting and increases 'line of sight' by monitoring leading and lagging indicators of overall corporate performance.

Hyperion® Business Modeling helps organizations become more efficient in execution of corporate strategy. A strong business model allows executives—down to the analyst level—to test operational and financial planning assumptions for the purpose of strategic decision making.

As the foundation of an effective performance management system, Hyperion Business Modelling helps organizations gain a broad understanding of processes, value drivers and delivers the mechanism to model, measure and optimize resources, operations and behaviour.

Hyperion Business Modelling supports many performance management solutions:

- *Economic profit* Cost of capital included for the calculation of economic profit, partnering with: Stern Stewart Economic Value Add (EVA).

- *Activity-based management, budgeting and planning* Delivery of activity-based budgeting with Hyperion's budgeting and planning applications.

- *Strategic decision analysis and support* Validation of strategic plans and assumptions.

- *Operational planning and resource capacity management* Run scenarios to determine whether sufficient capacity exists and determination of the best use of that capacity.

- *Target costing* Determining the best cost solution for new products.

- *Customer and product profitability* Model total profitability by customer or product down to the activity level.

- *Integrates with Hyperion's strategic analytic platform* Using the power of Hyperion Essbase for extended reporting, analysis, modelling and planning.

- *Web-enabled* Fast and easy enterprise deployment to engage a broader range of users.

For further information, please visit the Hyperion website at www.hyperion.com.

i2 TECHNOLOGIES, INC.

i2 Technologies, Inc., offers solutions that impact the key business processes and power the bottom line. i2 solutions enable collaboration and decision support inside a single company, between multiple enterprises and across private or public marketplaces. Offering integrated solutions on a ready e-commerce platform, i2 delivers more value than any other solution provider today.

i2 Supply Chain Management™

i2 SCM™ helps businesses optimally plan and execute the movement of goods and materials through the supply chain. With i2 SCM, a business can estimate future demand for its products, enabling planners to position supply resources, inventory and capacity to best effect. When an order arrives, the supply chain is able to respond with speed and execute the most profitable delivery of goods to the customer. i2 SCM extends this to consider not only the finished goods delivery, but also how to optimally plan and execute the service needs of a company's customers.

i2 Supplier Relationship Management™

i2 SRM™ is an integrated suite of business-to-business (B2B) design, sourcing and procurement capabilities that enable companies and their suppliers to collaboratively create and manufacture better products faster, at lower cost. SRM brings true collaborative commerce technology to the forefront with its unique enabling architecture that supports both strategic decision optimization and high velocity collaboration across the extended supply chain. During product development, i2 SRM optimizes designs by considering sourcing and supply constraints, and design collaboration when outsourcing manufacturing. For procurement, i2 SRM enables companies to define the optimal sourcing strategy to reduce supply risks and costs, negotiate the best terms and streamline the requisitioning and buying of both direct and indirect materials.

i2 Customer Relationship Management™

i2 has extended CRM solutions to include the planning and execution of all customer value cycle processes (marketing, sales, fulfilment and service) across the demand chain. i2 CRM™ enables not only process automation, but transaction management to include all elements of the order life cycle—capture, brokering, administration, logistics execution, settlement and service. In addition, i2 CRM provides robust decision-support solutions beyond marketing analytics to include demand forecasting, pricing optimization, order promising and planning, and service asset planning. Finally, i2 CRM supports the often-overlooked customer-facing process of order fulfilment to include order planning, promising and physical execution.

- *i2 Platform*™ enables companies to design, deploy, run, and monitor e-marketplaces with maximum security, reliability, and scalability while minimizing costs. It is a flexible, open, standards-compliant, integrated system that provides the infrastructure, administration services and intelligence for marketplace owners.

- *i2 Content*™ provides content management and publishing capabilities for products and suppliers in all major industries, as well as custom database development for enterprises and e-marketplaces.

- *TradeMatrix Open Commerce Network*™ is the only B2B network that addresses the e-marketplace and partner connectivity challenges faced by global enterprises. It meets the needs of any supplier—no matter what size—to participate in both private and public marketplaces.

Strengthening the Links in the Value Chain in all Industries

With i2 solutions, companies can attack whatever part of the value chain they want—no matter how far they have progressed with an e-business strategy. Today, a complete suite of i2 solutions for supplier relationship management, supply chain management and customer relationship management along with content and a technology platform, enable customers to make better decisions faster in every phase of business.

i2 serves companies in the following industries: aerospace and defence, automotive, chemicals, construction, consumer electronics, consumer packaged goods, durable goods, energy, finance, healthcare, high technology, industrial, logistics, metals, maintenance, repair and overhaul (MRO), packaging and printing, paper and forest products, pharmaceuticals, public sector, retail, semiconductor, soft goods, tele-communications, transportation and utilities.

For further information, please visit the i2 website at www.i2.com.

IDONS-FOR-THINKING SOFTWARE: NEW PARADIGM THINKING

Changing Needs for Challenging Environments

For most of us it is hard to make changes unless we have to and when we do they are often reactive. When complexity overwhelms operation we often reach to 'do more', 'or less', 'increase efficiency' 'put in new systems' or 'replace people'. This is a hard time to study what went wrong, but if we did we would probably find that *the mode in which we were operating* was stuck in linear or sequential assumptions.

Operating sequentially or even through parallel processing is no longer adequate: there are too many new, interconnected and changing needs to be satisfied quickly; too much information which must be rapidly converted into *meaning and results*.

We must Understand Emergent Patterns

While we can link effective use of resources with productivity we may not adequately have understood the importance of expanding our capacity for recognizing patterns. The ability to think creatively in new ways, expand awareness of overview, understand cause and effect and identify relationships all relate to patterning.

In Collective Situations this must be Shared

To shift from a reactive approach to a proactive one, we must take up the challenge of learning to think and communicate better, quickly, flexibly and holistically in patterns—both alone and interactively. Tools that help us develop these skills deliver proactive solutions and competitive advantage.

New Needs require Appropriate Tools

Idons-For-Thinking software offers 'A new way of organizing structured and unstructured thoughts' according to *Information Week*.

A unique software medium for thinking and communication, Idons-For-Thinking acts as an extension of the mind to reflect our ideas, provoke innovation, structure thinking tasks and monitor alignment of action agendas. Ideal for organizing complexity from multiple perspectives and as a knowledge management tool, Idons-For-Thinking additionally offers a customizable, user friendly, visual modelling environment.

An easy to use inspiring visual interface provides a modelling arena where methods, tutorials and model examples help collect information in diverse forms and convert it into shared meaning and action that can be tracked.

As a customized live capture tool Idons-For-Thinking supports facilitation, meetings, workshops and conferences with a full trail of thinking and modelling.

As a knowledge resource and learning reservoir the software offers multiple ways to represent information, and so more meaningfully link to the web, other programs and direct communication, e.g. interactive modelling between individuals or groups at a distance. It is an ideal environment for shared thinking, exchanging meaning, monitoring change and exposing new patterns.

How it Works

Deceptively simple—ideas are surfaced, formulated, made explicit and diagrammed through creatively combining words, images and patterns while modelling frameworks guide the thinking process.

Applications include:

- Personal modelling.
- Meetings support.
- Decision support.
- Mapping ideas for structure.
- Best practice database and knowledge management.

- Distance interactive modelling and tracking.

- Customized front-end driving all programs.

Manuals and on-line tutorials provide a host of modelling approaches, methods and model examples for a variety of applications. These include strategic thinking with scenarios, business development, quality management, creativity, problem solving, knowledge management, advice on application and meeting support, theory on Visual Thinking, facilitation hints and tips, original contribution from experts and more.

For enquiries, sample screens and software, and more information, please visit the Idon website at www.idonresources.com.

INPHASE *PERFORMANCEPLUS*™ VERSION 3.2 WEB

PerformancePlus™ is an Enterprise Performance Management and Balanced Scorecard application that helps nurture the Performance Culture essential for world-class organizations, developed by specialist performance management company, INPHASE.

A Background of Expertise and Practical Experience

INPHASE developed the first Balanced Scorecard software for NatWest in 1992, alongside KPMG Nolan Norton's research and publication in *Harvard Business Review* by Professors Robert Kaplan and David Norton.

Through continued involvement delivering organizational management systems to some of the world's leading organizations, INPHASE identified a requirement for a holistic approach to support the introduction of a Performance Culture.

Client experience with companies such as Barclays, Booker Foods, Whitbread, Department of National Savings, DuPont, Lloyds TSB, Wigan County Council, Atomic Weapons Establishment and Superdrug, alongside industry research indicated that a minimum of five of the following performance management approaches were being deployed *simultaneously* in major corporations: Activity Based Costing; Balanced Scorecard; Best Value; departmental budgets; plans and objectives; Economic Profit model; EFQM Business Excellence Model; Investors in People; Kaizen; continuous improvement; Management by Objectives; process re-engineering; supply chain reengineering; team and personal performance management; Total Quality Management; Value Based Management.

Rather than address these approaches as separate systems, INPHASE created TOMAS™, a framework concept for enabling the delivery of an integrated Enterprise Performance Management system, which is fully embedded into *PerformancePlus*™.

What is TOMAS™?

TOMAS™ stands for Team Objectives Management And Support. The framework, with the key common denominators identified in bold, can be described as:

> *An organization has* **teams** *contributing* **skills** *and* **competencies** *towards achieving shared* **objectives** *each of which can be assigned an* **owner** *and specific* **measures** *of performance to assist their* **management**. *Objectives are related in different ways.*

The consistent use of these common denominators enables TOMAS™ to be used to integrate any chosen best practice approaches into a holistic overarching framework. This makes it possible to realize an integrated Enterprise Performance Management approach, reducing operational costs and creating a consistent performance methodology for an organization.

PerformancePlus™ Supporting a Performance Culture

The TOMAS™ framework is embedded in *PerformancePlus*. This provides support not only for the integration of management approaches, but for the entire performance management process, helping organizations achieve a Performance Culture, from strategy through operational excellence, down to individuals and the integration of capability management.

Software Benefits
- Deliverable out of the box.

- Full integration with MS Office®.

- Leverages the latest Microsoft technologies for ease of data automation from operational systems.

- Also supports manual data entry over the web.

- Easy configuration and evolution by users straight over the web.

Business Benefits
- Overall business performance improvement at all levels of the organization.

- Support for the entire performance management process.

- Interactive mapping of strategy at any level of the organization.

- Visualization of cause and effect at every level.

- Consistent and effective communication throughout the organization.

- Focused leadership.

- Improved motivation of staff.

- Improved business planning process.

- Integrated policy and strategy development.

- Improved customer satisfaction.

- Rapid roll out of new or revised strategies.

- Improvement in the way business processes are identified and performed.

- Greater flexibility.

- Faster responsiveness to change.

- Superior organizational development.

- Stronger organizational coherence.

- Greater levels of empowerment.

- Higher levels of staff satisfaction and motivation.

- Improved transparency of performance.

- Reduced operational costs.

- Greater competitive advantage.

PerformancePlus™ and TOMAS™ together help companies around the world achieve a Performance Culture, one in which:

- Staff improve organizational performance because every individual wants to deliver their best, and is enabled to do so.

- Individuals and teams take much of the responsibility for monitoring and managing their own performance, against agreed objectives, measures and targets ... and receive the coaching and support that they need to do this.

For further information please visit the Inphase website at www.inphase.com.

MATRIX V3 STRATEGIC MARKETING SOFTWARE

MATRIX V3 helps competent marketing practitioners to analyse the potential of target market sectors and develop winning strategies. By using a combination of industry statistics, historical and forecast sales data and qualitative research information, users are able to build realistic business models. The result is a clearer understanding of the marketing environment, a more balanced product/market portfolio and lower risk business decisions. MATRIX V3 reflects the most recent thinking in marketing, is very powerful, very fast and very easy to use. It has become the *de facto* standard PC software application for strategic marketing.

Striking a Balance

- Markets are becoming increasingly competitive.

- Market lifetimes are becoming shorter.

- Typically over half of the market is shared by the top two suppliers.

- The costs of market entry can be enormous.

- Getting it wrong can be a disaster.

Executives are now coming under increasing pressure to adopt a more rigorous approach to the analysis of strategic problems. They need structures to describe their markets. They need to break down complex problems into component issues and apply judgements where necessary. They need a transparent decision-making process in which they can frame and win their arguments. And they must be able to point to evidence in support of their strategic proposals.

What MATRIX Does

MATRIX V3 brings together economic objectives, existing 'product line' performance data, market statistics and qualitative data from research campaigns to help the practitioner reach informed decisions about business potential. It provides a structure that will help the user to 'think through' the underlying issues relating to competitiveness, market potential and corporate objectives. Once populated with the necessary data, MATRIX V3 will provide a valuable insight into:

- *Life Cycle Analysis*, growth and potential within each segment.

- *Market Share Analysis*.

- *Segment Attractiveness*, based upon a range of criteria stemming from the proximate and long-term objectives of the enterprise.

- *Competitive Strengths and Weaknesses Analysis*.

- *The Boston Matrix*, illustrating which segments should be cash-rich and which require funding through growth.

- The *Directional Policy Matrix* illustrating which segments should be included within the portfolio and which should be divested.

- Multidimensional *Perceptual Maps*, for competitor analysis and off-line studies.

- *Gap Analysis* based upon revenues and gross margins. (Can also be linked to the *Ansoff Matrix* to establish the trend of core and new business opportunities).

- *Risk Analysis* using a unique algorithm developed by Market Modelling Ltd which enables the user to compare the risks and returns of different opportunity portfolios.

The information thus provided will help the user to decide upon the overall direction of the business and provide a feeder into lower level marketing plans.

Product Features

MATRIX V3 is a stand-alone PC application running under 32 bit Microsoft* Windows environments (e.g. Windows 9x, NT, 2000). Models can be produced either on a stand-alone PC, or on a network via a shared network drive. The application supports an unlimited number of business models, products, markets and competitors.

Data is entered into the model via a range of simple dialogues and scorecards, or optionally prepared in Microsoft Excel for direct import.

Analyses are exported to the Microsoft suite to enable the preparation of reports, spreadsheets and presentations to integrate into strategic plans or share with colleagues and sponsors.

The application comes documented with an on-line Help system, Tutorial Model, Manual, Case Study and Algorithms documents in Microsoft Word format.

The Benefits

- A structured approach to solving strategic problems.

- 'Best of breed' marketing practice.

- Reason and logic replace whim and dogma.

- A living framework (not 'shelfware').

- Transparency in the decision-making process.

- Better informed, lower risk business decisions.

- A more profitable business.

Organizations that have Purchased MATRIX V3

The following represents just a small cross-section of the organizations that have purchased MATRIX V3.

- ABB Alstom power UK Ltd.

- Cranfield School of Management.

- DERA.

- Ernst & Young Management Consulting.

- GUS.

- Gerber Foods.

- IBM UK.

- ITNET.

- JCB.

- Marketing Management Services International.

- Pfizer Limited.

- Prudential Annuities.

- Royal Bank of Scotland.

- Shell Europe.

- Valor Heating.

For further information please visit the Market Modelling Website at www.market-modelling.co.uk.

ORACLE

Oracle Balanced Scorecard, article bylined to Colin Addison, product marketing manager, Oracle Corporation UK Ltd.

Two essential keys to all successful ventures are strategy and management. Not having a strong combination of these elements may not only hamper an organization from achieving its goal of market dominance but also its ability to compete.

Oracle Balanced Scorecard is a tool that helps translate strategy into action. It helps companies determine what impact a potential change will have on the rest of the organization, looking at it from the four perspectives of finance, customers, internal processes and innovation and learning for employees.

When companies look to set strategies and goals, they typically only set the financial objective of increasing the revenue or return on investment. But Balanced Scorecard finds that this is a backward view and that companies need to be more proactive. Oracle Balanced Scorecard analysis takes into account financial and non-financial measures, internal improvements, past outcomes and ongoing requirements as indications of future performance.

The tool examines performance in four areas. Financial analysis, the most traditionally used performance indicator includes assessments of measures such as operating costs and return on investment; customer analysis—looks at customer satisfaction, retention and growth; internal analysis—looks at production and innovation, measuring performance in terms of maximizing productivity; learning and growth analysis—explores the effectiveness of management in terms of measures of employee satisfaction and retention and information system performance.

Unlike most analytical tools, Balanced Scorecard enables managers to see how one of the above performances impacts the other.

The key performance indicators of the above might be measured somewhere in a company's IT system but Oracle Balanced Scorecard tool draws all the up to the minute data together on managers' desktops. This allows them to gain a clear picture of the business and identify direct and quantifiable targets. Oracle Balanced Scorecard analysis helps give managers a clear understanding of how their decisions impact both their direct area of responsibility and overall company strategy. By being able to best analyse the information drawn together in this way, a company will be better equipped to maximize its profitability and performance.

An example of where Balanced Scorecard method can be applied is to a company's new eCommerce initiative. For the initiative to be successful, a company cannot rely alone on the eCommerce platform. Starting with that customer-facing goal, the balanced scorecard approach can define goals in other areas: internal processes, employee impact and finance. This might result, for example, in a company's IT department getting the associated systems euro compliant in the internal processes category, implementing an IT career structure in the employee learning category and meeting overall budget commitments in the financial category.

As a structure, balanced scorecard methodology further breaks broad goals down successfully into vision, strategies, tactical activities and metrics. As an example of how this might work, an organization might include in its mission statement a goal of maintaining employee satisfaction. This would be the organization's vision. Strategies for achieving that vision might include approaches such as increasing employee management communication. Tactical activities undertaken to implement the strategy could include, for example, regularly scheduled meetings with employees. Finally, metrics could include quantifications of employee suggestions or employee surveys.

Oracle Balanced Scorecard is used across all industries, including manufacturing, service, public sector and non-profit organizations. Many of the world's largest corporations that have successfully been utilizing Oracle Balanced Scorecard tool include Mobistar and Kemper Insurance. This has enabled them to assess the full impact of their corporate strategies, searching out any unintended consequences to their employees, their customers or their bottom lines that could occur when they alter, for example, a production process.

These businesses have experienced the benefits a Balanced Scorecard brings them as it has enabled them to link strategy to quantifiable and measurable metrics; link strategy to the planning and budgeting process; provide enterprise wide deployment capabilities and provide rapid prototyping and setup features.

Those organizations that have implemented Balanced Scorecard methodology have helped put themselves ahead of the game and stand a really good chance of successfully achieving their goals of gaining competitive advantage and market dominance.

For further information please refer to the Oracle website at www.oracle.com.

PEOPLESOFT

What Makes a Business Intelligent?

Business Intelligence. Without it, your enterprise is blind. Your strategy is untested. Your people are without clear direction.

To be truly intelligent, your business must empower its people with the right information and the ability to make decisions. It must make everyone accountable for translating the company vision into business actions.

PeopleSoft Enterprise Performance Management collects volumes of data on your customers, suppliers, and employees and makes sense of it. Who is your most profitable customer? Does your workforce make up fit your business strategy? Are your suppliers meeting your needs? Get the information you need, then act on it. PeopleSoft empowers your people to make better decisions. More profitable decisions.

Software does not make business decisions. People do.

The Only

PeopleSoft Enterprise Performance Management is the only end-to-end business analytics solution. Integrated data acquisition, data bmanagement and data analysis technologies are just the beginning. Enterprise Performance Management delivers the information your employees, customers and suppliers need to be proactive and prosper in an eCommerce world.

With the Internet, you can give your enterprise—your employees, customers and suppliers—the information they need to predict and proactively respond to your requirements and industry trends. You give them the power to make decisions. Organizations who use

Peoplesoft Enterprise Performance Management include Danske Bank, Société Generale and Pfizer.

Data Warehousing Integration

PeopleSoft was one of the first to integrate data warehousing capabilities directly with business analytic applications. PeopleSoft Enterprise Warehouse is the main repository of enterprise information. It draws from PeopleSoft applications, and third-party and legacy systems, to stage, store and make information available for analysis. You can exploit this information to gauge your success and create a competitive advantage.

Manage Your Investments

You invest heavily in your customers, employees and suppliers. Is it smart to invest in something you do not understand? With Enterprise Performance Management, you get to know them. How effective is your sales team at winning business? How will a salary and benefits change affect your workforce? How do your inventory problems affect your suppliers? When you know your enterprise, you understand the impact of your investment.

Be Proactive

Enterprise Performance Management puts the power to make smart decision in the hands of those who need it most—those who make decisions every day, not just at the end of the quarter. PeopleSoft's pure Internet technology is the vehicle by which business intelligence is disseminated to your workforce. All enterprise data is collected in the PeopleSoft Enterprise Warehouse, and becomes business intelligence upon request. The data is there. Just ask for it.

Always Think Strategically

A successful strategy takes into account how one department's actions affect another, and defines each person's role in turning corporate vision into reality. PeopleSoft Enterprise Performance Management makes your corporate vision tangible. It enables you to set departmental targets by which you can gauge their performance. As a result, everyone becomes an active participant and vested stakeholder in the execution of strategy. Everyone is accountable for your success.

Focus on Strategy

Your numbers for the quarter are falling short of expectations. Everything is a fire drill. Your CEO is asking why no one is doing what was expected of them. Does everyone understand the corporate strategy and how they impact it? Do they understand the effect they have on other departments?

Your corporate strategy is your lifeblood. To be successful, you must know what affects customer satisfaction, profitability and shareholder value. Each line of business, region or branch must work towards the same goals. You must track and measure performance of your entire organization—workforce, financial, opportunity management or supply chain. According to the Balanced Scorecard Collaborative and *CFO* magazine:

- Less than 10 per cent of all strategies are effectively implemented.

- Only 5 per cent of the workforce understands the strategy.

- Only 25 per cent of managers' incentives are linked to strategy.

- 60 per cent of organizations do not link budgets to strategy.

- 85 per cent of executive teams spend less than 1 hour a month discussing strategy.

More often than not, when a strategy fails, the problem does not lie in the strategy. It is in the execution. Learning how to weave your strategy into every part of your organization is the objective of the PeopleSoft Balanced Scorecard.

As the backbone of PeopleSoft's strategy management solution, Balanced Scorecard is your central nervous system for strategy execution—communication, measurement, reporting and analysis. It gathers data from your various operational systems, calculates performance and enables you to compare current and expected performance to your corporate objectives. Information can be tailored to both high-level strategy and line-level performance.

For further information, please visit the PeopleSoft website at www.peoplesoft.com.

IMPROVING ENTERPRISE PERFORMANCE USING PRODACAPO

Even large and well-established organizations can face harsh treatment at the hands of the financial markets. Survival often depends on the value an organization can create.

But the fact of the matter is that value is created at the point where a decision is made. It follows that value is more likely to be created in a business where management decision making is better informed and better aligned at all levels of the organization. Prodacapo is an Enterprise Performance Management system that is particularly good at helping to visualize the extent to which decisions could either create or destroy value by creating 'One solution, bringing it all together'. Managers throughout the business can access an integrated management information database where internally consistent information appropriate to a wide range of management decisions can be accessed easily, on demand.

This analytical, decision-support system includes Activity Based Costing, Process Management, Balanced Scorecard and Business Planning.

Activity Based Management information provides a cornerstone to better informed management decision making and the Balanced Scorecard creates a coherent framework by which to direct, coordinate, focus and control the business. Creating visibility of the 'cause-and-effect' relationships of what drive performance and the need for resource within a business, and how processes and activities add value and contribute to its outputs is at the foundation of better informed management decision making.

Prodacapo is not just another software progressively extended over time in response to the latest 'hot buttons' via addition of other suppliers' software packages. From the beginning it has aimed at providing a *single database* for managing all aspects of business improvement, resource allocation, performance management, profitability analysis and management reporting in a *fully integrated* manner.

Prodacapo is uniquely designed to provide the following functionality from within the same database:

- Financial reporting and resource analysis by cost centre.

- Organization charting and ISO 9000 documentation.

- Process Mapping and Process Costing.

- Process Improvement and Change Management.

- ABC, Output Costing and Profitability Analysis.

- Performance Measurement and Management through the Balanced Scorecard.

- On-going, operational activity accounting and cost centre capacity management.

- Planning and 'what if?' analyses.

- Web access to results across both Intranets and Internet.

It is a *total system* making a difference to the performance of the organization, rapidly and with minimum effort with the following benefits:

- Uniquely based around a very strong concept of Business Improvement and Performance Management, significantly reducing the effort required for effective implementation.

- Integrates seamlessly with other financial, operational and ERP systems.

- Wholly scalable allowing small implementations to migrate upwards in size, easily.

- Powerful, flexible and user-friendly analytical and reporting capability.

- Flexibility allowing organizations to implement progressively.

- Designed with the end-user in mind so that line managers find it *easy to use*.

- *Web-enabled* removing the need to publish routine financial and performance management information manually if required.

We believe our support is second to none. Our clients tell us so. For example, our Helpdesk was recently voted by one of our most experienced clients as 'the best Helpdesk she had ever come across' and she has been using ABC tools for over five years.

That this support philosophy is attractive to Prodacapo clients is witnessed by the fact that Asea Brown Boveri (ABB), the global engineering group which is probably the leading implementer of ABM, made a corporate decision some five years ago to implement the Business Improvement and Performance Management concept and the associated software developed by Prodacapo. This is currently being rolled out worldwide across all units within ABB. Over 250 ABB units have already implemented the first stage of the Business Improvement and Performance Management programme, using Prodacapo. ABB have also committed to further implement the on-going, activity-based accounting and capacity management by the year 2002.

Clients we have worked with include Skandia Life, Consignia, Ricoh, Hagemeyer, ABB and British Airways. Prodacapo itself is implemented in over 460 clients in 58 countries.

More information on Prodacapo can be found at <u>www.bellis-joneshill.com</u>.

SAS STRATEGIC VISION ™

Creating Shareholder Wealth by Optimizing Strategic Performance

How do you communicate strategy in a way that has meaning to thousands of employees? How do you ensure that day-to-day activities are aligned to the strategic vision? How do you measure performance based on 'intangibles' that are difficult to quantify? How do you communicate performance so that individual employees can respond quickly to changing circumstances?

Perhaps most important of all: how do you draw on corporate knowledge to ensure that strategy decisions are based on hard facts, not fiction? And communicate value-creation to shareholders, also based on hard facts?

Executing the Strategy

No matter how visionary the strategy, if it is not effectively implemented, it is devoid of practical meaning. Organizations can only achieve success when employees 'live' the strategy as part of their day-to-day jobs.

SAS Strategic Vision™ draws on SAS's years of experience in implementing many successful performance management projects in organizations such as ING Bank, Quaker Chemical, Siemens AG Austria, Telecom Italia, Haburi.com and Duke Hospital. It brings together the three critical elements that are required to ensure quick wins and sustained success. These three elements are world-beating business intelligence technology, a proven implementation methodology and industry specific key performance indicators.

Power to Collaborate and Communicate

The technology behind performance management must also combine the flexibility to meet your organization's particular needs with the power to achieve rapid, demonstrable successes. Strategic Vision software can be applied to any performance management approach such as the Balanced Scorecard. It translates the philosophy into metrics, fuels these metrics with real-world information from the knowledge store and facilitates the distribution of strategy maps and actionable targets to the appropriate individuals.

Strategic Vision consists of the following components:

- A map to define corporate direction and to document strategic objectives, measures, targets and initiatives.

- A compass to measure and manage progress towards strategic goals.

- A knowledge base for exploring new opportunities.

- Supporting applications to analyse and surface information relevant to each performance perspective.

- An easy-to-use web interface, enabling rapid deployment

throughout the organization, and enabling users to identify and review indicators with just two mouse-clicks.

Performance Management in Days, not Weeks

A performance management project needs to achieve rapid gains to create and sustain momentum. We therefore offer the SAS Methodology for Strategic Feedback Systems, an iterative, phased approach summarized in the phrase 'think strategic, start focused'. Each phase is broken down into Assessment, Requirements, Design, Construction, Final Test and Deployment stages. At the end of each phase, the results are analysed, reviewed and fed back into the loop. Each iteration embraces more of the organization until all business units, departments or functions have their own performance management solutions.

Selecting the Appropriate KPIs

The tough challenge is identifying what you need to measure and how to measure it. Financial indicators are effective measures of past activity, but to achieve sustainable success, you have to be able to measure your present course and predict future directions based on a variety of indicators.

Based on our experience on many projects, we have documented the KPIs required by industry, and the cause-and-effect linkages between these KPIs. Of course, we recognize that both your organization and its strategy are unique so there is no 100 per cent ready-made solution.

Strategic Vision gives you the key elements you need to get a performance management solution up and running in the shortest possible timeframe.

For further information, please visit the SAS website at www.sas.com.

ACTION DRIVEN BALANCED SCORECARD (ADBS)

ShowBusiness Software/Lotus

The Performance Management system includes knowledge management, action management supporting improvement and learning across organizations and supply chains.

The ADBS extends beyond measuring performance to managing performance. It has proved effective in support of organizational and cultural transformation, integration of quality management with business management, modernizing government and tracking e-business and e-government projects. The ADBS is uniquely suitable to large or distributed performance management applications based on the following attributes:

- *Strategic alignment*   Create a shared understanding of Goals, Critical Success Factors (CSFs) and Key Performance Indicators (KPIs) so that strategy is clearly defined, shared and understood.

- *Totally secure*   Based on the proven, distributed security model of Lotus Domino ™, each KPI has its own Reader List, meaning the right people get the right information and nothing else.

- *Exceptional collaboration*   ADBS has a strong focus on collaboration and action tracking. Collaboration means easy sharing of knowledge and achieving results together.

- *Action management*   ADBS highlights what is important using the Action Attention List—showing overdue actions. ADBS provides workflow for Corrective, Preventative and Breakthrough Actions, supporting people in making, monitoring and delivering on promises.

- *Speed of implementation*   Deploy a Scorecard in two weeks, including elearning, classroom training and embedding of best practice in performance management processes.

- *Organizational learning*   Learning is automatically captured and shared to help KPI owners learn from experience.

- *Peer-to-peer approach*   'Plant' ADBS in any organization unit to create a knowledge-sharing and learning community and let it grow. Include a new unit by simply including it in the ADBS organization tree and giving one person the security privileges to invite others into their Scorecard. It is so easy to share when technical and administrative barriers are removed.

- *Anytime, anyplace*   Barriers of scale, time and place are removed.

Access Scorecards via a Web browser or Lotus Notes$^{(TM)}$—either way review and manage performance wherever you are!

* *Absolutely scalable*   Deploy at any organizational level to 10 or 10 000 users. Reports provide quick and easy management information complete with 'Traffic Lights'. Sophisticated data analysis functionality lets users *ad hoc* query and drill-down into detail.

* *Totally open*   Uses existing infrastructure and incorporates data from multiple sources (ERP, Business Intelligence and data warehousing tools).

Clients include some of the largest organizations in the world, both corporate and government. For example, Philips has over 10 000 user licences of ADBS:

> *Our aim for adopting the balanced scorecard solution is to consistently communicate strategy deep down into Philips' 80 businesses and support more than 10 000 managers with tools to turn strategy into action by sharing knowledge, aligning actions, monitoring progress and learning.*
>
> (Peter Geelen of Philips Corporate Control)

For further information please visit the ShowBusiness Website www.ShowBusiness.com.

SIEBEL SYSTEMS

Siebel Systems, was founded in 1993 to address the growing need of organizations of all sizes to acquire, retain and better service their customers. Today, Siebel Systems is the world's leading provider of eBusiness application software with more than 7000 employees who operate in more than 38 countries and 144 offices around the world.

Siebel eBusiness Applications

Siebel Systems provides the industry's most comprehensive family of multichannel eBusiness applications and services, enabling organizations to sell to, market to, and service customers across multiple channels, including the Web, call centres, field, resellers and dealer networks. With best of class *e*Business application software, coupled with a broad array of around-the-clock global services, Siebel Systems delivers a single source of customer information that organizations can use to tailor their offerings to meet the unique needs of each customer. By using Siebel *e*Business Application suite of products, organizations can develop new customer relationships, serve existing customers profitably, and integrate their systems with those of their partners, suppliers and customers regardless of their locations.

- *Siebel .COM Applications*   Enable organizations to immediately leverage the Internet to acquire new customers and enhance each and every customer relationship. By implementing Siebel .COM Applications, companies can create and execute Internet-based marketing campaigns to identify and acquire new customers, develop customized product and service offerings that meet customers' unique requirements and expectation, facilitate unassisted selling over the Internet, provide 24-7 customer service and support, and manage channel relationships to ensure optimum effectiveness and efficiency.

- *Siebel Call Centre Applications*   Enable organizations to deploy the marketing leading call centre solutions, encompassing state-of-the-art customer contact centres that include intelligent call management, sales and service automation, workflow and business process optimization, and real-time legacy integration capabilities.

- *Siebel Field Sales and Field Service Applications*   Provide market-leading field automation capabilities that enable organizations to deploy the most functionally complete and scalable mobile field solutions on the market today. With Siebel Field Sales and Field Service Applications, sales and service personnel can synchronize with corporate databases, enabling them to better respond to time critical sales opportunities and service requests.

- *Siebel Marketing Applications*   Enable organizations to align campaigns with appropriate target audiences; plan and execute highly personalized campaigns with the right message at the right time; use preferred communications channels; and measure, monitor and refine campaign performance to ensure optimal return on investment.

● *Siebel Channel Applications* Provide the industry's leading partner relationship management (PRM) solution that supports the entire process of managing of partners over the web. Siebel Channel Applications automate the business processes between organizations and their partners by enabling them to work collaboratively to market to, sell to, service and retain customers.

● *Siebel Industry Applications* Deliver comprehensive, out-of-the-box *e*Business functionality that is uniquely tailored to the specific business practices across a broad range of industries. Developed in close collaboration with customers and partners, Siebel Industry Applications enable organizations to manage and coordinate all customer touchpoints, including the web, call centre, field, retail and distribution channels. With Siebel Industry Applications, organizations can lower customization and maintenance costs and shorten implementation timeframes.

Siebel *e*Business Applications and complementary service offerings enable organizations to develop new customer relationships, profitably serve existing customers and integrate their systems with those of their partners, suppliers and customers regardless of their locations.

Customer Focus

We have an absolute commitment to customer satisfaction. In independently audited surveys, our customers report average increases of 12 per cent in revenue, 20 per cent in customer satisfaction, and 20 per cent in employee productivity, directly as a result of using Siebel *e*Business Applications.

Customers in the UK include leading organizations in their field, such as BT Wholesale Services & Solutions, Cable & Wireless Communications, Consignia, Gartmore, Guinness, Knight Frank, Leeds City Council, Marks & Spencer, Reuters, United Distillers and Vintners, West Bromich Building Society and Yorkshire Electricity.

For further information please visit our website at www.siebel.com.

YGNIUS

Ygnius is a software tool for personal productivity which is revolutionizing the way people work. It deploys computer-aided thinking to help release the natural genius within all of us, so that we can get ahead in our working lives and work smarter.

Ygnius is based on the principles of mind mapping, but is much more than a mind-mapping tool, allowing mind mapping to have many practical applications within the workplace. Now information contained within mind maps can be manipulated and analysed, producing knowledge bases, reports, presentations, project plans, web files and much more.

The Education sector have used mind maps for years, based on the pioneering work of Tony Buzan, because they help students learn and remember new areas of knowledge and it effectively accelerates their thinking power. Ygnius is ideal for mind mapping, but its major benefit is that it also facilitates the reverse process—getting information and knowledge out of your head. With Ygnius you take your existing knowledge and experience, record and organize it visually, and apply it to the task in hand. Ideas and solutions are presented, communicated and delivered quickly and effectively, in your other business applications.

For example, in order to tackle any task you need to access the knowledge and experience in your head. This may sounds simple, and usually is for the obvious information. Where is becomes difficult, however, is when you are searching for those crucial details—risks, assumptions and other peripheral information.

With Ygnius, you use mind-mapping techniques to extract and build the framework for the task in hand in a visual layout which stimulates your creativity and comprehension.

You will need to make sense of your thoughts to identify the best way forward. You can view your map in different layouts for better understanding. You can reorganize and add to your thoughts, linking them to other sources of information and creating a portal for future reference. You can apply intelligence to your map and set filters to see only the information that is relevant to your needs.

As we know only too well, no task is complete until we have passed it on to a colleague, manager or client. Any work outlined in Ygnius can be saved directly into Microsoft Word, Powerpoint, Project, Outlook and HTML among others, for fast, effective reports, presentations, project plans, web pages, etc.

Ygnius is not just a software tool, it is a whole new way of working, and the software is so easy to use that, not surprisingly, it has found many customers, particularly among the large blue-chip companies.

Honeywell International use Ygnius, discovering that the product could 'set fire to the way they work' and 'remove 2–3 weeks from their project time frames'.

Users of Ygnius include Microsoft's American headquarters in Redmond. Ygnius links with Microsoft Word XP such that procrastination and mental blocks when writing in Word are detected by a 'smart tag' and cured by the instant launch of Ygnius — the troublesome topic is brainstormed and explored in Ygnius and the outline then returned into the original Word document.

Ygnius is available in both an English and Spanish language version.

To download a free 30 day evaluation of the software, please visit www.ygnius.com.

Appendix 2

GMAS COLLABORATIVE AND MMSI HELP SUPPORT AND ASSISTANCE

The GMAS Collaborative is a user group and forum that facilitates the exchange and reportage of the user's findings on what works and what does not. It is designed in such a way that allows users of GMAS theory to develop the concepts further and learn from each other as well as get information on consultancy, software and system providers. In addition to this, users have access to the latest developments, academic research and new module designs.

Chapter 7 described how to develop your own GMAS modules and the Collaborative offers a platform to trade or sell your modules.

MISSION OF THE GMAS COLLABORATIVE

To develop the GMAS model so that it becomes one of the leading strategic management theories of the 21st century.

The mission will be achieved by ensuring that managers are provided with access to the best practice, academic research and practical examples.

Website

The core of the collaboration is its website located at www.riding-thestorm.net. The website allows access to the range of service as well as links to providers.

Newsletters

A newsletter is published montly on the website and if you would like to contribute, please send your submission to editor@ridingthestorm.net.

Seminars and Conferences

The current programme of events, seminars and conferences are listed on the website.

Benchmarking

Benchmarking questionnaires and dynamic reporting are available so that registered users can see how well they are doing compared to others in deploying and utilizing GMAS.

Help and Support

There is a range of help and support available including:

Free Updates

Books take time to write and things move on so the latest on the GMAS theory and its deployment can be found on the website.

Research Services

Some research samples will be available on the website as well as the latest versions of the GMAS quality control forms.

Consultancy Support

The forum and its notice board allows members to share experiences and by working together, overcome some of the inevitable problems organizations will face in deploying GMAS or its associated modules.

Knowledge Base

The knowledge base is where registered users can place their own GMAS modules and gives others the opportunity to try them. All modules will have to satisfy a three F review and a quality control process before being made available for others' use.

The aim of the knowledge board is to provide a genuine forum for sharing knowledge and experiences so that GMAS can become more effective in providing its users with a global marketing advantage in their specific market.

Glossary

Activity Based Costing (ABC)

This, very basically, measures activity costs based on the process driver and the resources consumed. All activities have a purpose: inputs and outputs. It measures the activity and allocates costs to the outputs. It differs from traditional costing models in the level of detail and accuracy it provides. This detail and accuracy allows management to make process improvements to meet cost objectives and provides performance measures.

Arthur D. Little Life Cycle Matrix

This model builds on the product life-cycle model by adding another avenue of investigation—'competitive position'. This is a rather intricate model because of the complex nature of life-cycle planning and competitive position. This model is best applied to companies whose market is fast changing because changes to product life cycles can have a weighty impact on them.

Balanced Scorecard (BSC)

Balanced Scorecard (BSC) converts a company's operations and strategy into an inclusive list that supplies the structure for a tactical assessment and control system. It supplies an organization with expertise which it needs to guide potential triumph. It offers an organization's corporate level personnel with a complete structure that interprets its operations and strategy into a logical set of performance indicators.

(a) The financial view   The ultimate objective of this view is to 'improve shareholder value'. Improved shareholder value comes as a consequence of the offsetting of income growth against increased productivity within the company. The factors of income growth and productivity both consist of two main subsections. Within income growth, the contributing factors are the expansion of the market and the increasing of income from the present client base. The two factors that lead to increased productivity are increased efficiency and better use of current resources combined with large investments being replaced by gradual investments.

(b) The customer view   Kaplan and Norton describe this section as 'the heart of the strategy'. This area outlines the exact strategy for gaining new custom or for enlarging the current customers' division of business.

(c) The internal view   This view outlines the corporate processes and exact actions that company must perfect in order to maintain the customer view, which as has already been said is fundamental to the model.

(d) Learning and growth view   Kaplan and Norton outline the 'unquantifiable' resources that are necessary in order to allow the goals of organizational actions and client/company interaction to be carried out at increasingly sophisticated levels, to be achieved. There are three main sections to be considered within the learning and growth view. The first is that of strategic capabilities. This section encapsulates the knowledge and abilities demanded from the staff in order to maintain the strategy. The second section is that of 'strategic technologies' (Norton and Kaplan, 2001:93). This part is concerned with the technological requirements that are necessary to maintain the strategy. The third and final area that contributes to the learning and growth view is that of environment for activity. Within this part the effect of shifts in the social atmosphere of the organization are taken into account as the optimum environment in which to maintain the strategy is examined.

Benchmarking

Benchmarking is the strategy of studying the competition's products, services, or practices to improve your own company or business.

Boston Consultancy Group Growth Share Matrix

This model presupposes that the quiescent cash flow of a particular product is proportional to the enlargement of the market as a whole in relation to its competitors and its present market share. One clear advantage of this model is its universal application, which allows parallels and contrasts to be drawn between widely differing products.

Critical Assumptions

The 'facts' on which the strategic plan is based. In order to make a decision, in the absence of perfect information, assumptions are made. If these assumptions turn out to be erroneous and these would have a substantial material impact on the organization, they are considered critical.

Citicorp Interaction Analysis

Because neither top-down nor bottom-up strategic planning models fully encapsulated Citicorp's style, they adopted a more complex matrix model.

The first step in the Interaction Analysis is to recognize important assets of each business unit and identify any overlap between these. Second, all major responsibilities of each business unit must be established and any overlap pinpointed. The third and final step in the analysis is to judge the level of interdependence that exists between the business units and to establish the strategic consequences of this.

Closed Domain Market

This is a market in which all prospective customers can be identified.

Customer Relationship Management (CRM)

Customer Relationship Management (CRM) is a system that gives a complete overview of the client/company exchange. It involves itself in every means of communication and exchange between the organization and the customer. A CRM programme is customized to effectively meet the needs of any individual organization's customers' requirements.

Dow-Corning Strategy Matrix

The Dow-Corning model's starting point is placed in the hands of senior members of management who are obligated to formulate objectives. Because objectives can often straddle a number of borders (be they departmental or systematic), the manager who formulates the objective then goes on to navigate the objective's path through the company maze until it has reached its implementation point. This ensures that critical strategies are completed effectively.

Dynamic Reporting

GMAS provides reporting systems using a system developed in-house called Dynamic Reporting. This system allows research results to be delivered securely and dynamically, so that users can request whichever survey and the period they want to look at, and have the results generated in real time. From the broadest results overview, respondents can drill down to find out who gave a particular response to a particular question, at a particular time. The purpose of Dynamic Reporting is that it gives authorized users access to research being gathered in real time at the right time in the right format for the users purpose.

Enterprise Neuron Trail (ENT)

The critical internal communication channels within an organization encompassing formal and informal means of exchange.

Enterprise Resource Planning (ERP)

The term 'enterprise resource planning' was created by the Gartner Group in the last decade of the twentieth century to relate company software applications. Resource System (ERP) involves the consolidation of all units and operations across an organization into an individual computer application that can assist specific needs and enable contact within the organization as well the common use of data that is produced by the application.

Fuzzy Logic

Enables imprecise approximations to be interpreted and reasoned in a manner that strongly resembles human thought processes. Fuzzy logic does not see information as merely 'true' or 'false', it can distinguish gradations of truthfulness to lead to a conclusion that indicates that something may be, for example, 70 per cent true and 30 per cent false.

General Electric Matrix

This model follows a similar line as the Boston Consultancy Group (BCG) Growth Share Matrix. The BCG's model used two main factors to measure the appeal of the market and the infallibility of the company. However, in contrast, the General Electric Matrix employs a large number of determinants to measure these. The result of employing a large number of determinants is that General Electric's matrix is not as rigid as BCG's and can be adapted by varying the determinants to allow effective utilization in the most unusual of sectors.

Harrigan-Porter End-Game Analysis

Harrigan and Porter developed this model that would provide a number of substitute tactics for companies placed in receding industries. In addition to this, the model can assist the organization in establishing the most suitable strategy in at that particular time. This model can help, in addition to companies in declining industries, those with products entering the last stage in their life cycle.

Irrefutable Research

Research that is valid and free from bias is irrefutable. The concept can be summed up using the formula $M = R + B$ What we measure (M) is equal to the real answer (R) plus the bias (B). There is always bias of some kind or another, e.g. interviewer, question design, and sample. Irrefutable research aims to eliminate as much bias as possible therefore reflecting better the true result.

King's Strategic-Issue Analysis

This model allows managers and analysts to come to a point of broad agreement. In addition to this, the model facilitates the improvement of decision making on issues and the incorporation of dissection of those issues within the normal planning system.

Local Area Network (LAN)

A computer network that is confined to a small area (such as a building or ship, for example). Although the LAN exists only across a small space, it can be attached via telephone lines to other LANs over a greater distance. A group of LANs connected in such a way is referred to as a Wide Area Network (WAN).

McKinsey and Company 7-S model

The model considers the following elements, which are all interrelated:

(a) Strategy   Strategy can be described as a means to ensuring an organization has a market advantage over the competition. This advantage can be manifested in a number of ways, but ultimately advantage is achieved through being, in at least one characteristic, unique. As the Harvard Business School puts it (1996) 'Strategy is, or at least ought to be, an organization's way of saying: "Here is how we will create unique value".' President and fellows of Harvard College, *Organizational Alignment: The 7-S Model* (Lecture notes).

(b) Systems   The term 'systems' refers to the entire menagerie of methods and procedures put in place within an organization in order to assist the managing of it. The main objective of systems is to sharpen up the focus of the management team and therefore increase the effectiveness of them along with the organization overall.

(c) Structure   Structure prescribes how people within an organization are grouped and indicates where control of that organization is located. The main reason why structure is put in place is because it can help to increase the efficiency of the business by concentrating the staff's minds on the tasks to be undertaken. When building a structure, the need for division in order to aid depth of specialist knowledge must be offset against the need for maintaining a unified firm. Structure can be manifested in the four main forms of network, matrix, functional and divisional (for a full description of these forms, please refer to appendix?).

(d) Skills   This refers to the particular talents that are held within an organization. These talents can be held not only by individual members of staff, but can also be embedded into the ethos of the company. In the latter scenario it is the company as a whole that possesses and represents good practice in the given area.

(e) Style   Style is not a measurement of the output of an organization—it is an assessment of the manner in which output is produced. What do managers spend their time doing—for example, are they participating in meetings or supervising the staff? Where is the focus of the managers—is it fixed internally or externally? How are decisions taken—in a top-down or bottom-up manner? The answers to all these questions will point to a certain style that in turn lays down the cultural norms of that organization.

(f) Staff   How a company selects, integrates and develops its staff of course differs greatly between different companies. However, these processes coupled with the demographics of the people the organization chooses to employ and deployment of particular people to particular areas has a profound effect on the overall performance of it.

(g) Shared values   Shared values refers to the beliefs that are central to company's ethos and mould the approach that those within the organization apply in the everyday situations they are faced with. Shared values are useful as they help to maintain concentration on the focal point of the organization and furnish a feeling of there being a common goal that everyone is working towards.

Neuro Linguistic Programming (NLP)

This is a theory of human behaviour and communication that is applied to study a person's own individual experiences, and seeks to discover why a certain person will do what they do. The NLP can assist in developing a personalized method of therapy, where the brain is thought of as a computer. This 'computer' can be programmed to feel or act in a different way than before. By doing so, the person can be assisted in accomplishing their own specific objectives.

Orchard Matrix of Market Attractiveness

The Orchard Matrix of Market Attractiveness should be employed when a company is considering a move into a previously uncharted market. The purpose of the model is to provide a tool with which firms can measure the appeal of the options available.

Paradigm Shift

A paradigm shift is fundamentally a shift in the basic rationale upon which a market is based. For example, computer speed may be considered a rationale for purchasing a computer. If this rationale was replaced by design, this would mean that a shift in paradigm had occurred. The classic example of this is in the disk drive market with the move away from density in the days of mainframes, to size in the era of the portable and handheld.

Pareto Principle

The Pareto Principle is defined as a theory that states that a tiny number of causes are responsible for a large percentage of the effect. This ratio is usually 20 per cent to 80 per cent.

PEST Analysis

It is very important that an organization considers its environment before beginning the marketing process. In fact, environmental analysis should be continuous and feed all aspects of planning. The organization's marketing environment is made up from:

1   The internal environment e.g. staff (or internal customers), office technology, wages and finance, etc.
2   The micro-environment e.g. our external customers, agents and distributors, suppliers, our competitors, etc.
3   The macro-environment e.g. political (and legal) forces, economic

forces, sociocultural forces, and technological forces. These are known as **PEST** factors.

Political factors   The political arena has a huge influence upon the regulation of businesses, and the spending power of consumers and other businesses. You must consider issues such as:

1 How stable is the political environment?
2 Will government policy influence laws that regulate or tax your business?
3 What is the government's position on marketing ethics?
4 What is the government's policy on the economy?
5 Does the government have a view on culture and religion?
6 Is the government involved in trading agreements such as EU, NAFTA, ASEAN or others?

Economic factors   Marketers need to consider the state of a trading economy in the short and long terms. This is especially true when planning for international marketing. You need to look at:

1 Interest rates
2 The level of inflation and employment level *per capita*
3 Long-term prospects for the economy gross domestic product (GDP) per capita, and so on.

Sociocultural factors   The social and cultural influences on business vary from country to country. It is very important that such factors are considered. Factors include:

1 What is the dominant religion?
2 What are attitudes to foreign products and services?
3 Does language impact upon the diffusion of products on to markets?
4 How much time do consumers have for leisure?
5 What are the roles of men and women within society?
6 How long are the population living? Are the older generations wealthy?
7 Do the population have a strong/weak opinion on green issues?

Technological factors   Technology is vital for competitive advantage, and is a major driver of globalization. Consider the following points:

1   Does technology allow for products and services to be made more cheaply and to a better standard of quality?
2   Do the technologies offer consumers and businesses more innovative products and services such as Internet banking, new generation mobile telephones, etc?
3   How is distribution changed by new technologies e.g. books via the Internet, flight tickets, auctions, etc?
4   Does technology offer companies a new way to communicate with consumers e.g. banners, Customer Relationship Management (CRM), etc?

Porter's Value Chain Analysis

This model is complex, but the basic tenets of it can be grasped fairly easily. The model's main use is in the refining of company strategy in order to compare favourably with that of the competitors. The model seeks to provide competitive advantage through establishing the areas where the organization makes profit. Within this model the emphasis is shifted from placing a cost on everything in a traditional way, to calculating the potential to make money or the value. The advantage of this system is that it exposes the areas where companies compare and contrast effectively, thus highlighting areas of competitive advantage.

Product Life Cycle

The time span over which a product exists from the initial phases of design until close-out.

Random Walk

The idea that all factors are open to an unpredictable future where the value of those factors can increase as well as decrease with equal probability.

Real Options

The ability to choose to make a decision, at some point in the future. As the future is uncertain and market conditions can change unpredictably, making one decision can be better or worse than making another. Sydney Howell *et al.* (2001) define it, in their book *Real Options*, as 'real option analysis helps to decide: a) how much money we should spend to acquire an economic opportunity, and b) when (if ever) we should commit ourselves to one of the available decisions'.

Return Material Authorization (RMA)

The process under which faulty goods are returned to the manufacturer.

Spherical Vision

Spherical Vision provides a 360-degree view of the organization and its internal and external relationships.

STORM

At the heart of the GMAS system is the STORM. This is a meeting chaired by the strategic planning team which provides the human input into the interpretation of both real- and right-time market intelligence and supplies the initial decisions. The STORM (Strategic Tactical Operational Review Meeting) is the central key of the principal GMAS module groups: Strategy, Operations, Staff, Real-Time Critical Assumptions, Monitoring, and Testing.

Strategic Business Unit (SBU)

Product lines or businesses that have been tied together inside a company because they share markets, competitors or strategies. SBUs bring under one management various product groupings that had previously been administered separately and were very common in the 1990s. And their staff support services such as accounting and technical development can be brought in, too.

SWOT Analysis

SWOT analysis (Strengths, Weaknesses, Opportunities, Threats) is a tool for auditing an organization and its environment. It is the first stage of planning and helps marketers to focus on key issues. Once key issues have been identified, they feed into marketing objectives. It can be used in conjunction with other tools for audit and analysis, such as PEST analysis and Porter's Five-Forces analysis. It is a very popular tool with marketing students because it is quick and easy to learn.

SWOT stands for strengths, weaknesses, opportunities and threats. Strengths and weaknesses are internal factors. For example, a strength could be your specialist marketing expertise. A weakness could be the lack of a new product. Opportunities and threats are external factors. For example, an opportunity could be a developing market such as the Internet. A threat could be a new competitor in your home market. During the SWOT exercise, list factors in the relevant boxes. It is that simple.

A word of caution, SWOT analysis can be very subjective. Do not rely on it too much. Two people rarely come-up with the same final version of SWOT. So use it as guide and not a prescription.

Transactional Research

Research conducted looking at the customer experience and satisfaction with a specific service or purchase event.

Value-Added Retailer (VAR)

A company that sells items that have been produced by another company but prior to retailing the goods, adds something of worth to the package. For example, a company may purchase computers for resale, but prior to selling them installs some software, thus increasing the value of the computer.

References
and Bibliography

Bank of Scotland (2001) *Report on Scotland 2 July 2001*, Henley-on-Thames, NTC Research.

Brodeur, E. (2001) *Integrating ABC and ERP Systems*. BetterManagement.com. www.bettermanagement.com/lib.../library.asp?mode = printversion&libraryid = 408&A = 1.

Buzan, T. (2000) *Use Your Head*. London, BBC Consumer Publishing.

Christensen, C. M. (1997) *The Innovator's Dilemma: When New Technologies Cause Great Firms to Fail*. Boston, MA, Harvard Business School Press.

Cusumano, M. A and Markides, C. C (eds) (2001) *Strategic Thinking for the Next Economy*. San Francisco, CA, Jossey-Bass.

De Bono, E. (1970) *Lateral Thinking – Creativity Step by Step*. London, Perennial Library.

De Kare-Silver, M. (1997) *Strategy in Crisis: Why Business Urgently Needs a Completely New Approach*. London, MacMillan Business.

Dietz, L. R. (1999) *What Every Business Needs to Know About SAP*. Rocklin, CA, Prima Tech.

Fink, A. (1995) *The Survey Handbook*. Thousand Oaks, CA, Sage.

Foster, T. R. V. (1993) *101 Great Mission Statements: How the World's Leading Companies Run Their Business*. London, Kogan Page.

Foust, D. and Lavelle, L. (2000) *CEO Pay: Nothing succeeds like failure*. Business Week Online, 11 September 2000. www.businessweek.com/2000/00_37/b3698111.htm.

Galt, M., Chicoine-Piper, G., Chicoine-Piper, N. and Hodgson, A. (1997) *Idon Scenario Thinking: How to Navigate the Uncertainties of Unknown Futures*. Pitlochry, Idon.

de Geus, A. (1999) *The Living Company*. London, Nicholas Brealey Publishing.

Hiam, A. (1990) *The Vest-Pocket CEO: Decision-making Tools for Executives.* Paramus, NJ, Prentice-Hall.

Howell S., Stark, A., Newton, D., Paxson, D., Cavus, M., Pereira, J. and Patel, K. (2001) *Real Options: Evaluating Corporate Investment Opportunities in a Dynamic World.* London, Prentice-Hall.

Huff, D. (1991) *How to Lie with Statistics.* London, Penguin Books.

Kahaner, L. (ed.) (1996) *Competitive Intelligence: From Black Ops to Boardrooms—How Businesses Gather, Analyze and Use Information to Succeed in the Global Marketplace.* New York, Simon & Schuster.

Kaplan, R. S. and Cooper, R. (1998) *Cost and Effect: Using Integrated Cost Systems to Drive Profitability and Performance.* Boston, MA, Harvard Business School Press.

Kaplan, R. S. and Norton, D. P. (1996) *The Balanced Scorecard.* Boston, MA, Harvard Business School Press.

Kaplan, R. S. and Norton, D. P. (2001) *The Strategy Focused Organization: How Balanced Scorecard Companies Thrive in the New Business Environment.* Boston, MA, Harvard Business School Press.

Knowledge@Wharton (2001) *Making Customer Relationship Management Work.* BetterManagement.com. www.bettermanagement.com/li.../ library.asp?mode = printversion&libraryid = 1345&A = 1.

Koch, C., Slater, D. and Baatz, E. (Enterprise Resource Planning Research Center) (2000) *The ABCs of ERP.* www.cio.com/forums/erp/edit/122299_erp_content.html.

Koch, R. (2000) *The Financial Times Guide to Strategy: How to Create and Deliver a Useful Strategy,* 2nd edn. London, Prentice-Hall.

Kotler, P. and Scheff, J. (1997) *Standing Room Only.* Cambridge, MA, Harvard Business School Press.

Leipziger, D. (2001) *SA 8000: The Definitive Guide to the New Social Standard.* London, Prentice Hall.

Mabert, V. A. (2001) *Enterprise Resource Planning*: Common myths versus evolving reality. www.findarticles.com/cf_dls/m1038/3_44/75645903/print.jhtml.

McKenna, R. (1997) *Real Time: Preparing for the Age of the Never Satisfied Customer.* Boston, MA, Harvard Business School Press.

McQuarrie, E. F. (1996) *The Market Research Toolbox: A Concise Guide for Beginners.* Thousand Oaks, CA, Sage.

Meyer, C. (1993) *Fast Cycle Time: How to Align Purpose, Strategy and Structure for Speed.* New York, Free Press.

Mintzberg, H. (1994) *The Rise and Fall of Strategic Planning.* London, Prentice-Hall.

Moore, G. A. (1995) *Inside the Tornado.* New York, Harper Business.

Moore, G. A. (2000) *Living on the Fault Line: Managing Shareholder Value in the Age of the Internet.* New York, Harper Business.

Moore, G. A., Johnson, P. and Kippola, T. (1998) *The Gorilla Game: An Investor's Guide to Picking Winners in High Technology.* New York, Harper Business.

Nadler, G. and Hibino, S. (1994) *Breakthrough Thinking: The Seven Principles of Creative Problem Solving,* 2nd edn. Rocklin, CA, Prima Publishing.

O'Leary, D. E. (2000) *Enterprise Resource Planning Systems: Systems, Life Cycle, Electronic Commerce and Risk.* Cambridge, Cambridge University Press.

Oppenheim, A. N. (1996) *Questionnaire Design, Interviewing and Attitude Measurement,* new edn. London, Pinter Publishers Limited.

Pande, P. S., Neuman, R. P. and Cavanagh, R. R. (2000) *The Six Sigma Way: How GE, Motorola and Other Top Companies are Honing Their Performance.* London, McGraw-Hill.

Porter, M. E. (1980) *Competitive Strategy,* Free Press, New York.

Price, F. (1984) *Right First Time: Using Quality Control for Profit.* Aldershot, Wildwood House.

Reichheld, F. F. (1996) *The Loyalty Effect: The Hidden Force Behind Growth, Profits and Lasting Value.* Boston, MA, Harvard Business School Press.

Siebel, T. and Malone, M. (1996) *Virtual Selling: Going Beyond the Automated Sales Force to Achieve Total Sales Quality.* New York, Free Press.

Silvon Software Inc. (2001) *The Bottom Line of CRM: Know Your Customers.* BetterManagement.com. www.bettermanagement.com/lib.../library.asp?mode = printversion&libraryid = 1327&A = 1.

Smith, D. and Dexter, A. (2001) 'Whenever I hear the word "paradigm" I reach for my gun: how to stop talking and start walking'. *International Journal of Market Research,* **43**(3): 321–340.

Tooker, R. N. (2001) *The Many Faces of CRM.* www.bettermanagement.com.

Von Altrock, C. (1997) *Fuzzy Logic and Neurofuzzy Applications in Business and Finance.* New York, Prentice Hall P T & R.

Index